The Wages of Affluence

The Wages of Affluence
Labor and Management in Postwar Japan

Andrew Gordon

Harvard University Press
Cambridge, Massachusetts
London, England
1998

Library of Congress Cataloging-in-Publication Data

Gordon, Andrew, 1952–
    The wages of affluence : labor and management in postwar Japan /
Andrew Gordon.
        p.   cm.
    Includes bibliographical references and index.
    ISBN 0-674-80577-1 (cloth : alk. paper)
    1. Industrial relations—Japan—History—20th century.
    2. Labor policy—Japan—History—20th century.   I. Title.
HD8726.5.G56   1998
331'.0952—dc21   98-18610

For Jennifer and Megumi

Acknowledgments

Writing often feels like a solitary endeavor, but I have been able to think through the issues addressed in this book, however imperfectly, only because of the help of numerous people. It is a great pleasure to acknowledge their contributions.

I am especially grateful to the men and women in Japan who so generously made time available for interviews, and so thoughtfully and frankly answered my questions. I thank Professor Okuda Kenji for opening the door to so many of these interviews and for sharing his own rich experience of labor and management at NKK, and I am grateful to Professor Nimura Kazuo and the entire staff of the Ohara Institute for Social Research for their critiques, friendship, and practical assistance over many years.

I thank colleagues on three continents for valuable advice and criticism of written drafts and oral presentations of work in progress: Arif Dirlik, Ronald Dore, Daniel Foote, Sheldon Garon, Lawrence Goodwyn, Hyōdō Tsutomu, Gregory Jackson, Sanford Jacoby, Horst Kern, Alex Keyssar, Karl Lauschke, Richard Locke, Charles Maier, Ruth Milkman, Corrado Molteni, Walter Mueller-Jentsch, Tag Murphy, Nitta Michio, Ōsawa Mari, Wolfgang Streeck, Watanabe Etsuji, Thomas Welskopf, Yamamoto Kiyoshi, Jonathan Zeitlin. I am particularly indebted to Sheldon Garon for engaging me in a critical and constructive dialogue for some twenty years. Joyce Seltzer at Harvard University Press deserves special thanks for greatly improving the manuscript with thoughtful critiques of several drafts. I thank Jeffrey Bayliss, Jonathan Dresner, Stefano von Loe, and Chitose Sato for their capable aid as research assistants; Paul Talcott for preparing the graphs; and Margot Chamberlain for excellent help in preparing the final draft of the manuscript.

Between 1987 and 1997 numerous institutions provided funding that allowed me to conduct this research, and I am pleased to acknowledge them: the Fulbright fellowship administered by the Japan–United States Education Commission in Tokyo, the Japan Foundation, the Abe Fellowship of the Center for Global Partnership and the Social Science Research Council, the Duke University Faculty Research Council, and the Reischauer Institute for Japanese Studies at Harvard University.

Through it all, as ever, my wife, Yoshie, and my entire family have supported and inspired me. I dedicate the book to my children, who have provided such delight throughout the years of my obsession with this project. On the occasion of my fortieth birthday, at an early stage in the research, my sister, Betsy, brother, Bill, and his wife, Marcy, prepared a song that changed the way I have written this book. To the tune of the refrain from "I've Been Working on the Railroad," they sang "Brother, write a book that we can read." I look forward to discovering if I have succeeded.

Contents

The Wages of Affluence

Prologue

I began work on this history of labor and management in postwar Japan during the heady years of the "bubble economy" of the late 1980s. This was a moment when a commentator on National Public Radio described the astonishing spectacle of wealthy young Tokyo-ites downing sushi wrapped in gold leaf at $40 per slice, and business reporters in the United States marveled at the stunning performance of the Japanese economy. They often explained this performance as a result of the remarkably productive and harmonious system of industrial relations in Japan, a land where efficient and cooperative teams of men and women apparently worked long hours with little complaint. Many observers in the United States, echoed by an ever more confident chorus of boosters in Japan, argued that flagging economies worldwide could be rescued by adopting the Japanese model of industrial relations. Two assumptions lay behind these attitudes: that the Japanese economy was more dynamic and more productive than those elsewhere; and that Japanese workplaces were kinder and gentler places for employees.

Reacting to these assumptions, I examined the recent history of labor and management in Japan in a contrarian frame of mind. Japanese practices of labor-management relations did offer some important competitive strengths to managers. But it did not follow that working for these corporations was an enviable fate. I discovered—and determined to explain—the oppressive political and ideological processes that enabled the Japanese system of "cooperative" labor-management relations to emerge and to endure. At the same time, I hoped to rescue from oblivion the alternative initiatives and visions that did not prevail. The historical evidence undermined the common wisdom of the 1980s that employees can only benefit by emulating a

Japanese model said to offer the best of all possible worlds, a glorious future of flexibility, harmony, and cooperation.

Then the bubble burst. The Tokyo Stock Exchange crashed, Japanese land prices fell sharply, the GNP stopped growing, and from 1991 to 1994 industrial production in Japan actually fell by about 10 percent. The chorus of praise for Japanese management turned flat as pundits announced that dramatic "restructuring" was the order of the day. Japanese executives told us that existing managerial practices, including systems of labor relations, had to be transformed. Profound changes were predicted: lifetime employment was about to vanish, and seniority-based wages were following the dinosaur into oblivion. Far from being a status symbol of international envy, Japanese capitalism came to be seen as a clunky vehicle needing total overhaul. The sandy foundation of "the present" had shifted under my feet; Americans no longer needed convincing to view the Japanese economic system skeptically. In fact, they needed to be reminded that a political and economic system deeply rooted in modern history was unlikely to evaporate and was probably not entirely dysfunctional.

A history of labor and management in postwar Japan is in fact worth reading in times dominated by exaggerated prognostications of doom as well as times, certain to recur, of uncritical praise for an enduring Japanese system. The postwar history of the Japanese workplace told in this book contradicts the 1990s common wisdom of Japan-dismissal. It refutes rash predictions of the demise of long-term employment and other Japanese modes of organizing the workplace. At the same time this book contradicts the older conventional wisdom of Japan-veneration. It shows that the Japanese model owed as much to coercion as to happy consensus. My investigation of the past took place during two very different present moments, and it highlights the theme of the tension between capitalism and democracy. Managers and workers in postwar Japan created a dynamic economic system to mobilize the energies of workers on behalf of production and profit. In so doing, they undermined the democratic potential of postwar society.

The story is grounded in a close-up analysis of a single steelmaking complex in postwar Japan. I show that a system of so-called cooperative labor-management relations was established in Japan from the 1950s through the 1960s in a turbulent process, a postwar contest for the workplace. I expect most readers will be surprised at its intensity.

The early chapters explore trails partially blazed during this contest but ultimately not taken. They recreate a world of shop-floor activism in which organized workers raised serious challenges to an uncertain corporate hegemony, pursuing goals that demand attention and respect even if they were only achieved in part. These chapters also begin to describe the road eventually taken. I try to explain why "cooperative" labor-management relations prevailed. Why did the turbulent era of nearly two decades' duration after World War II give way to an enduring hegemony of the corporate-centered society? Answering such a question requires attention to the historical roots of the Japanese industrial relations system and constitutes one reply to predictions of its imminent demise.

Explaining this durability is at least implicitly a comparative task. The postwar history of workplaces in Japan has much in common with Euro-American histories, but it is more than a variation on a Western theme. In Japan's workplaces of the past fifty years, tensions that elsewhere erupted into political, economic, or social crisis were contained to an unparalleled extent. Since the 1960s the hegemony of the corporation has been more durable and less profoundly challenged in Japan than in any of the other major industrial nations. At several points I compare Japan to Europe and America and suggest what might account for the durability of the Japanese hegemony, or the fragility (or contentiousness) of labor-management relations elsewhere.

A history of the Japanese contest ultimately raises the difficult matter of assessing the mixed legacy left to later generations in Japan and around the world. Carving out spaces of dignity and security in a world of huge organizations devoted to efficiency and profit has not been easy for people in Japan; but one is hard pressed to identify anyplace where it has been easy. The Japanese experience offers no easy answers, but a cautionary, in some ways familiar, tale of trade-offs and hard choices in a difficult world. The fate of both victors and vanquished in the contest for the Japanese workplace contradicts a simplistic view of workers in Japan as uniquely exploited, working furiously for long hours while living in cramped apartments in distant suburbs. But the outcome of this contest also challenges those who would idealize the Japanese model. Working people had to compromise institutions of democratic self-determination in pursuit of the wages of affluence.

1   *Japan Reborn*

On August 15, 1945, the Emperor of Japan stunned his subjects with a radio broadcast announcing the nation's surrender to the Allied forces. Eight years earlier Japan's rulers had launched a full-scale war in China. They had exhorted the Japanese people endlessly to sacrifice for the sake of a great and certain victory to liberate Asia from the tyranny of the "British and American devils." In the name of Greater East Asian Co-Prosperity, countless millions had been killed throughout Asia and three million out of seventy million Japanese people had perished. Despite his stilted language, Emperor Hirohito made it clear that the most destructive war in history was over, and Japan had been utterly defeated. Many Japanese later recalled that August noon as an instant of rebirth, a moment when past experience and values were discredited and a totally new course, both personal and national, was to be charted. In the years that followed, in an unprecedented context of crisis at home and reform imposed from outside, millions of people struggled to realize new visions of equality and democracy.

Nakamura Kōgō's remembrance of August 1945 powerfully invokes just such a story of postwar democratic commitment. Nakamura was born in 1924 in a village in Miyagi Prefecture in Northern Japan. After elementary school, he came to Tokyo in 1938. He attended an industrial high school with funds sent by his father, a clerk at the village office. His studies were interrupted first by the labor draft that pressed him into service in a munitions factory, and then by the military draft. Hired by the NKK steel company in 1947, Nakamura soon became a union activist. He tells an archetypal tale of rebirth, polished in the frequent retelling and shaped by the shared language of postwar Marxists and modernists.[1] At the time of surrender, "the emperor system that had enveloped me and all of Japan was

4

exposed. A brand new era began. Democracy was an entirely new experience and concept. August 1945 was a new departure for me, spiritually and ideologically. I felt that way then, and I still feel that way now" (1991).[2]

Although Nakamura recalled democracy as an "entirely new experience" of the postwar era, many other prewar Japanese, from intellectuals and journalists to factory laborers and tenant farmers, had accumulated important experiences with democratic practice from the late nineteenth century to the 1930s. The reforms of the Allied occupation enabled such activists to regroup and join hands with novices such as Nakamura. They vastly expanded the constituencies supporting a democratic and egalitarian political system.

A fearful experience of deprivation gave special urgency to these new endeavors. For several years after the war, millions of Japanese faced starvation. Thousands indeed starved to death.[3] Atomic bombs had destroyed Hiroshima and Nagasaki, and virtually every other major city had been devastated by firebombs. Inflation surged out of control. Companies found it more profitable to sell raw materials on the black market than to process them, so much of the industrial plant that had survived stood idle. One American recalled that "for four years after the war, the great inflation hung over Japan like some immense, brooding presence. . . . By 1949, when inflation was finally contained, the price level had risen 150 *times* in four years." Workers crowded onto trains for the countryside to barter kimonos for cabbage, and "shedding clothes to buy food was first compared to the snake's shedding of its skin, then to the peeling of an onion, because it was accompanied by tears."[4]

By the spring of 1946 poor harvests and a paralyzed rationing system had produced a serious urban food crisis. The average household spent 68 percent of its income on food in 1946, and the average height and weight of elementary school children decreased until 1948.[5] Ordinary citizens joined unions and the parties of the left in taking to the streets. In Tokyo, hundreds of thousands jammed the plaza in front of the imperial palace, demanding rice and democracy on May Day 1946 and again on a so-called Food May Day demonstration two weeks later. Smaller groups attacked former military storehouses in search of rice. Decades later, older Japanese watched with pained memories the numerous TV specials on the postwar march from poverty to prosperity, which predictably began with 1945–46 scenes of massive demonstrations and emaciated youths with distended bellies. The young watched in disbelief and embarrassment: "This doesn't seem like my country," they would say; "it looks like Bangladesh."[6]

The United States governed Japan for seven years, acting through the offices of General Douglas MacArthur, the Supreme Commander for the

Allied Powers (or SCAP). The acronym refers to both the man and his organization. Until 1947 SCAP was singleminded in pursuit of its mission to demilitarize and democratize Japan. It was only slightly concerned by the failing economy. It welcomed, or at least tolerated, much of the popular activism. Members of the old guard in Japan battled to retain their authority. They were led by a canny and strong-willed career diplomat named Yoshida Shigeru, who viewed the American revolution from above with alarm and anger. He and his colleagues charged that SCAP had been taken over by communists, and Yoshida is said to have once asked MacArthur directly if he intended to "turn Japan Red."[7]

Prime Minister Yoshida first tried to stimulate the economy through subsidies. He and his predecessor, Shidehara Kijurō, paid out huge sums to businesses for outstanding war contracts, expecting the latter to invest for peacetime production. Businesses instead used the payments to hoard and resell scarce raw materials whose value was climbing sharply with inflation. Under American pressure, the government finally halted the subsidies by the autumn of 1946, but production continued to decline, while inflation rose. To head off an impending crisis, the government worked out a more carefully focused Priority Production subsidy program. This funneled capital and materials to the coal and steel industries, and it enjoyed some success by 1948. The crisis of shriveling production and soaring inflation had been averted, although the economy stood on shaky ground until the 1950s.[8]

Economic crisis coupled with fears and hopes for revolution was by no means unique to Japan at this time. The Communist Party was moving toward power in China. In Europe, a respected observer in late 1945 pronounced that believers in "the American way of life—that is, in private enterprise" were "a defeated party."[9] Only in retrospect is it clear that such predictions misread the ability and willingness of the United States to underwrite recovery and find allies in a project of more modest reform. As the Americans moved in 1946 and 1947 toward such a role in Europe through the Marshall Plan, their shifting policies similarly defined the context for the strivings of people in Japan.

The Americans sent a clear initial message that democracy should be the cornerstone of a new Japan. The core reform was a constitution. This was drafted by a committee of occupation officials in the winter of 1946, vigorously discussed and ratified that spring in the Imperial Diet (still in existence until the new constitution replaced it), and promulgated that November, to take effect in May 1947.

The postwar constitution downgraded the emperor from absolute monarch to a "symbol of the State and of the unity of the people." It granted to the people of Japan an array of "fundamental human rights" that included the civil liberties of the American Bill of Rights, such as freedoms of speech, assembly, and religion. It then boldly extended the concept of rights into the social realm. The new constitution guaranteed rights to education "correspondent to ability" and to "minimum standards of wholesome and cultured living." It assured the right (and obligation) to work, to organize, and to bargain collectively. It outlawed discrimination based on sex, race, creed, social status, or family origin, and it gave women explicit guarantees of equality in marriage, divorce, property, inheritance, and "other matters pertaining to marriage and the family." Finally, its Article 9 committed the Japanese people to "forever renounce war as a sovereign right of the nation and the threat or use of force as means of settling international disputes."

Japanese elites were stunned by these sweeping guarantees, especially when the Americans insisted that the Japanese government present them to the people as the government's own recommendation; but the draft document met an enthusiastic popular response. As officially sanctioned goals or ideals, its ambitious provisions framed the discourse and institutions of contemporary Japan.

SCAP reformers went well beyond redesigning the basic law of the land. They disbanded the oppressive "thought police" and for a time decentralized the national police force. They disestablished the official state Shinto religion. They freed Communist Party members from jail. Indeed, they allowed a greater range of political expression than was possible in the United States at the time. They attacked the sprawling business empires called *zaibatsu*, taking away ownership and control from holding companies dominated by the zaibatsu families (Mitsui, Sumitomo, Yasuda, Iwasaki, Asano, and others) and breaking up some of the larger firms. They encouraged and advised unions, and at first they welcomed the extraordinary drive of organizing and strikes. They imposed a program of land reform that revolutionized the distribution of social and economic power in rural Japan, essentially expropriating the holdings of landlords and creating a countryside of small family farms. These sweeping measures changed the climate of ideas and the distribution of economic and social power, and a fever of democratization swept Japan. The projects of democracy and equality were understood in extremely expansive terms by their advocates; they meant far more than voting and land reform. They implied to many— and this was both promise and threat—a remaking of the human soul. Talk of renovating and remaking and transforming echoed throughout Japan, and one heard it clearly in the workplace.

Scattered labor organizing began within weeks of the surrender, and this effort surged forward when the Americans announced their support for unions in October 1945. Union membership rose from about 5,000 in October to nearly 5 million by December 1946, over 40 percent of the nation's adult wage earners. Fueled by the deprivation and anger of masses of workers, union activists were militant in their tactics and often radical in their goals. Through June of 1946, 157,000 newly organized men and women engaged in 233 instances of "production control." They locked out managers and ran factories, railroads, or mines on their own when demands for wages and the democratization of the workplace were denied.[10] This tactic usually won the union its demands, and it had revolutionary implications. Workers were challenging fundamental notions of private property and managerial authority.[11]

However close the workers were to launching a revolution, they were not close enough to overcome American opposition. The occupiers had attacked the old order with radical reform to root out what they called feudalistic militarism, but they sought to remake the nation in their own image as a capitalist democracy. In May 1946 SCAP condemned production control as well as mass demonstrations such as the Food May Day. A newly confident Japanese cabinet suppressed further takeovers. Production takeovers fell from roughly 50 events involving over thirty thousand workers each month in the spring of 1946 to about 25 monthly actions involving five to six thousand in early 1947.[12]

Labor was forced to change tactics, but the enthusiasm for organizing was not dampened. People in Japan were straining to define the meaning of their postwar democracy in a shifting international and domestic context. Their efforts made the fifteen years after World War II a uniquely contentious era marked by a battle of ideas as well as work stoppages.

In the 1940s and 1950s, the dominant position among workers active in labor unions was a radical one. Their ultimate political goal was a socialist revolution. They saw unions allied to either the socialist or the communist party as the most important building blocks of a new society. At the industrial level, these unionists initially joined the Sanbetsu federation (Zen Nihon *Sangyō Betsu* Rōdō Kumiai Kaigi, or Japan Council of Industrial Labor Unions), dominated in both its national councils and plant unions by the Japan Communist Party. When Sanbetsu collapsed, they joined in creating the Sōhyō federation (Nihon rōdō kumiai *sōhyōgikai*, or General Council of Trade Unions of Japan) in 1950. They typically demanded large annual pay increases indexed to the cost of living and reflecting employee needs. Through activism at corporate headquarters and in the workplace, union leaders sought veto power over personnel decisions and a voice in day-to-day operation of firm and factory. In short, they challenged the legitimacy of the managerial chain of command.

A second important position was that of the venerable Sōdōmei federation (Nihon Rōdō *Sōdōmei,* or Japan Federation of Labor), founded in 1919, which carried the message of the cooperative wing of the prewar labor movement into the postwar era. In name and in ideology, Sōdōmei resembled the mainstream of the postwar union movement in the United States. Its member unions accepted the basic framework of a capitalist society and saw their role as the defense of workers within it. While their goals were not revolutionary, Sōdōmei tactics could be militant. Their leaders argued that labor and management had a common general interest in making a capitalist system viable, but that predictable differences separated the two sides, though these differences could normally be settled through good-faith bargaining.

After the production control movement was suppressed, thousands of unions in both these camps shifted to more conventional tactics. They won huge wage increases and contracts, giving them a substantial voice in matters previously reserved to managers. The Sanbetsu federation led this drive, which culminated in the 1946 "October struggle" of over 100 strikes involving 180,000 workers nationwide. These actions won guarantees of job security and wage systems designed to reflect employee needs. Then, the unions in both Sanbetsu and the rival Sōdōmei federation, spurred by popular fury over economic collapse and the complacent policies of the Yoshida cabinet, joined hands to plan a national general strike of about 6 million workers, public and private, for February 1, 1947. In the weeks building to the strike, the members of the Sanbetsu-Sōdōmei Joint Struggle Committee, dominated by Communist Party leaders, believed themselves on the eve of revolution.

Their hopes proved false. At the last moment, on the afternoon of January 31, MacArthur ordered the Committee leaders to call off the strike. This was a giant step in the American turn from agent of antifeudal revolution to supporter of capitalist recovery. Realizing the rank and file would not defy MacArthur, the strike organizers complied with the ban.[13]

Despite this debacle, unions remained vigorous over the next three years. Just six days after the aborted February 1 strike, Sanbetsu, Sōdōmei, and the

Keizai Dōyūkai, a new organization of reform-oriented capitalists, formally launched an Economic Recovery Council. This provided a new framework for unified labor activity. Strikes were still numerous, workers continued to organize new unions, and the unionized proportion of the workforce continued to rise to an all-time peak of 56 percent in 1949.

But as the Japanese idiom has it, the two union federations were "sleeping together but dreaming separately." The Economic Recovery Council collapsed after just over one year. Despite continued growth, by mid-1948 the labor movement was on the defensive. In July 1948, MacArthur advised the Japanese government to revise its labor laws, and the Yoshida cabinet eagerly obliged with a new law that denied public sector unions the right to strike. In 1949 SCAP implemented the Dodge plan (named for its architect, American industrialist Joseph Dodge) to promote recovery through an extremely austere fiscal and monetary policy. Tight money and state pressure on firms to restrain wage costs led enterprises nationwide to dismiss thousands of workers, and provoked numerous, invariably unsuccessful acts of union resistance. In June 1950, Americans directed the Japanese government to fire over 12,000 union activists identified as Communist Party members or sympathizers, and Japan's rulers happily complied. By the end of 1950, the number of union members had fallen from 6.7 million to 5.8 million, and the unionized proportion of the work force had dropped by nearly 10 percent.[14]

Japan's unions gradually regrouped once more, building toward a peak of confrontation at the end of the decade. The newly founded Sōhyō union federation surprised Japanese critics and dismayed occupation officials, who initially expected the group to become a cooperative, noncommunist alternative to Sanbetsu. Sōhyō instead came to support the left wing of the socialist party in national politics, aggressive wage bargaining at the industrial level, and militant day-to-day actions in the workplace.

Corporate managers faced with this varied and vigorous labor insurgency were divided in their response. Some hard-liners never came to terms with the occupation reforms; they continued to treat unions as a threat to be suppressed.[15] Others, particularly in firms with relatively unchallenged monopolies in an industry, for a time made their peace with radical unions.[16] But the majority of Japanese managers groped their way toward a strategy of attacking such unionists and nurturing their cooperative opponents, who could help them manage the workforce. As they did so, they helped bring to power a third major stream of postwar unionism.

This was a revised cooperative position that emerged in the 1950s and came into its own in later years. Its adherents saw the interests of workers and managers as fundamentally the same and assumed managers would normally act in the mutual interests of both employees and the company. Only in rare cases when managers were unusually venal or selfish would a union need to confront them in tough bargaining. The union's primary function was to cooperate to mobilize worker energies on behalf of the firm and help the company work smarter, prosper, and grow, thereby serving the employees in the long run. Such unionism emerged first in private firms that were competing for shares of domestic and export markets. Critics have condemned it as the ultimate perversion of anything resembling true unionism; advocates laud it as the perfection of pragmatic Japanese industrial relations and a model for the world.

This new brand of cooperative unionism eventually won out over the radical vision as well as the relatively militant prewar and early postwar cooperative position. In the process, managers became ever more comfortable with unions. By the late 1970s they were so confident of the wisdom of their policies that they began proselytizing on behalf of Japanese-style management to Westerners and other Asians.[17] Firmly consolidated at home, Japan's corporate-dominated system now had a global reach.

In the conventional telling of this story to the English-speaking world, the early postwar contest for the Japanese workplace was brief and easily won. The radicals were unrealistic, dogmatic outsiders with only superficial support among workers. They left nothing significant to posterity.[18] The moderates were practical and farsighted. Their victory was inevitable and fortunate for themselves, for later generations of Japanese, and even for the world.

This is a myopic view. It fails to understand the promise and the legacy of the early postwar union challenge, which sought unprecedented equality among employees and new forms of participation in workplace and corporate decisions. This drive had widespread appeal. Ultimately it fell short, and this narrowed the scope of postwar democracy in Japan; but even in defeat the ambitious union challenge of the 1940s and 1950s had a significant impact: managers and their union allies incorporated portions of the early postwar agenda into the new cooperative order.

The factories of the city of Kawasaki were among the most energized sites of postwar union activism. They offer a unique vantage point to gain a sense of its character. They received extensive attention from the Japanese intellectual world, the media, and the government. Sandwiched between the occupation army's headquarters in Yokohama and SCAP headquarters in Tokyo, labor in Kawasaki also received special attention from the Americans.

One of the most scrutinized sites in the city was Japan's second largest steelmaker, Nippon Kōkan (NKK). Events at the NKK mill could influence national policy. On January 26, 1946, members of NKK's Tsurumi mill union roughed up the company president and zaibatsu leader, Asano Ryōzō, at a tumultuous negotiating session. This incident prompted four government ministers to outlaw all production control takeovers on February 1, 1946, a decision that SCAP promptly overturned.[19] To Japan's rulers, this incident was a shocking sign of the apparently unlimited American support for Japanese unions in the first months of the occupation.

Until the early twentieth century, Kawasaki had been a quiet place, a thin finger of territory stretching several miles inland from a short, marshy coastline (see Figure 1). It emerged as an industrial center when a major landfill project allowed the construction of several huge plants on the coast. In addition to NKK, these included the Asano zaibatsu's shipyard and steel mill just across the Tsurumi river toward Yokohama, and the bulb factory of Tokyo Electric Company (which merged with a rival to become Toshiba in 1939). Well before World War II, Kawasaki had become one of Japan's quintessential blue-collar towns, with an image as a tough and dirty place. At its wartime peak in December 1943, the city's population had swollen to 390,000, over double the 1933 total of 180,000.[20]

Nippon Kōkan (Japan Steel Tube) was founded in 1912 by two university classmates. Imaizumi Kiichirō, until then an engineer at the Yahata Ironworks, provided the technology, and Shiraishi Genjirō provided the money, drawing on the considerable resources of his father-in-law, Asano Sōichirō. In the company's founding myth, these two men were moved by a dream of showing their countrymen that a private steelmaker could flourish in Japan. In fact, both competition with and dependence on the state's Yahata facility are motifs of NKK's entire history.[21] By the end of World War I, the Kawasaki mill employed several thousand steelworkers. In 1936 NKK fired its first blast furnace, making the Kawasaki mill an integrated facility that produced a comprehensive sequence of iron, steel, and rolled metal products. By the end of World War II, the Kawasaki mill boasted five blast furnaces, a workforce of 18,000, and a peak annual output of about 2.3 million tons of iron and steel. Along the way, NKK in 1940 strengthened its rolling and platemaking capacity and gained a captive customer by absorbing the Asano zaibatsu's nearby Tsurumi steel mill and shipyard.

The steel industry in general, and NKK in particular, can be seen as both representative and strategic cases in the postwar history of the Japanese workplace. They are representative in that what happened in steel mills was remarkably similar to what happened in most major industries. In addition, the story at NKK was more or less identical to that at the rest of the Big Five steel companies (Yahata, Fuji, NKK, Sumitomo, and Kobe Steel). This holds true whether one speaks of the ideology of the contestants, the outcome of disputes, or the innovations in technology and labor management.

The industry's representative character is not coincidence. It stems from the economic and political impact that rippled out from the steel industry. Throughout the postwar era, steel executives were fond of quoting the maxim "Whither steel, so goes the nation" *(tetsu wa kokka nari)*. For decades, wage settlements in the steel industry served as benchmarks for other industries, as did innovations in work organization and quality control. Likewise, steel unions led the way toward a new political coalition that later promulgated cooperative unionism nationwide.

The strategic position of NKK as an enterprise is less apparent than that of the industry as a whole. In some respects NKK was a follower, overshadowed from its founding in 1912 by the nation's first modern steel mill, the government-run giant at Yahata that had started production ten years earlier. Although Yahata became a private company in postwar Japan, it was always the biggest of the big. NKK people, from top executives to furnace workers, nursed the mentality of the number two who must try harder. NKK trailed Yahata by several years in key innovations, such as the introduction of a hot-strip mill and an American-style foreman system. But it led the way in other new steelmaking technologies. The same managerial policies and labor responses can be studied there.

NKK nonetheless occupied a strategic niche. Kawasaki's proximity to the academic and journalistic capital of Tokyo and to the American occupation headquarters not only encouraged close scrutiny of the mill and left a rich documentary record of observers' reports from the 1940s through the present. In addition, the 49-day strike at NKK and Fuji Steel in 1959 was the last hurrah of activist unions in steel. Its outcome opened the way to the ascendance of cooperative unionism in the steel industry and throughout the economy.

Accounts of the individual lives of steelworkers in the 1940s and 1950s enrich our appreciation of the labor struggles of postwar Japan. In these workers' conflicting visions one sees the complex understandings of "true" labor unionism that crystallized into factions and ideologies, causing a fierce contest for the workplace in the 1950s.

Kamimura Hideji was born in 1915. His formal education ended in sixth grade. Childhood memories of his father's humiliation as a tenant farmer powerfully shaped his social conscience. In December each year, his father would take a day off from work in the fields to bring the rent rice to the landlord. Handing it over, he would bow low and thank the landlord. In 1992 Kamimura remembered watching this little ceremony of 65 years earlier and "thinking as a child 'What the hell is going on? Why thank the landlord?' This seemed to me such a contradiction."[22]

Kamimura's first and only industrial employer was NKK. He entered the mill in 1935 and worked as a crane operator in the materials section, unloading shipments of coal and iron ore. A skinny youth, he was overwhelmed at first by the twelve-hour shifts and the "heavy work, heat, oil." He was also stubborn and proud. In 1941, he and about fifty others in his section demanded output premiums on a par with the furnace workers, and at the start of one evening shift they walked out the gate. Loudly scolded by the assistant section chief, they returned to work around midnight. The premium rate was raised, but the base wages of the individuals involved were lowered as punishment, leaving the activists with no net gain.

Kamimura's sense of grievance remained with him after the war: "I was truly discontent with my place in the company's hierarchy. If we ever complained we were put down. I deeply desired to change this." He was unhappy with the domineering foremen, assistant foremen, and crew bosses within the category of production worker *(kōin)*, and he detested the high status of white-collar staff *(shokuin)* compared to production workers. "There was so much discrimination. I felt extraordinary animosity toward the white-collar staff."

Kamimura's commitment emerged from long years of workplace experience. That of Nakamura Kōgō, the young man who had experienced August 1945 as a moment of spiritual and ideological rebirth, had a more bookish grounding, spurred by his sense of betrayal by the wartime regime. Living in Tokyo from 1945 to 1947, he supported himself with money sent by his parents and by odd jobs, such as selling black market rice in front of Kawasaki station. He had always been an avid reader, and he now read voraciously, roaming the used book stores and stalls, seeking new ideas. He was profoundly moved by Kawakami Hajime's pioneering Marxian writings on the prewar economy and a book on law by Takikawa Yukitoki, a professor fired from Kyoto University in 1937 for his liberal political beliefs. "Kawakami taught me about economic issues and Takikawa about political rights. I developed a sense of myself, awareness, confidence, ability to speak out. Those books were precious. I still keep them on my shelf in the order I read them. It's like a physical intellectual diary. I hate it when people move them around, and I won't donate them to a library if they will be separated, mixed in with other books."[23]

Nakamura joined the Socialist Party in 1946. When he heard in April 1947 that NKK was hiring workers, he applied but was refused because the company wanted production workers with no higher education, not even in an industrial high school. Three months later he reapplied successfully, this time omitting his schooling from the application. He immediately threw himself into the union movement and, on the urging of the labor section employee who hired him, he stood for election as union official in September 1947 and won a post as head of the union's education section. Nakamura had spent just three months as a full-time NKK employee. He would spend the next thirteen years as a full-time union officer, a stalwart of NKK's radical forces.

Nakamura's cantankerous personality was unusual. He was also an unusual stickler for procedure. One of his co-workers joked that union meetings lasted three times as long when Nakamura was there. But he was typical of the radical stream in his idealistic commitment to the triad of peace, democracy, and socialism. Another typical sign of this era in which authorities were forced to act democratically and sometimes did so with zeal was the support of the manager in the personnel section who hired Nakamura. He knew of the young man's radicalism, yet encouraged his union ambitions.

Kudō Shinpachi, a third steel worker active in the early postwar union movement, was profoundly different both in work experience and in ideology. He is typical of that early stream of unionists who hoped to cooperate with the company, but supported militant actions on occasion. He would later throw in his lot with the ultracooperative stream of the 1960s, occasionally complaining that the cooperative leaders had given away too much.

Like Kamimura, Kudō was born to a tenant farming family, in Northern Japan in 1918. He completed only an elementary education. Around age fourteen he began working on his family's rented fields where he remained for several years, then entered NKK at age twenty in 1938. He was then drafted and spent the years from 1939 to 1942 with the army in China, at which point the army designated him "qualified technical personnel" and sent him back to NKK. He stayed on at the Kawasaki mill through the war's end and the occupation, eventually rising to the rank of foreman. He retired in 1973 at age fifty-five, and moved on to supervise operations at an NKK subcontractor.

Kudō helped set up the Kawasaki union in 1946, and he remained active in union affairs until 1949. He was then promoted to crew boss, and he quit his official union posts in the belief that younger rank-and-file workers should lead it. Kudō presented himself in later years as a "true labor unionist" who opposed both exploitation by the company and domination of the union by the communist party or the left wing of the socialist party. "What the union was supposed to do, I thought, was increase the workers' share of the fruits of our labor. Wage bargaining was the heart of the matter for me ... I felt the company was selfish and would not give large enough wage increases to avoid a strike, and I wanted the union to keep more distance from the company than other cooperative unionists did."[24] Kudō's actions undermine this claim of independence from both company and left-wing unions. Beginning in the 1950s he would seek above all to combat Communist Party strength in the union, leaving little time or energy for promoting a positive program to combat what he later called corporate "selfishness."

Somewhere between the positions of Kamimura and Nakamura on the one hand and Kudō on the other was Isobe Toshie, who also called himself a "labor unionist." In Japan as elsewhere union politics often revolved around a fight to define one's own stance as "true" unionism. Isobe eschewed the socialist party affiliations of Nakamura and Kamimura, but compared to Kudō he drew a much sharper line between his interests as a unionist and those of the company.

The son of a well-to-do landlord in Japan's snow country of Niigata, Isobe recalls a childhood of militaristic education (through middle school) that led him to volunteer for the army in 1938, at age nineteen. After a year's training, he spent six years in China and on various islands, including Okinawa, building airports or shoring up defense positions, before returning to Japan in late 1945. Like Nakamura, Isobe after the war was obsessed with the "need to understand what had happened to Japan."[25] Influenced by his recollections of tenant protests observed in a nearby village before the war, he looked to socialism both to explain Japan's recent disaster and as a guide to the future. Unable to find food in the city, he returned to the family farm in early 1946 and spent a year in self-directed study, reading books sent by a university-student cousin in Tokyo. After the land reform, Isobe rejected the prospect of taking over his father's much-reduced farm and, in October

1947 via the introduction of a friend, he secured a job as a furnace worker in the number 2 pipe rolling mill at NKK's Kawasaki plant.

Isobe was a small man, about 5 feet 2 inches, perfect posture, quick step. He recalled: "This [1947] was my first time in a steel mill. I was astonished. Twelve-hundred-degree heat from the furnace. This was real man's work, but I figured if I had survived the army I could handle it. When I entered NKK we were busy producing gas pipes for reconstruction projects." Isobe says that he applied himself "quietly" to his work for about six months but was quickly drawn to the union. "We were demanding food. Management was basically absent in the workplace and had no vision for the future." He stood for election to a local union office in the spring of 1948, and for five years served in various positions in the local of the #2 rolling section while working full time. In 1952 he was elected to a full-time union post, and he eventually served as union vice-chairman from 1964 to 1968.

Isobe saw his independent unionism as shaped by a "sense of mission" to promote unity among workers and defend them by seeking fair distribution of profits, wage increases, and reasonable staffing levels and work hours. He describes his days from 1948 to 1952 in the rolling mill as a constant round of union meetings, complaints about the workload, negotiating sessions, more meetings. He felt the only way to realize his mission was to energize the union from the bottom up, building militance by encouraging the rank-and-file union members to speak out. In the 1950s he would go a good distance toward achieving this goal.

These four men entered the union movement through differing sorts of chemistry: childhood humiliations and subsequent life on the job informed Kamimura's sense of righteous anger and will to act; a sudden political awakening informed by self-study catalyzed Nakamura; work experience and status as a skilled young shop-floor leader prompted Kudō; and youthful idealism, enthusiasm to give meaning to postwar democracy, and harsh workplace experience combined to spark Isobe. Socially far removed from the world of university-trained managers, and often resentful of them, these men were central figures in the workplace struggles of the early postwar decades. They were not quite experienced or prominent enough to serve as the earliest postwar leaders of the union movement at NKK, but they were among those attending assemblies, debating the status system, and voting to strike. They vigorously embraced unions as vehicles to improve their material lives and win social respect and equality, and to build a varied and promising new tradition of democratic practice in postwar Japan.

Recalling the Unimaginable

In a 1973 memoir of his career as a personnel manager, Orii Hyūga wrote this important retrospective view of early postwar turmoil:

> [During negotiations] large crowds of union members were present, in addition to the union and management committee representatives who sat at the bargaining table. It was a sort of mass bargaining, probably a strategy to intimidate management with the force of the crowd. But on the other hand, the union leaders at the time had not yet built sufficient authority, and the mass of union members would not necessarily accept the results of bargaining carried out [privately] by union and management representatives, so it was common practice for a mass of onlookers to join the negotiations.
>
> In such bargaining, union members would shout at the top of their voices, "Take a look at the workers' dining hall. We haven't seen a grain of rice in days. Do you think we can do heavy labor to rebuild the nation's industry drinking soup that doesn't even taste of *miso*, with maybe 4 or 5 dumplings in it? Prices are going up. Even rationed goods have doubled or tripled in price. We want a cup of rice a day! We want the money to buy it!"[26]

Orii was a university-educated personnel manager, a self-described "modern, scientific" administrator. Men like him were at the forefront of the managerial ranks at similar tumultuous bargaining sessions at hundreds of large workplaces in Japan in the late 1940s and throughout the following decade. Orii's subordinate in the labor section at NKK was Konda Masaharu, a hardheaded corporate warrior described by his wife as "the last soldier of the Imperial Japanese Army." Konda tells of sleeping on a cot in the personnel office for two weeks at the height of the NKK strike in 1959. One day the union threatened to bring 120 people to the next day's bargaining session, but finally agreed to limit the delegation to 20. Yet at daybreak, 120 union members showed up after all, and Konda's superiors had not yet arrived. "I stood and faced them, resigned to a beating. Besides August 1945, when I was stationed at Atsugi Base awaiting the American arrival, these were the tensest days of my life."[27]

In the Japanese workplace of 1949 evoked by Orii, managers and unions held deeply opposed ideologies, and they clashed in nearly equal battle. Through the 1950s, this conflict was acted out on the shop floor until finally, in the 1960s, that order of things that critics call the "corporate-centered society" established itself as hegemonic. By 1973, when Orii wrote his memoir, he felt the need to tell readers that "negotiations back then were menacing to an extent impossible to imagine today." He realized that just two decades after this turbulent era, most Japanese would view such furious confrontation in the workplace as unnatural. They would consider early postwar society part of another world and regard militant actions of employees toward employers as relics appropriate to a bygone day, if not a foolish stance in any era.

One veteran director of Nikkeiren, Japan's major business federation concerned with labor issues, neatly summed up this tremendous change in the labor movement from the 1950s through the 1970s: the mainstream of organized labor had adopted management's position.[28] Japan had become a place where the vast majority of people assumed that the good of the enterprise normally coincided with the common good of employees, of managers, of consumers, and of the public at large. The story of steel was at the heart of this postwar transformation, a change that endures and remains relevant to readers at the end of the 1990s.

It is important to recognize that this radical transformation of the Japanese workplace involved more than a simple defeat of a working class movement by capitalists. Although grassroots democracy was compromised, the specter of its return was one reason managers offered substantial benefits to some working people. In establishing hegemony, corporations absorbed important elements of the union agenda. As junior partners in the power structure of contemporary Japan, union leaders helped mobilize their members to produce efficiently, and managers who appreciated this help respected the union call for job security in particular.

Nonetheless, as the corporate-centered society came to permeate the thinking and daily lives of Japanese people, it began to limit what seemed possible, imaginable, or natural. It constricted the boundaries of legitimate democratic action from expansive political goals and activism claiming a voice in the workplace to a narrow defense of the economic interests of a shrinking unionized minority. This narrowing vision has a significance beyond the borders of Japan. It is at the center of a paradigmatic twentieth-century tale of the benefits and the costs of the triumph of capitalism.

2 *Organizing the Steelworkers*

The call to democratize the workplace was everywhere in early postwar Japan. For many workers, democracy meant winning a voice in making decisions about their jobs, whether by direct actions, such as electing supervisors, or through representation on management councils. Democracy at the same time embraced a powerful desire for equality, both among workers and between workers and managers. The twin call for voice and for equality had roots in the prewar past. It was further shaped by the occupation reforms and took on specific meaning in a context of economic crisis and the crumbling of established authority. Union programs or speeches rarely paused to define the word, but the details of organizing at places like NKK convey what democracy meant to Japanese workers as they began to build institutions of economic self-determination in a remarkable moment of hope mixed with despair.

The link between democracy and equality reached back to some of Japan's earliest labor disputes. In the 1890s workers went on strike to demand new job titles that would convey respect; they made it clear that the symbols and policies of status-based discrimination offended them deeply.[1] The prominence of postwar demands for status equality and the emotional resonance of this goal flowed from the workers' heritage of resistance to discrimination.

Also from the past came a view of the factory as the natural unit of action and a primary source of identity and community. A decision to organize labor unions in workplace units rather than by trade or locality—indeed the fact that this was hardly a conscious decision at all—was a defining characteristic of early postwar organizing. Working people elsewhere have organized unions on the basis of categories other than the workplace, such as craft, trade, or region, but Japan's industrial workers since the late nineteenth century have rarely done so. Indeed, no word for "trade union" exists in the Japanese language. One could yoke together a word for trade (such as *shokugyō*) and the word for union *(kumiai)*, but the term would confuse most people. Lacking traditions of craft or regional organizing comparable to those in Europe, Japanese union organizers before and after World War II felt it so natural to create factory unions comprised of workshop locals that they rarely considered other organizing principles.

Union founders who organized in workplace and factory units undertook a broad range of activities to enable employees to survive the desperate postwar years. They pressed employers to improve company-specific welfare benefits, and they also sought a voice in corporate governance. The drive to participate through management councils in particular had historical roots in foreign imports of prewar vintage. In the 1920s, managers at three fourths of Japan's largest heavy industrial enterprises, those employing over 500 people, had created "factory councils" or "works councils." These were made up of manager and worker representatives in equal numbers, the former always appointed, the latter sometimes elected.[2] American shop committees, the Whitley Councils in Britain, and the works councils of Weimar Germany were all noted as models by Japanese advocates, and state bureaucrats pushed managers to create these bodies as alternatives to labor unions.[3] They were to be safely controlled forums to hear the voices and address the needs of workers, and they often served this role during labor disputes from the mid-1920s.

Then, in the 1930s and during World War II, the Japanese state turned to a new model of participatory, nonunion organization of labor, that of the Nazi Law for the Organization of National Labor, which created advisory "Councils of Trust" in all German factories of twenty or more employees.[4] The institution that emerged in Japan from this endeavor of bureaucrats, managers, and social policy intellectuals was called the Industrial Patriotic Service Association. As in Germany, factory-based advisory councils of employee representatives were the basic units of the organization. Until 1940, companies were merely encouraged to set up these groups; thereafter participation was legally required. Unlike the earlier factory councils, these wartime bodies denied the division of worker versus manager; every employee, including the company president, was a member of the broader "association" from which council representatives were drawn.

The tendencies of postwar unions to demand status equality, to organize inclusively in workplace units, and to seek a voice in managerial affairs drew on all these past practices, but the past cannot fully account for the subsequent journey. Much of the postwar framework for labor-management relations was new. The American occupiers imposed a new legal system that protected unions. The Japanese authorities, seeking to rein in the tiger of labor demands for managerial authority, encouraged the formation of management councils to embrace unions rather than to exclude them as before the war.[5] And in the immediate postwar crisis, workers went far beyond their prewar efforts in the scope and the success of their demands.

Considerable labor organizing took place in the 1920s and early 1930s at factories throughout Kawasaki. At Nippon Kōkan steelworkers in the 1920s had organized a local of the Sōdōmei federation and carried out several strikes; but within several years NKK had crushed the union. By the eve of World War II, almost all unions in Kawasaki, as throughout Japan, had collapsed, and a state order dissolved the few remaining unions in 1940.

Within two months of surrender, union organizing revived in Kawasaki. Communist Party members led some of these efforts, while prewar Sōdōmei unionists led others. At NKK's Tsurumi mill, Hayashi Takeo, a Communist Party member and veteran of the student and union movements of the 1920s, played a leading role in organizing a union. At the Kawasaki plant, men in several work sites separately began to discuss forming a union, and Sōdōmei veterans were active in pulling these impulses together by January 1946.[6] Independently of each other, strikes took place at each mill in 1946. In these activities of the first two postwar years, workers began to build institutions of self-determination focused on the dual goals of participation and equality.

When organizing began in October 1945, the city of Kawasaki was physically devastated and economically depressed. Firebombing had destroyed 46 percent of the city's housing, and Kawasaki's population stood at less than half the wartime peak. It was easier for authorities to count houses than people, so precise data on unemployment is harder to come by than that on bomb damage. But in Kanagawa prefecture, dominated by the cities of Yokohama and Kawasaki, 18 percent of all factory workers had quit or been dismissed within six weeks of the surrender, and 41 percent of the prefecture's factories had stopped operating.[7] In addition, NKK's managers in 1945 and 1946 were paralyzed by uncertainty over three American steps: the purge of executives for wartime collaboration, the trust-busting plan to divide NKK into several independent companies, and the ceiling placed on

Japanese steelmaking capacity by the war reparations plan. Further, SCAP and the Japanese government controlled access to materials and capital, and even if managers had wanted to refire the blast furnaces, they needed official approval.

The work sites of Nippon Kōkan in 1945 and 1946 could hardly be called steel mills. When the first unions were formed in late 1945, the company's seventeen open hearth furnaces and five blast furnaces all stood idle. A few rolling machines processed those ingots in stock, and workers produced tertiary products such as buckets, pots, and pans.[8] Managers responded to the collapse in demand by dismissing most of the workers. Attrition and dismissals reduced the force at Tsurumi from 6,000 at the wartime peak to 2,000 by early fall 1945 and at Kawasaki from 18,000 to under 4,000. Even so, there was precious little for the remaining employees to do. As Hayashi Takeo, the first head of the Tsurumi mill union, later wrote:

> In September 1945, burnt-out enemy shells lay scattered around the Tsurumi mill. The scorched fields of the town had not been touched. The blast furnace was shut down. Work commenced with a trickle from the steel section. With the first round of dismissals, the work force was cut by two thirds. With prices going up daily, those of us left could not eat on our wages. Some of the workers would use the mill's electric furnaces to bake sweet potatoes they had bartered for in the countryside. They would sell these to supplement their pay. Others made eating utensils from the company's stock of sheet iron and sold them. People who went by the rules [and did not trade on the black market] could not live. If things continued this way the company would lose [money] as well. If we did not start up production so the workers could work and eat, the company and Japan's economy would collapse. This is why I set out to build a union.[9]

NKK's managers, like those elsewhere, sought to preempt this initiative and form a captive union. Hayashi's group got wind of this plan and quickly proclaimed itself a "Union Preparation Committee." Caught off guard, the mill director recognized Hayashi's group. With little time to spare, the organizers recruited influential veteran workers from as many different workshops as possible, even if they were foremen. The union held an inauguration ceremony on December 12, 1945, and immediately presented demands for a pay raise, recognition of the union, and control of company welfare facilities.[10]

The Tsurumi union was typical in building on workshops as the local unit of a factorywide union and in giving ranked workers, even foremen, leading positions in locals and the executive committee. These features of union building were even more pronounced at NKK's much larger Kawasaki mill (nicknamed Kawatetsu). The union creation story there brings into sharp relief central social and ideological features of the workplace: the extraordinary antagonism of production workers toward staff, and the crucial place of the factory as a source of community identity and action.

A tentative drive for a union at Kawatetsu began with blue-collar production workers. In mid-September, a worker in the battery-charging room of the transport section named Iijima Kiyoshi started talking up the idea of a union as a means to get the mill going again and so secure worker livelihoods.[11] This was several weeks before SCAP gave public blessing to union organizing, and Iijima met a cool, worried response from those he talked to. To allay these fears, he first secured a promise of noninterference from staff members in the labor section, who apparently expected SCAP to legalize unions shortly. But private assurances were not enough for the nervous Iijima. He decided he needed a public display of company approval before employees would give him a hearing, so he insisted a labor section staffer walk around with him as he promoted the union in various workshops.

With help from a few workers with prewar experience in Sōdōmei unions at NKK and other companies, Iijima gradually drew together a corps of organizers from around the mill into a Committee to Form a Union. By late October, these men were meeting each day in the battery room. Their early discussions were conducted in fearful whispers, but as reports surfaced of unions formed elsewhere, their anxiety gradually subsided.[12]

One young man drawn into the preparatory committee with little prompting was Kamimura Hideji, the tenant farmer's son who had been so outraged at his father's humiliation before their landlord. Unhappy with domineering foremen, and even angrier at the deep status divide between blue- and white-collar men, Kamimura joined the Committee to Form a Union as a representative of the transport section. This group intended to create a union for blue-collar workers only. It consisted of representatives from all the workshops in the mill, especially veteran skilled foremen. Many, like Kamimura, viewed staff as the chief exploiters of workers and argued that a union with staff in it would be worse than none at all. By mid-December, the committee was ready to hold a public meeting to announce plans to found a union.

The steel mill's staff of managers, engineers, and technicians consisted of graduates of universities and relatively prestigious vocational high schools. Until the end of the war their positions had been far more secure than lowly production workers, and their social status far higher. However, in the fall of

1945, a prestigious white-collar position at NKK no longer offered a livable wage or a secure job. According to Nakajima Hideo, the key activist on the staff side, "in September and October the company had been aggressively cutting back by firing assistant section chiefs and even section chiefs, so the emotions of the white-collar men were quite stirred up."[13]

The story of the staff's organizing drive is best told by Matsuda Takezō, principal author of the union's *Ten-Year History*.[14] Matsuda grew up in northern Japan, graduating from the Morioka Industrial High School with training as a machinist. In 1939 he entered NKK as a white-collar employee. He recalls that with this status, at the tender age of seventeen he could wear a yellow stripe on the arm of his uniform and give orders to skilled foremen three times his age. He was given the title of machine supervisor and assigned to the maintenance shop of one of the mill's blast furnaces. Nakajima Hideo was from the same town, had gone to the same school, and studied construction. He entered NKK one year after Matsuda, in the same job and position. Matsuda recalls Nakajima as a man who "really worked well with people." He was a "boss with a sense of righteousness" who looked after his employees. He came to believe that improving the lives of workers was necessary to enable economic recovery, "that one couldn't just go to work and follow company orders as in the past, but that workers themselves had to join together to act, somehow." The Kanagawa headquarters of the recently revived Sōdōmei federation was located just outside NKK's main gate, and Nakajima developed close ties with the federation's leaders.

Nakajima took his first public step late in the fall. With permission from the labor section, he made a plea over the company's PA system for white-collar staffers to form a union. The gist of his broadcast was that "workers at companies all around the area are forming unions. We should form a union, join all our strength to break out of this uncertain situation."[15] A group of staff members formed around Nakajima, identified in the union history by their work site: "Uno of transport, Kawagoshi of machine shop."

Like the blue-collar men, Nakajima's group by mid-December had formed a "preparatory committee," and Matsuda Takezō was sufficiently committed to become a member. As with so many postwar activists, he began with no knowledge and learned about unions on the job. A handful of men with an intellectual bent served as mentors to these inexperienced activists. At Kawatetsu, a largely self-taught blue-collar worker named Takeda Ryūsuke played such a role and articulated the Kawasaki mill version of a cooperative union ideology.

The white-collar activists considered forming their own separate union, but decided they could be more effective by joining with the blue-collar men to create a single union. On December 25, they approached the latter group to discuss this possibility. Iijima was sympathetic, for he saw the union as a vehicle to promote the recovery of the mill, and he envisioned a common organization of production workers and staff. But he faced an uphill battle; as the union's *Ten-Year History* put it: "At Kawatetsu up until then, the status discrimination of staff and worker was awful. Staff wore yellow stripes on their arms as signs of their supervisory status, and workers were not even allowed to wear the NKK mark on their uniforms. Dining halls were separate. Even utensils were different. The position of worker *(kōin)* was humiliating. They hated the staff."[16]

Indeed, Iijima's blue-collar group had already convened a meeting open to all comers in mid-December to test their support, but fewer than thirty people had attended, and a few workers complained that "we can't talk freely with workers and staff together." In deference to such sentiment, on December 23 the preparatory committee held a meeting limited to blue-collar workers. It was a huge, lively affair in a packed room. Iijima spoke on behalf of unity, but the overwhelming sentiment of the meeting was for a union of workers only.[17]

When the staff group two days later proposed a union embracing white- and blue-collar employees, a tense round of negotiations began. A group of three staffers and four workers held the first session. One sign of the social distance between worker and staff is that Nakajima had never before met the four worker leaders. He describes his anxious first impression of "the huge Nikaido and fierce Arai, the latter standing guard at the entrance to the conference room, shouting at others to 'keep out!!'"[18] The meeting produced no decision.

Despite their own reservations and in the face of the strong opposition expressed by those at the December 23 meeting, Takeda Ryūsuke and Iijima nonetheless supported the joint plan. Takeda expressed animosity toward the staff, but he felt a need to work together to overcome it. Iijima felt that staff brains and worker brawn would be a powerful combination. Those blue-collar leaders who opposed a unified body countered that with 75 percent of employees being production workers, they could form a union on their own. They felt tremendous animosity toward staff over "status discrimination" and ruled out common action. They believed that letting in staff would allow the company to capture the union.

On the other side, Nakajima and his white-collar allies strongly believed that a union was necessary to ensure both personal and company survival.

As one engineer noted: "We were like a deflated balloon in those [immediate postwar] days. But at the same time, we were all chafing to take action by our own hands to somehow open a path toward survival. I think we expressed this in the form of the union movement."[19] Nakajima argued that the section chiefs were as desperate economically as their subordinates. Despite their relatively high status, the white-collar men suspected the motives of top management and feared the company would form a captive union if they failed to act. They wanted employees up to the level of section chief *(kachō)* to be union members.

After several days of intense debate, the blue-collar leaders overrode strong opposition and accepted a joint union on the condition that it make "unity of worker and staff statuses" and abolition of status discrimination top priorities.[20] The staff leaders accepted this condition. The blue-collar side particularly wanted to remove the ceiling that made foreman *(kumichō)* the highest supervisory position to which a man hired as a "worker" could aspire.

Unresolved tensions carried over into the new year in a rancorous dispute about the ratio of staff to workers among delegates to the union assembly. Should there be separate balloting for worker and staff delegates to ensure each group's representation, or a single election for all? The union organizing committee eventually decided to hold a single election, with delegates chosen in a ratio of one for each twenty employees regardless of status. On January 15, 1946, a section chief and union official, Aoki Fujio, presided over a grand founding ceremony in the workers' dining hall attended by 1,500 union members.[21] Eight of the twelve members of the union's first executive committee were white-collar staff, and even Iijima was annoyed at this unbalance.[22]

Almost all the members of this new union's blue-collar preparatory committee had ranked positions: foremen, sub-foremen, crew bosses. Although they had little formal management power, these men held much informal, day-to-day authority concerning work assignments and discipline, and they advised staff on the performance of subordinates and promotions or pay raises. At the same time, most of these men had in common with unranked workers a rural upbringing and limited elementary education. They had typically spent ten to fifteen years as unranked workers before promotion. Their humble origins combined with seniority and skill to give them legitimacy among their subordinates as both fellow workers and leaders. This allowed the ranked men to mobilize collective action on the basis of a shared worker consciousness.

Although these workplace bosses deeply resented the privileges of white-collar staff, their supervisory role also gave them an ambiguous attitude toward their superiors. In the face of intensive and evidently sincere appeals by the white-collar group, they accepted the proposal for a joint union of white and blue collar, so long as the union committed itself to seeking a less discriminatory workplace. They debated at length the divisive issue of admitting white-collar staff to the union, but they ultimately sought to build an inclusive organization.[23] Rather than organize a union that would crystallize a division between positions of worker and manager, they wanted the union to erase this division.

In this orientation, they inherited the spirit of prewar workers who had used unions to demand respectful job titles and treatment on a par with white-collar staff. The ranked men's focus on building an inclusive, egalitarian workplace also reflected a belief particular to the postwar crisis that working people at all levels had to join hands to rebuild the company on behalf of personal and national survival.

The two mill unions at NKK built on the enthusiasm of these founding drives and quickly took action. Demoralized managers resisted union demands by calling for sacrifice in the name of the nation and country, but unions were not persuaded. They won unprecedented power and gave practical meaning to slogans of "democratization" and "equality."

Two days after its founding, on December 26, 1945, the Tsurumi union presented five demands to the company and negotiations began immediately. Managers quickly accepted the demands for the rights to bargain collectively and to strike, but they resisted demands for a wage increase, a promise of no dismissals, and union control of welfare facilities. At one negotiating session, a vice-president told the union negotiators that although their wage demand was reasonable, the company simply lacked the money to pay. Challenged as to "how are we then to survive?" he imprudently suggested that the workers supplement their pay by trading on the black market. Negotiations broke off in an uproar. Representatives of each of the mill's work sites were waiting at union headquarters, and they immediately voted to launch a production takeover.[24]

For over two weeks the union ran the mill in a well-ordered action.[25] The union paid wages in accord with company standards and concluded contracts to sell sheet metal and tin for houses for bombing victims. (It obtained the informal consent of supervisors for such major decisions.) It implemented an eight-hour day and raised both output and attendance by about 5 percent.[26] But order broke down at the tumultuous end of the strike on January 26. Over 1,600 workers surrounded NKK headquarters in Tokyo, and union leaders literally forced the executives present to accede to all their demands. Among other indignities, a worker hit Kawada Jun, the head of the labor section, in the face with a wooden pole. As NKK's president in later years, Kawada would take his revenge.

In this dispute, the union successfully drew some men of managerial rank to its side. A group of assistant section managers became the "production committee" that took charge of plant operations during the takeover. The union allowed the mill director to move about freely, but did not allow him to issue any orders. It allowed middle managers (section chiefs) to enter and leave the plant's main office, but restricted their access to the production site. At first the section chiefs remained neutral and kept a low profile, and some activists proposed bringing even them into the union. This plan was dropped when some section chiefs began to actively oppose the production takeover.[27]

During this action, the union's blue-collar members were particularly enraged at ongoing symbols of status discrimination. One worker recalled his anger at the contrast between his own ragged military clothes and the suits worn by executives, and at the discovery that the corporate headquarters' dining hall served such luxuries as rice curry. And when the elegantly attired, Harvard-educated president, Asano Ryōzō, addressed the workers massed outside the head office after giving in to their demands, somebody shouted, "Take off your hat!" Asano complied.[28]

Heady with their triumph in this dispute, the Tsurumi union followed up by demanding that workers be allowed to take "votes of confidence or no confidence" in their section managers *(kachō)*. Those failing the vote were to be removed from their posts. While negotiations on the demand were still under way, the union conducted its own poll. Several managers received votes of no confidence. Although the company refused to remove these men, the union pressure was sufficient to force the offending supervisors to apologize to their subordinates. The union called this the "shell purge," after what some activists described as an ancient Greek practice in which the populace purged dictatorial leaders by writing their names on shells.[29]

In these early moments of conflict, workers challenged hierarchies of social status and class. They briefly realized a mode of participation that radically challenged the existing capitalist order. They were making factory-based unions into democratic institutions responsible for self-help as well as economic reconstruction.

Such efforts accelerated in the second half of 1946 with a focus on the economics of daily life, as a national food crisis reached its peak. Deliveries of rationed food to the cities were chronically late. Workers took unauthorized leaves to barter for food in the countryside. The Kawatetsu and Tsurumi unions, like others throughout the city, each set up a Committee to Overcome the Food Crisis. In cooperation with the company's welfare section, it entered the risky business of black marketeering. It first secured permission from the mill director to manufacture salt on the premises. Workers formed teams to raise sea water and boil it down in the mill's gigantic kettles. The union then devised an incentive system in which employees received salt rations in proportion to team output, which they traded for food on the black market.[30]

The committee also negotiated with the company for paid "food supply" holidays, which workers used to travel to the countryside and barter for food. Cooperation between company and union was no doubt facilitated by the fact that an assistant chief in the personnel section was also head of that section's union local. He arranged for the planting of crops on unused company land and distributed coal and other company supplies to union locals, to be given to workers as bartering material.[31] The head of the Kawatetsu committee contacted nearby farmers' cooperatives along the Tama river in 1946 and arranged for the union to exchange pumping equipment for food. He remembered shedding tears of gratitude when these co-ops donated cartloads of potatoes during the strike later that year. The union president recalled that local gossips called Kawatetsu "not a steel mill but the Kawasaki Salt Mine."[32]

All the major steel mills in Japan produced salt in 1946 and 1947, and the economics of bartering were complex. At Tsurumi, except for two shops that made buckets, pots, and pans, the entire workforce was engaged in salt-making in mid-1946. Some of the product was given to the electric company to pay for power, some was sold to the Japan Salt Monopoly (in theory *all* salt was to be sold through this monopoly), and the rest was distributed to the workers. The union even paid visiting lecturers with packages of salt![33]

In addition to a food crisis committee, the Tsurumi union set up its own welfare section. This body supervised the gathering of shellfish and seaweed from the bay. It negotiated salt-for-sweet-potato "exchange rates" with farmers, begged Kanagawa authorities for permission to import food from another prefecture, and (illegally) traded metal barrels for rice with a village agricultural cooperative in Niigata. In this last instance, a rival agricultural association leaked information on the deal to the press. Headlines screamed of "NKK Black Marketeering," and a union member was jailed briefly for violating the economic control laws.[34]

These episodes marked the nation's general regression from a money toward a barter economy in the immediate postwar crisis. Links between farmers and workers sometimes developed in the radical direction of union-controlled circuits of production and exchange, as in a case involving workers at a chemical plant in Niigata; another in Tokyo; farmer associations in Niigata, Tohoku, and Hokkaidō; and coal miners.[35] In Kawasaki, the labor-farmer connections were at that point limited to serving the cause of survival, with occasional gestures of solidarity; but the union's role in setting up bartering networks was nonetheless unprecedented.

NKK employees also treated the mill as their community when the union pressed the company for a "ceremony fund" to provide marriage, birth, and funeral allowances. In August 1947 the Kawasaki mill union's Women and Young Men's Division drew up a proposal for a "marriage allowance." The NKK union federation, at this stage a loose alliance of the company's several mill-based unions, then began negotiating in earnest for a more comprehensive companywide schedule of marriage, childbirth, and funeral allowances, as well as paid leave on such occasions. A first agreement was reached in November 1947 and renegotiated the following summer. In this agreement the union also successfully expanded the group of eligible workers to those with at least one year, instead of two years, of employment.[36]

Clearly, union members in 1945 and 1946 were conferring a broad mandate on their organizations. They expected them to do more than bargain over the exchange of labor for money. As blue-collar men vented their fury at the arrogance and privileged status of white-collar staff and sought to remake the workplace hierarchy, and as young workers demanded marriage and other allowances, they were using unions to negotiate the terms of membership in a community.

The strike at the NKK Kawasaki mill in October 1946 shows how this broad union mandate could be a source of strength even for a relatively moderate union. The Kawasaki union's platform, adopted in January 1946, proclaimed the "principle of the mutual prosperity of labor and capital" to be the guiding spirit of the contract the union hoped to conclude. It then spoke of "raising our skill, increasing our efficiency" so as to "dramatically increase steel production, the motor of national reconstruction." It went on to echo a rhetoric reaching back to some of Japan's earliest prewar unionizing efforts. "We hope to build a healthy workers' culture, by raising our social status and forging our character in a spirit of freedom, equality, [and] fraternal love, and by enlightening ourself and perfecting our skills."[37]

The first wage demands put forward by this group reflected this moderation. On February 8, 1946, the Kawasaki union presented and won a demand for a 200 percent average pay raise just two weeks after the Tsurumi mill union's production control tactic had achieved a *300 percent* wage hike. The Kawasaki union reportedly accepted the company's contention that the Tsurumi settlement had been so costly that NKK could afford no more than this for Kawasaki mill workers. In negotiating sessions, union representatives spoke of "our burning love of company, which is the true reason for presenting these demands for improved pay to protect our livelihoods" and claimed, in a neat reversal of paternal rhetoric where the company was usually the loving father, "we love the company as we love our wives and our children. Please [grant this raise] so we can revive Japan from this tragic condition."[38] Not surprisingly, Tsurumi and other unions denounced NKK-Kawasaki as a co-opted "company union."[39]

Given this reputation, the Kawasaki union's successful week-long strike in October drew national attention and surprise. The willingness of the Kawasaki workers to risk this strike clarifies their proclamations of loyalty and love for the company as partly instrumental, conditional statements, rhetorical strategies to elicit material support and win social respect. At issue in the strike was not wages but the terms of the union contract with NKK. Workers across the ideological spectrum were seeking at least an equal voice with management in planning for economic recovery.

The company had objected adamantly to demands for a closed shop and a union veto over any decisions to fire, hire, transfer, reward, or punish workers. Company negotiators argued that to sign such a contract would surrender their fundamental "personnel authority." They promised instead to "consult" on such decisions and take disputed cases to an in-house management council composed of company and union representatives.[40] A final company offer then conceded a union veto on transfer and firing decisions, except for section chiefs, but the union refused this exception because section chiefs were also union members.[41]

The strike began on October 4. The two sides immediately quarreled over responsibility for protecting the furnaces and blame for impeding recovery. The company blasted the union for betraying recovery by shutting down the coke furnace after all the effort to start it. (With government inspectors standing by this designated "state industrial facility," the strikers had managed to shut the furnace down without damage.) The key sticking point remained the position of section chiefs. Union negotiators claimed that since the union stood for "mutual prosperity of company and union," there was nothing to fear in having section chiefs covered by the contract. The company insisted it had given away too much already. On October 9 a mediator from the government's newly created Regional Labor Mediation Committee proposed that disagreements on closed shop issues be brought to an outside "labor committee" and that the company accept a union veto over dismissals and transfers but not in hiring, rewards, or punishments. Both sides agreed to the first proposal, but the union held out for its original demand on the second point. Sometime past midnight, the company agreed that the union would have a veto on general policy concerning even hiring, rewards, and punishments, but no veto over individual decisions. The union accepted this.[42]

Justifiably enough, the Kawasaki mill union leaders presented this settlement to its members as a great victory. The union assembly happily ratified the agreement and ended the one-week strike. The union's *Ten-Year History* boasts of the members' pride in having repudiated the label of "yellow union." One worker in the research section grandly proclaimed that "harmony without struggle is the road to death. Harmony backed by struggle is the great ideal."[43] The statement exemplified the Sōdōmei brand of cooperation backed by strength and a willingness to strike. It neatly represented the militant tone that lay under the surface of cooperative unionism in this era.

The extraordinary surge of organizing and strikes reached a nationwide peak in early 1947, with the drive for a national general strike. The American decision to forbid this action, and concurrent U.S. moves to scale back the scope of war reparations and allow managers to organize their own national federations, put organized labor on the defensive for the first time since the surrender. Even so, workers continued to make vigorous use of unions in calling for equality among employees and a voice in decision-making.

At the Kawasaki mill, eliminating status discrimination had been a condition for founding a joint union of white- and blue-collar workers. As soon as the inauguration ceremony of January 1946 had finished, the head of the union's planning division (a white-collar employee) began work on a proposal to reform the status system. The union history notes that the issue's "complexity" slowed his progress.[44] We can read "complexity" to mean both disagreement between union and company as well as sharp disagreement between white- and blue-collar people within the union over what equality or "abolition of the status system" meant in practice.[45]

The heart of the matter was the structure as much as the level of pay. As before and during the war, the manner of calculating wages for worker and staff differed fundamentally. The former received a combination of a basic daily wage, an output premium, and a few allowances, the latter a monthly base salary plus a more generous array of allowances, one linked to output. The difference was magnified by calculating bonuses and retirement pay as unequal multiples of the base wage. A staffer's bonus would be several months of extra salary, while a worker's would be two or three weeks' wages. Both staffers in supervisory positions, such as section manager, and supervisory workers, such as foreman or crew boss, received "rank allowances," but the staff allowances were far higher.

Some in the union favored integration. They wanted to abolish the separate categories and place everybody in a single new category, such as "employee," with a uniform wage structure. Others wanted separate but equal status, making both the structure and the level of wages the same for blue- and white-collar employees. The dynamics of decision-making within the union and negotiating between union and company on this issue are murky, but it appears that some combination of company resistance to abolishing status distinctions and continued antagonism between workers and staff within the union kept negotiations focused on the separate-but-equal course.

Shortly after the Kawasaki mill strike, in November 1946, the nine factory- and shipyard-based unions at NKK's far-flung operations joined together to form an NKK Labor Union Federation whose objective was to bargain with the company on issues of common interest.[46] In April 1947, this federation raised the status issue in the context of that spring's wage negotiations by demanding an end to the status system in addition to an increase in the average worker's monthly income from 1,500 to 2,700 yen. Specifically, the federation demanded the company eliminate the categories of staff *(shokuin)* and worker *(kōin)*, create a unified wage structure, and adopt a monthly salary system.[47]

Despite the status-related demands, the major issue that spring was clearly the pay raise. The company for several weeks would not budge from an initial offer of a 2,000-yen average monthly wage. The union threatened a strike and won a 2,300-yen average by the end of May, but the status issue was not resolved. The union accepted continued separate wage structures for staff and worker.[48]

In these years of intense inflation, most unions negotiated basic wage levels at least twice a year. At NKK the fall 1947 talks began in late October, just four months after the spring round ended. Once more, the Kawasaki mill's union demanded both a pay raise and a "unified wage structure" that would eliminate separate worker and staff status. But this time the dispute played out differently; younger, more radical workers, including several Communist Party members, were joining union activities and calling for greater attention to rank-and-file sentiment. Probably hoping both to use and to control this new energy, the union chairman took the unusual step of forming an ad hoc "struggle committee" of fifteen workplace representatives to lead negotiations, and those elected included six Communist Party members. The committee organized a vigorous drive from below in support of the demands. Seeking to bring union leaders closer to the rank and file, the Kawasaki union was acting independently of the relatively weak new companywide federation. The Kawasaki struggle committee successfully demanded that the negotiations be held at the mill, not at NKK's corporate headquarters. The mill's electrical workers rigged up microphones to broadcast the negotiating sessions to workers outside the meeting room.[49]

Despite this grassroots pressure, the Kawasaki union ended up accepting an offer it had rejected two weeks earlier as grossly inadequate. The young members of the struggle committee were furious with the cautious senior leaders of the union. Although the wage level had been set, negotiations continued over the status issues. A companywide settlement was finally reached the following March 1948. The union federation and NKK agreed that the pay of all employees, *shokuin* or *kōin,* would be composed of the same array of allowances and premiums. The largest single component, the "base wage," would now be paid to all employees as a monthly wage. At the same time, the workforce would continue to be divided into categories of "worker" and "staff," and the amounts of some of the pay components would reflect this difference.[50] The shift in structure to a monthly salary for all was a major change in the direction of status equality in the workplace, one being made in similar fashion in companies nationwide. At NKK, this system stayed in place for almost twenty years.

The status issue remained controversial among the employees even after this settlement. In the summer of 1948, several blue-collar workers petitioned the union's executive committee to push the company to re-designate them as white-collar staff due to their high levels of education.[51] The issue of this upgrade came to a head at a tumultuous July 1948 union assembly. Members angrily denounced the executive committee. Opponents shouted, "Have you forgotten our founding slogan?" They argued vociferously that an upgrade would betray the more basic goal of eliminating the status system and discrimination.

The matter came to a vote at a union assembly in mid-August. A bare majority of 164 to 152 voted in favor of requesting the upgrade, and the company agreed to it. While the union's *Ten-Year History* claims this decision "closed the book" on the status issue, the angry debate and close vote make it clear that differential status designations remained attractive to those in staff positions and repugnant to blue-collar workers.[52]

While they brought greater equality to the workplace, unions continued to pursue the goal of sharing in the management of the economy and the enterprise. Recovery councils at the national level and management councils at the company level were the forums in which this action took place. As early as the spring of 1946, Sōdōmei had called for a Movement for Industrial Recovery to Overcome the Production Crisis, in which unions would participate in corporate and national economic planning for the purpose of "democratizing industry" and realizing a "planned economy." Over the next six months, Sōdōmei and the new business federation of Japan's young, so-called reform capitalists (the Keizai Dōyūkai) hammered out agreement on plans for an Economic Recovery Council. For Sōdōmei, the Council was a step toward union participation in economic planning. For the Keizai Dōyūkai, it was a means to build a "reformed capitalism": a high-productivity, high-wage economy that could afford to avoid strikes by nurturing cooperative labor-management relations.[53]

To the left of Sōdōmei, the Sanbetsu federation warily observed these negotiations. Sanbetsu's vision of recovery was far more radical: workers would participate in a recovery controlled by laborers, scientists, and technicians. With considerable misgivings, Sanbetsu made a temporary strategic peace with the capitalists. It joined the Council as a means to strengthen labor unions and build toward ultimate victory in a class struggle. This goal was utterly at odds with the cooperative program of Sōdōmei, not to mention Keizai Dōyūkai.[54]

Thus, three strange bedfellows come together on February 6, 1947, to found the Economic Recovery Council. At the apex of a complex structure stood a national council with a central committee of delegates from member organizations, an executive committee, and various specialized planning and policy committees, carefully balanced between union and industry representatives. Below this stood about two dozen prefectural and industrial recovery councils. In theory at least, company-based management councils, composed of union and management representatives, were to be the basic building blocks of the edifice or, to switch metaphors, a motor pushing recovery ahead. The organizational pyramid was remarkably similar to that of the wartime Industrial Patriotic Service Association, with the important exception that almost no bureaucrats sat on the national or local committees. The Council sought to influence state policy via discussions with government ministers and vice-ministers and presentation of formal policy proposals. Yet it achieved relatively little by the time of its dissolution in April 1948.[55] The recovery movement is important primarily as a sign of the immediate postwar aspiration of national union leaders for a voice in economic policy-making.

Important signs of similar aspirations at the local level, which left a greater legacy, were the ubiquitous company- and factory-based management councils. Almost all labor contracts negotiated in the early postwar years, including those concluded by NKK's Sōdōmei and Tsurumi mill unions, provided for such councils.[56] Typically, they were composed of equal numbers of worker and company representatives, the former chosen by the union, and the body would be authorized to discuss labor management, wages, production, company finances, and long-range business planning. In most cases, the council's approval was required for all matters brought before it. This gave unions huge formal power.

A noteworthy attempt to use such a council took place at Tsurumi in 1948, when year-end bonus negotiations foundered and the Tsurumi union announced it would find the money itself. It began to investigate company-supplier relations to expose unnecessary entertainment expenses, and ordered workplace locals to survey material use to expose waste and hidden goods. As the investigation proceeded past the new year and into February, managers apparently panicked and agreed to pay a bonus.[57]

Building on this momentum, the union announced a Draft for a Movement to Revive Production. Its goals were to revive production "by and for workers," protect jobs in the process of recovery, and ensure a "fair" division of profits among labor, management, and capital while strengthening discipline at work. To this end, the union proposed to undertake three types of activity: (1) business decisions on product mix, production volume, marketing, purchasing, and quality; (2) labor management initiatives to raise morale and increase efficiency (improved discipline, awards for efficient use of materials); and (3) "rationalized" operations and improved work conditions (wages), which would remove "obstacles to production." Through this movement the union sought to dominate the management council by setting up its own shadow cabinet composed of a production council, a management council, a labor management sub-council, and workplace councils.[58]

The core concept of this movement was that the union should act to raise, even "rationalize," production and fairly distribute the fruits to labor, management, and capital. The term "rationalization" in this context meant increasing the productivity of labor through new technology or more efficient use of existing machines. In the 1950s, managers would be the champions of this term, and many unions would condemn it as a code word for exploitation by speeding up the work pace. But for union leaders in the late 1940s who had faith in their ability to control corporate planning, rationalization was welcome. Although union members ultimately lacked the time and access to information to make this shadow cabinet work, the attempt reveals how determined the union was to join managerial decision-making.[59]

At Kawasaki, the union's claim to a voice in plans for recovery was less ambitious, but nonetheless significant. The focus of Kawatetsu's Economic Recovery Movement was the brand-new, undamaged number 5 blast furnace, completed in 1944 but never fired due to the scarcity of raw materials at the end of the war. In February 1947, union locals in four workshops petitioned the union executive committee to push to fire the furnace. They argued that the furnace was in perfect condition, and that they needed only the go-ahead from authorities to start it up.

In the ensuing weeks, the union convened rallies to build public support, and for about a year it worked with NKK management and the Kawasaki city council to lobby the ministries of Commerce and Labor, the Economic Stabilization Board, and other authorities. In the drive to restart the Kawasaki furnace, the union invoked a rhetoric not only of cooperation but willingness to sacrifice for the sake of recovery.[60] Some on the left cautioned that such attitudes would play into management hands and constrain demands for better conditions. But at a time when NKK's union leaders could realistically imagine they might hold the upper hand in reviving the firm and the industry, or at least have a voice equal to that of management, such cautions apparently were not convincing. Permission was finally granted in early 1948, and 700 guests from the Japanese government, SCAP, and the local community attended a grand firing ceremony on April 1.[61]

A speech by blue-collar activist Takeda Ryūsuke on the eve of the drive to restart the blast furnace conveys the spirit that moved the Kawasaki union:

> Industrial recovery and increased production are the only ways to save the Japanese race from destruction. We are proud that steel is Japan's star industry and NKK is a champion of steel. We have already created a man-

agement council and made it into a decision-making, not advisory, body. *We are not merely hired hands as in the past. With an awareness of ourselves as participants in management, we are determined to bring about recovery by the hands of the workers themselves.*[62]

Once liberated and encouraged to organize, Japanese working people drew on past experience to act in unprecedented ways. At NKK, after the two famous strikes of 1946, no work stoppages longer than twenty-four hours took place until the mid-1950s, but on several occasions credible threats drew in SCAP and Japanese mediators and forced the company to make concessions. The union remained militant. The left was gaining support among younger workers, even at the Sōdōmei stronghold of the Kawasaki mill. Within the union, many of the senior union leaders, veteran foremen, and staff supervisors were gripped by a fearful sense that they were losing control.

The extent and the ambition of this labor offensive has few parallels in world history. Within sixteen months of surrender, 40 percent of industrial workers in Japan had joined unions. In contrast to the prewar era, where managers set up factory councils to ward off unions, after the war organized workers demanded the creation of management councils, and their demands predated state promotion of such councils.[63] In addition, no prewar unions had included blue-collar laborers and white-collar staff in a single body, the way so many postwar unions did.

One finds a new *totality* in the postwar labor offensive. This can be seen in the membership of the unions (staff and worker), in the bodies employees created (management councils as well as unions), and in their ideals of status equality and participation. Many activists, even technical staff never before part of the labor movement, saw management and technology not as enemies of the working class, but as tools by which Japanese people, using new institutions, could build a new nation whose bywords would be democracy, peace, science, and culture.[64] Although rooted in previous experience, the totality of the aspirations of activists in the workplace was new, a product of an unprecedented war and its awful aftermath.

The crises of war and reconstruction engendered concerns with issues of production and planning that one would expect to find in workers in the other defeated powers, Germany and Italy. To some extent, one does. Even in the last years and months of war, as well as in the wake of defeat, workers in both these nations energetically set out to organize or revive labor unions. People in both countries set forth ambitious programs of participation and democratization through their unions. In contrast, the labor-management accords already in place in Britain and the United States were not as profoundly shaken.

But a shared experience of war and traumatic defeat offers only a partial explanation for these nations' postwar history. Events in Japan were shaped by prewar anger over status differences, diverse prewar practices of organizing unions and factory councils, and wartime programs of labor control. They unfolded through a postwar conjuncture of economic and political crisis, reforms imposed from above and without, and widespread enthusiasm for national and individual rebirth. Radical and militant unionists shared something important with loyal company men, and certainly with the many who saw themselves as both militant and loyal: they hardly ever viewed the workplace as just a place to earn a wage in the detached manner of many of their Anglo-American counterparts. They rather saw it as a site for the creation of enduring community and meaning in daily life.[65] Workplaces and companies became sites where employees sought respect and social identity as well as higher wages. They began to make their unions into institutions that would enforce equality and allow both participation in management and a voice at work.

3 Restoring Managerial and State Authority

In the late 1940s, managers at Nippon Kōkan faced a hostile world, and their siege mentality was in no sense paranoid. The company confronted a two-front assault on its integrity as an enterprise. The enemies within were unionists intent on seizing managerial authority. The foes without were Americans determined to purge executives and break up the corporation.

The union offensive was real and powerful. It sought equality in the workplace and demanded a voice in management decisions. In theory, the logic of this union challenge offered an opening to managers sharp enough to see it. NKK's workers connected their personal fate with the survival of the company, and a rhetoric of common interest of managers and workers occasionally surfaced even at moments of harsh conflict.[1] Managers were tempted by the workplace-centered goals of the unions to argue that a free hand to pursue corporate goals could best serve the entire community of employees.[2] But in the early postwar era, this appeal was unconvincing. The attitude of members of independent-minded and militant factory-based unions ranged from suspicious to scornful of executives who pushed to regain unimpeded authority over personnel decisions or long-range planning.

At the same time, a three-pronged American attack threatened to break up the company into its constituent parts, purge its leaders, and confiscate its plants as war reparations. The American government's Initial Post-Surrender Plan for Japan of September 1945 called for the dissolution of "excessive" concentrations of industry and finance. The Asano zaibatsu, with intimate personal and financial ties to NKK, received a dissolution order immediately. Trading of Nippon Kōkan stock was frozen in December. In February 1948 NKK itself was designated for dissolution.

41

In addition, SCAP purged over 20,000 Japanese "militarists and ultra-nationalists" from public positions in 1946 and 1947. While 80 percent of the targets were military men, the purge also included top leaders of businesses judged to have played critical roles in the war effort. In April 1946 NKK tried to preempt the purge of its leaders by replacing a vice-president and the wartime president, Asano Ryūzō. This step had little effect. In May 1947, Asano's replacement (Watanabe Masato) and six other executives were purged by SCAP. Although NKK was the only top steelmaker whose equipment was not targeted for war reparations, until 1948 the fear that the company might be added to the list heightened managers' uncertainty. In addition, the overall ceiling on Japanese steelmaking capacity imposed by the reparations program inhibited recovery plans.[3]

SCAP tightly constrained NKK's strategy for three years. The company replaced purged president Watanabe with Kawada Jun, manager of the labor division, who had been the point man in the riotous negotiations with the union in 1946. NKK went along with the trust-busting program by drawing up plans to reorganize.

Then, from 1947 to 1948, the famous "reverse course" in U.S. policy intervened. The Americans had decided the emerging Cold War made revival of a junior industrial partner in Asia their top priority, and they now viewed democratization measures such as trust busting as obstacles to this goal. In November 1948, as the Americans sharply scaled back both zaibatsu dissolution and the reparations program, they revoked NKK's designation as an "excessively concentrated" enterprise. NKK executives were liberated from extensive American control and were relatively free to draw up their own blueprint for revival. They happily abandoned plans for deconcentration. They envisioned NKK as a unified enterprise drawing strength from the interdependence of steelmaking and shipbuilding. By 1949 both SCAP and the Japanese government approved plans to keep the firm together and reorganize financially by writing off losses, reevaluating assets, and recapitalizing the company at 1 billion yen.[4]

Taking back control of the workplace and the corporation from organized workers proved a far more difficult and lengthy struggle than winning independence from SCAP. With little choice but to accept some union presence, corporate leaders attacked not unions as such, but "excessive" union demands. But NKK managers gave away far more than they wished to, both in granting personnel authority to the Kawasaki union and in agreeing to management councils with substantial powers at both mills. Just as unionists differed over how to use their new power, and to what ends, NKK managers seeking to regain the upper hand differed on strategy and basic objectives.

Takemura Tatsuo was a leading hard-liner, believing in suppressing the union to the greatest extent possible. He was born in 1902, the son of a middling landowner on the southern island of Kyūshū.[5] He moved to live with relatives in Fukuoka, Kyūshū's largest city, to attend middle school, and his father sold timber from family land to finance his education at Kyūshū Imperial University in the mid-1920s. Upon graduation, Takemura entered the general affairs section of Asano Shipyard in 1928 and became an NKK employee in 1940 when the latter absorbed the Asano yard and steel mill in Tsurumi. During the war he was shifted to a position in personnel. He served as assistant manager, then manager, of NKK's labor division in the occupation era, before being promoted to a director's post in the 1950s.

Takemura attended the Kyūshū Imperial University at a time of intellectual ferment. His university experience decisively shaped his later thinking. He recalls that "Marxism was very popular then, and there were lots of Reds on the faculty . . . but even though everyone is attracted to communism in their youth, to ideals of justice and right, I couldn't sympathize with the Reds. . . . I don't know why. It must have been my personality. I didn't think it could work." In 1992 Takemura was a remarkable ninety-year-old who still came to the company daily for several hours, using his corner "senior consultant" office at the Kawasaki mill's main building, a rare prize for decades of service. He wore his NKK work jacket over a shirt and tie. His voice was vigorous, his posture erect, and his testimony equally forceful: this man had no use for unions in the 1940s and 1950s. He and his superior in the labor division, Kawada Jun, "were terribly afraid when the union was created in 1946. We had no idea what the Americans would do. The Japanese government was helpless. The Communists were strong in the union and getting stronger. There were numerous strikes and no food. We had nothing to give, but the union was demanding. Management had to deal with this on its own, defend itself, take responsibility."

Their first efforts at self-defense were not promising. They tried but failed to preempt formation of independent unions at Tsurumi and Kawasaki by encouraging hand-picked loyalists to form company unions. Kawada and Takemura also tried and failed to take a hard line in the production control dispute. Kawada suffered a blow to the head and a bloody nose, SCAP repudiated President Asano's direct appeal to the Yoshida government to outlaw this tactic, and the union triumphed.[6]

Eventually their reactionary strategy gave way to a more sophisticated approach. By the 1960s Takemura had come to believe there *were* such things as good unions. But in the late 1940s, he felt there could be no responsible unions. "I met with a U.S. labor official [during the occupation], and he advised me to study and learn from the American labor movement. But the premise of the American union situation was that there was enough to eat, enough to go around. In Japan's crisis of scarcity, this wouldn't work. How could we have a union movement in such a time?" Takemura Tatsuo in the late 1940s was typical of managers who believed that paternalistic traditions remained a viable basis upon which to rebuild the industrial economy and defined cooperation to mean "sacrifice as usual" by workers.[7]

NKK's union policy and overall program to manage labor evolved through the occasionally tense interaction of such old-guard managers with a new breed of modern labor specialists. Their champion was Orii Hyūga. He was born in 1908 in Yamanashi Prefecture. In 1932 he graduated from the citadel of elite education in prewar Japan, the Law Faculty at Tokyo Imperial University, and began to work at NKK. In his education, Orii, like Takemura, was exposed to Marxist and liberal ideas, but he engaged them at a deeper level in theory and practice. Drafted to serve in the military, Orii was briefly a prisoner of the Soviet Union after the war. There he edited a newspaper for his fellow inmates, supervised by his captors, which introduced Soviet life and ideas. Upon repatriation, he returned to the personnel division at the Kawasaki mill. He advanced to section chief in 1949 and then rotated through increasingly responsible labor management positions at the Kawasaki and Tsurumi mills and at corporate headquarters in the 1950s and 1960s.[8]

Early in his postwar career, Orii developed a comprehensive, historically framed understanding of his goals and methods. Japan, he insisted, must overcome its feudal past, including its practice of labor management, by adopting the enlightened human relations techniques of American industrial sociologists. Writing in a 1954 publication of Japan's new postwar business federation, Nikkeiren, whose primary concern was labor policy, Orii offered this succinct appraisal of his place (and that of Takemura) in the history of labor management in his country:

> Long ago there was an era of so-called authoritarianism, when we constrained workers with penalties and regulations, and motivated them to raise productivity by making them fear dismissal or punishment. Next, the mode of warm-hearted paternalism was implemented. And recently the methods of industrial psychology or the fruits of research into labor phys-

iology have been applied in labor management in order to ameliorate the difficulties imposed on workers in the process of rationalization.[9]

Over the following two decades Orii acted as the model of a modern manager. He commissioned one of Japan's leading sociologists, Professor Odaka Kunio of Tokyo University, to conduct a series of attitude surveys of NKK workers between 1952 and 1963 because "my motto was 'no policy without data.' I stressed objective, scientific judgments." Orii sought to remake the corporation through a commitment to democracy as well as science. "I valued the process of free debate based upon this survey data. . . . We must strive for policies that will allow employees to raise their standards of living and expand their capabilities as well as develop the enterprise. Labor unions are indispensable as a disciplining force to ensure that management maintains this correct posture." Orii saw the corporation as "a cooperative body giving birth to social value," and he defined the role of the labor manager as nurturing appropriately cooperative employees.[10] At the heart of his modernism was a powerful belief in the compatibility of science, democracy, and capitalism.

In the 1950s and 1960s, differences between old-guard paternalists and younger modernists at companies like NKK were resolved in a way that allowed managers to tame the union. While retaining ultimate authority, they improvised systems of carefully controlled participation and equality of opportunity, and they convinced most workers to identify managerial goals as their own. By the end of Orii Hyūga's career, both the early enthusiasm of workers for their unions and the bitterness of their disputes were distant memories. But in the late 1940s, the hard-line response of Takemura and Kawada prevailed, and conflicts between union and company remained chronic and angry. In bargaining sessions of 1948 and 1949 union leaders shouted at personnel staff to shut up and insisted that they would speak as equals to no managers except the mill director.[11] In this era, the notion that Japan might present to the world a model of harmonious cooperation at work was unimaginable.

The Cold War Politics of Management and Labor

Gradually and in halting fashion, the weight of geopolitical pressures shored up Japan's increasingly corporate-centered social order, but even at end of the 1950s the international contest was far from over. Cold War ideological confrontations framed the politics of the labor movement and labor-management relations, as agents of both the United States and the Soviet Union sought to secure the allegiance of ordinary Japanese people through a wide array of initiatives, both open and covert. The policies of state ministries, union federations, and business organizations were closely implicated in Cold War politics. Managers as much as workplace activists understood their daily initiatives as part of this larger struggle. The Cold War antagonists even scrambled to control the leisure activities of factory workers by sponsoring competing sports leagues and associations of music appreciation circles and reading clubs.

Japan's American government began to retreat from unconditional support for unions within a year of the surrender, when Douglas MacArthur warned unions in May 1946 to cease "disorderly or violent" actions such as production takeovers or mass demonstrations. The following winter, SCAP more decisively suppressed the revolutionary hopes of labor movement leaders by prohibiting the planned general strike of 6 million workers.

Parallel to these shifts, SCAP abandoned its unblinking hostility toward management. It allowed business leaders to revive their prewar national federations. In April 1948 existing regional business federations quickly came together to found Nikkeiren (Japan Federation of Employers' Associations), dedicated to a "properly strong" stance in defense of managerial prerogatives.

The continued close links between the Japan Communist Party and the union movement, together with heightened tensions between the United States and the Soviet Union and the communist revolution in China, provoked further measures by the Americans and the Japanese government that shocked the young union movement. In 1948 General MacArthur instructed the Japanese government to limit the organizing rights of public employees. The resulting Public Corporations Labor Relations Law prohibited strikes by public employees such as railway, tobacco, postal, and telephone and telegraph workers and severely restricted their ability to bargain collectively.[12] Finally, in 1950 the Americans worked with Japanese government and business leaders to purge over 12,000 accused Communist Party members from their jobs and union posts.[13]

These measures had major impact. Production control ceased to be an important labor tactic after SCAP's 1946 declaration. Nikkeiren rapidly emerged as a powerful advocate of corporate interests in labor affairs. Public-sector workers were placed on the defensive by the new legislation of 1948. The chilling effect of the so-called Red Purge can hardly be exaggerated; unions throughout the country lost some of their most important national and local activists. In the aftermath of the purge, any worker who supported union militance had to weigh this commitment against the fear of being labeled a communist and fired. The national rate of union membership plummeted from 56 to 43 percent in two years.

Yet within several years activism among public-sector workers revived to sustain a militant, politicized union movement in the face of legal restrictions. Private-sector unions, including those at NKK, retained important legitimacy and maneuvering room, and within two years of the Red Purge, many workers supported a revived movement of workplace activism. Throughout the 1950s organized workers refused to restrict themselves to an American-style business unionism concerned primarily with economic issues. They demanded higher pay and continued to pursue equality and participation in the workplace. Without a positive strategy to incorporate or co-opt such demands, repressive measures alone could not contain the labor movement.

Slowly the outlines of such a co-optive strategy began to emerge. Parallel to similar initiatives in Europe, American policy toward labor in Japan moved beyond steps to repress radicalism to focus as well on nurturing pro-American, cooperative labor unions. In so doing, it provided important guidance to Japanese managers and the state. The Japan Productivity Center (JPC) was among the most significant sites of this initiative. Preliminary organizing took place in 1953 and 1954, and the JPC was officially founded in 1955, with funds provided by the United States in cooperation with the Japanese government and business leaders. JPC advocates claimed that new systems of union-company consultation would lead to effective use of new technology and increased productivity. A growing-pie politics of dessert for all would replace the fixed-pie politics of class confrontation. Proclaiming that increased productivity would "expand markets, increase employment, raise real wages and standards of living, and advance the common interests of labor, management and consumers," the Center reached out to factories across Japan. In its first two years, it sent fifty-three small groups of managers and union leaders on missions to learn the art of productivity from the American masters, and the pace of exchange increased thereafter. Back home, the Center promoted the movement with lectures, pamphlets, and a newspaper.[14]

The divided response of organized labor to the productivity movement reflected and reinforced prior divisions. Roughly parallel to the international split among labor federations, the Japanese labor movement had bifurcated sharply along Cold War lines in the early 1950s. On the left, favoring a socialist transformation of the economy and unarmed neutrality in place of the U.S.-Japan mutual security agreement, stood the Sōhyō federation, founded in 1950 and claiming the allegiance of roughly half of Japan's organized workers through the 1950s. On the right stood two federations, the venerable Sōdōmei and the newer Zenrō federation (All-Japan Labor Union Conference, or Zen Nihon Rōdō Kumiai Kaigi), comprised of four industrial federations that broke away from Sōhyō in 1954 in opposition to its positions of pacifism and a Soviet-leaning Cold War neutrality.

As American policymakers hoped, these latter two federations brought a portion of the labor movement into a newly cooperative relationship with managers and the state. They tried to put the dissenting Sōhyō unions on the defensive by calling them impractical, irresponsible, and obstructionist.[15] In 1955 Sōdōmei pledged to support the productivity movement in exchange for promises that productivity gains would be shared with workers in such forms as lower prices, higher wages, better working conditions, and expanded employment.[16] Despite some fears that the productivity movement was an excuse to hold down wages in favor of investment and to increase hours and overtime, the Zenrō federation soon added its support to the productivity movement.[17]

Corporate leaders and their political allies were building an important incipient alliance with labor, but in 1955 these two federations accounted for just 10 percent of organized workers. The majority of the labor movement, led by Sōhyō, would have nothing to do with the Productivity Center. Sōhyō embraced the largest single body of unionized workers throughout the 1950s (about 50 percent, or 3.4 million workers in 1957). Even NKK's union at the Kawasaki mill, previously affiliated with Sōdōmei, shifted to support the Sōhyō position. Although the United States had at first encouraged Sōhyō, whose founders were opposed to Communist Party control of the union movement, the Americans had failed to understand that noncommunists or even anticommunists could be both militant in tactics and radical in goals.

Sōhyō leaders expected their federation to clear a path toward a socialist remaking of Japan not by the ballot box but by activism in the workplace. Their strategy of shop-floor struggle aimed to overcome the weakness of enterprise-centered unions via industrial actions and by broadly diffusing tactics developed on the shop floors of Sōhyō's most active unions. The union organization at the workplace was to be the basic building block of a socialist transformation of Japan. By raising demands on the shop floor, unions would destroy the antidemocratic hierarchy of management that exploited workers. Workplace and community actions would "overturn the productive and social structure of Japanese capitalism from the bottom up."[18]

The Sōhyō drive to mobilize in the workplace won much support as unions in coal mines, railroads, and steel mills turned increasingly to shop-floor struggle tactics through the 1950s. The Japan Productivity Center reacted by calling on corporations and unions to replace struggle with cooperation and labor-management consultation.[19] Drawing on prewar American, German, and British precedents, as well as postwar initiatives of the International Labor Organization (ILO) in Geneva, the Center viewed the early postwar management councils as a false start. Unions too often used them as a vehicle to control a factory or firm. Proper consultation would rather allow "labor and capital to cooperate peacefully as equals to raise productivity" and fairly distribute the fruits of their joint efforts. To promote this system, the Center organized a standing committee of business and labor representatives and academic experts, which published pamphlets and magazines and sponsored lectures and seminars. The Center reported that by the early 1950s management councils of the earlier postwar type were fast disappearing, and that by 1958 over one third of unionized plants had consultative systems of a properly cooperative nature.[20]

While the Productivity Center initiatives stressed positive inducements to cooperate, the Nikkeiren business federation promoted a hard-line strategy to confront militant unions of the left. To avoid legal complications and charges of union busting, its publications carefully offered respect to "legitimate" union activities, but Nikkeiren in fact acted as a command center in the battle to destroy activist unions. The group's staffers compiled detailed analyses of the shop-floor struggle tactics of all the major Sōhyō industrial federations and offered specific advice on countermeasures, in particular "education" of foremen (who were also union members) on how to recognize Communist Party cells and how to cope with workplace union activism.[21] As managers at NKK dealt with the surge of shop-floor assertiveness in the late 1950s, they made good use of such advice.

Both the Productivity Center and Nikkeiren advocated an American style of business unionism. They presented the AFL-CIO as the model of a cooperative federation whose members bargained over wages while respecting managerial authority and agreeing that capitalism ultimately would deliver the goods. In addition to these U.S.-inspired initiatives undertaken by Japanese organizations, numerous Americans continued to promote their notion of cooperative "Free World" unionism directly in Japan as throughout the world. This foreign policy for labor proceeded through official and unofficial channels, both open and covert.

Leading actors and organizations involved in this effort included the labor attachés at the U.S. embassy in Tokyo, CIA personnel in the embassy or at front organizations such as the Asia Foundation, and American union federations as well as international labor federations aligned with the

United States. In a major diplomatic offensive beginning in the mid-1950s, these groups sponsored publications, seminars, study tours in the United States for Japanese union officials, and visits of American union leaders to Japan. From the 1950s through the early 1970s, over 5,000 Japanese labor leaders are estimated to have journeyed to America.[22] They visited factories, met counterpart union officials and studied their practices, and heard lectures from experts on labor law or industrial relations American-style. Sponsors included the Productivity Center, the Asia Foundation, and the Rockefeller Foundation. The office of the labor attaché in the American embassy in Tokyo helped to facilitate these exchanges, which were arranged with considerable political care. The left wing of the AFL-CIO (called "the Reuther group") tended to invite Sōhyō members, while the more conservative American unions ("the Meany group") cultivated ties to the Zenrō-Sōdōmei unionists.[23] In 1961 the attaché's office began publication in Japanese of a journal called *American Labor Review,* which preached the gospel of cooperative unionism, and those labor leaders who took advantage of American hospitality came to be dubbed "the embassy group."[24]

International union bodies took part in this activity as well. In 1949, the World Federation of Trade Unions (WFTU) had split over the issue of communist control of unions in the Soviet bloc, and North American and Western European unions that opposed communist influence formed the new International Confederation of Free Trade Unions (ICFTU). In 1953 the ICFTU opened an office in Tokyo and began to seek Japanese allies with some success. When a Japanese union decided to affiliate with the ICFTU, it was signaling its Free World alignment globally and a cooperative alignment in the workplace. By 1959, eighteen industrial union federations had joined the organization.[25]

The budding alliance with advocates of American and Free World unionism did not proceed unchallenged. In the United States, the United Electrical Workers (UE) consistently attacked the AFL-CIO and the International Metalworkers Federation for their red-baiting tactics and for supporting American Cold War policy rather than promoting independent unionism in other countries.[26] In Japan, the "embassy group" drew primarily on the minority of Sōdōmei and Zenrō unions, and the Sōhyō federation countered with frequent international labor exchanges with socialist states. In line with its neutral foreign policy, Sōhyō sent delegates to meetings of both the U.S.-aligned ICFTU and the Soviet-aligned WFTU from the early 1950s, but Sōhyō's leaders in fact saw workers in socialist countries as their natural allies.

Their ties to the communist world ironically deepened under the conservative cabinet of Hatoyama Ichirō in 1954. Hatoyama represented a substantial body within conservative political circles that wished to open economic and political ties to the People's Republic of China (PRC) and the Soviet Union in order to assert independence from the United States in foreign policy. Sōhyō took advantage of this stance to pursue its own initiatives. In 1954 and 1955 at least five large delegations, numbering well over 100 labor union leaders, made trips to WFTU meetings and conventions of industrial federations in the WFTU camp, as well as missions to Eastern Europe and Moscow, to the PRC, and to a conference of independent Asian unions in Burma in 1955.[27] The Tsurumi mill union at NKK enthusiastically supported these efforts, lobbying the government to expand trade with China (seen as a promising market for Japanese steel) and sending its vice-chairman on a visit to Europe, the Soviet Union, and China.[28] One energetic leader of NKK's Kawasaki mill union made nineteen trips to China from the 1950s to the 1980s.[29] Although the pace of exchange slowed from 1956 to 1958, another large delegation visited China in 1959, including the chairmen of the Japan Socialist and Japan Communist parties. On the occasion of this visit, socialist party chairman Asanuma Inejirō gave a memorable speech, in which he proclaimed that "American imperialism is the common enemy of the Japanese and Chinese people."[30]

These ties to the socialist world were important, but the sum total of union visitors to the Soviet Union and China numbered in the hundreds; those sojourning to the United States numbered in the thousands. Gradually, this traffic influenced the views of union leaders. Even Sōhyō officials were "impressed" by the assistance and support from Western unions in a Japanese dispute over the public-sector workers' right to strike in 1958.[31] The Japan Productivity Center, Nikkeiren, and American agents were finding support within the labor movement, as well as in government and management circles. But Cold War divisions remained deep within Japan, and corporate authority was sharply challenged. The Sōhyō federation retained by far the greatest number of members, and they initiated frequent and vigorous shop-floor struggles and opposed the productivity movement.

State, Society, and Labor

The bureaucrats and politicians who controlled the Japanese state in the postwar decades opposed communism and supported the institutions and ideals of capitalism. Despite some internal opposition, the Japanese government accepted a place in the postwar American imperium. It allowed American troops to remain in Japan under the terms of the United States–Japan Security Treaty of 1952. State officials were also delighted with

Korean War procurement orders, which spurred economic recovery. But as economic recovery turned to boom, their sense of how to support capitalism shifted in a way that reinforced Japan's evolving politics of productivity. The contending strategies of conservative politicians and bureaucrats ran parallel to those of NKK executives who argued over reactionary versus "enlightened" strategies of labor management, or those of the Americans who combined the stick of hard-line anticommunism with the carrot of the productivity movement. In all cases, programs of reaction gradually gave way to those seeking social order by integrating the labor movement into the postwar system.

An unprecedented fervor for consumption, for education, and for access to middle-class ways of life began to grip the Japanese population in the 1950s. The state responded by adroitly adjusting its emphasis from containing the anger of an impoverished working class to managing the aspirations of an emerging middle class. This effort to manage the social processes of the economic miracle to serve the evolving needs of industrial employers was quite effective. It shaped a distinctive postwar Japanese system that to this day is marked by ambivalence toward that holiest of capitalist ideas: competition. Encouraged to the utmost in some realms, such as the fierce scramble to enter good schools from kindergarten to college, competition in Japan has been discouraged or carefully regulated in others, such as interfirm markets for labor or products, in service of a larger commitment to social order.[32]

Industrial activity revived in Japan thanks to Korean War procurements, and it continued to surge thereafter due to massive investments in new plant and equipment, cheap energy, access to expanding world demand, and growing domestic demand. The real value of industrial production had matched the prewar standards of the mid-1930s by 1951, and it climbed to double that level by 1957. Gross national product, investment in plant and equipment, and individual consumption all returned to prewar levels in 1951, and then doubled by the end of the decade at the latest.[33] In the city of Kawasaki, heavy industries generated new jobs, as employment rose nearly 2.5 times between 1950 and 1960 and output increased nearly tenfold.[34]

The economic boom was in part the *result* of managerial efforts to retake authority that exacted a high price from workers. A hard line on wage increases in the early 1950s in the iron and steel industry helped businesses pay for investment in state-of-the-art facilities. As critics of the productivity movement predicted, the remarkable increases in output per person that followed resulted from a more intense work regime as well as from more productive machinery. In the city of Kawasaki, the average employee's regular working hours were longer in 1960 than in 1950, and average overtime per person had increased by roughly 50 percent.[35] Accident rates in the steel industry and throughout the city and nation were appalling. In 1960 factories in Kanagawa prefecture witnessed one death per day, on average.[36] A desire to change such conditions goes a long way toward explaining the enthusiasm of many Japanese workers for Sōhyō's call for shop-floor struggle in the 1950s.

Socioeconomic trends were at the same time *causes* of the eventual ability of managers to achieve hegemony. For the first groups of labor leaders who traveled to the United States for a crash course on the virtues of American-style unionism, the glittering dream of American material abundance seemed wholly out of reach. Kudō Shinpachi of NKK toured the United States in 1961 with a delegation of like-minded steel industry unionists courtesy of the Japan Productivity Center. He was "astonished at the huge steel mills in Pittsburgh, but I was even more amazed that workers drove their cars to the mill." His American counterparts "could not believe that the Japanese rode bikes to work."[37] Kudō was an important figure promoting cooperative unionism at NKK's Kawasaki mill in the 1950s and 1960s. The economic boom that began in the 1950s transformed the material and social context of workplace life, raising challenges to business managers, to state officials, and to unionists on all sides. During the years when Kudō led the battle to remake the NKK union in a less militant mold, the lifestyle gap that so shocked him was beginning to narrow in ways that helped his cause.

With peace and the repatriation of soldiers, a baby boom came to Japan as to all the combatant nations, but the soaring birthrate peaked in 1949 and began a long, steady decline thereafter. The mother in an average prewar family gave birth to five children, but this total dropped to just over two through the 1950s.[38] In cities especially, the nuclear family became both the statistical norm and a social ideal.

These smaller urban families began to eat and live better in the 1950s. The proportion of family income spent on food by Yokohama residents fell from crisis levels of more than 65 percent in the late 1940s to 48 percent by 1952 to roughly 40 percent by 1960.[39] With stomachs no longer empty, workers and their families were suddenly hungry to save and to spend as never before. In Yokohama the proportion of family income devoted to savings and other nonconsumer categories rose from 11 to 19 percent during the 1950s. At the same time throngs of shoppers crowded into department stores and small retail shops to buy the latest fashion in clothes, appliances, and consumer electronic goods. By 1959, 90 percent of Kawasaki households had radios, while 60 percent had televisions. Over two thirds of those TVs had been purchased within the previous 24 months.[40]

For all the change in birthrate, family size, and standard of living, the manner in which typical women and typical men spent their days changed little. The female homemaker was less often than before responsible for an extended family living under one roof, but she continued to manage the household while her husband worked outside the home. Few of these women were employed. A 1951 survey of workers at eight factories in the Tokyo-Kawasaki-Yokohama industrial belt reported that a mere 4 of 250 wives worked outside the home (13 percent took in piecework at home). This pattern seems more a matter of the husband's choice than the wife's. Many of the wives had worked before marriage, and most expressed a desire to work again, given decent conditions. But a strong majority of the husbands did not want their wives to work.[41] These trends suggest that a union or a company would win support to the extent that it satisfied the husband's desire to support his family, convinced his wife to take pride in her role as full-time homemaker, and allowed both of them to afford the enticing new necessities of the middle-class consumer lifestyle.

In the face of this shifting social landscape, the state indirectly but importantly sought to ensure the stability of private corporations and the predominance of management over activist labor unions in several arenas, including social policies, schooling, and labor laws. These efforts helped managers and cooperative unionists take advantage of socioeconomic changes and continuities and gradually erode the foundations of union activism.

The government's social policies helped anchor corporate hegemony in a foundation of traditionalistic male and female roles. The system of social benefits reinforced the dependence of women upon men for supports such as health insurance or old-age pensions. In addition, the government in 1955 supported a centrally funded national campaign called the New Life Movement. The inspiration for the project came in part from an initiative of the same name launched by managers at NKK two years earlier to train employee wives to be more competent and supportive, professional homemakers. Through the New Life Movement, the state and corporations reinforced a gendered division of labor that neatly joined employer, employees, and their families into a common endeavor defined as modern, scientific, and progressive. Women were to run "rational" and "efficient" homes, and this would allow men to realize the same ideals at work. By playing these complementary roles, women and men were expected to raise productivity and bring prosperity to all.

At the Ministry of Education, veteran bureaucrats with prewar experience remained powerful, and they were torn between an impulse to repudiate the institutions and ideas of postwar democracy and a pragmatic inclination to seek stability within the framework of the new order. The reactionary cast of the 1950s was hardly subtle. Education bureaucrats and their political allies wanted to strengthen central control by abolishing locally elected school boards and closely monitoring textbook selection, and they largely succeeded. They also sought to restrict teachers' political freedom and implement teacher evaluation as a tool of control, but with less success. At every turn they opposed cooperation with, or even recognition of, the left-wing Japan Teachers Union, and education officials in the 1950s wanted schools to inculcate discipline through preeminently political means. They tried to restore moral education to the school curriculum and bring back the official use in the schools of two controversial symbols of the prewar order: the national anthem and the flag. With public opinion divided, and a united Teachers Union fighting the ministry every step of the way, few of these changes were easily or fully implemented.

The politics of postwar education remained as contentious as those of the workplace through the 1950s, but beginning in the early 1960s, expert advisory committees of business leaders joined education bureaucrats in supporting a less blatantly political agenda. The educational aspirations of blue-collar workers were changing dramatically. In 1955 the proportion of middle school graduates who went on to high school passed 50 percent. The high school population continued to rise, and major corporations began looking to high schools for blue-collar recruits. They called on the Ministry of Education to design curricula that would secure a stable, competent labor supply. The education bureaucrats responded by making high schools the place where the future work force of blue-collar operatives, clerks, and low-level managers learned an impressive array of basic skills and was at the same time socialized to the demands of workplace life.

Bureaucrats in the labor field similarly rode and channeled the tide of reform. Japan's Labor Union Law of December 1945 was written at the behest of reform-minded American occupiers. The new law was a remarkably progressive document that granted unprecedented rights and protection to organized workers. But the law was drafted by veteran Japanese social bureaucrats who had supported legalized unions as a way to contain social conflict two decades earlier.[42] A close reading of its language and that of the Labor Relations Adjustment Law of the following year reveals that these men still saw the postwar legal system as a means to impose order upon unionized workers who might otherwise attack the capitalist system.[43] The law required unions to register and submit their constitutions to the government for approval, and it specified precisely what functions unions were to fulfill and how they were to be organized.[44] Through the Labor Union law, the state aspired to define the institution of "labor union" and administer it closely, rather than to regulate unions that were self-defined, pre-existing institutions, as is the case with Anglo-American law. The Japanese authors of the law were extremely careful to set up a legal system that would bolster social order.

The Labor Relations Adjustment Law of 1946 pursued this goal even more directly. It established a system of tripartite labor relations commissions at the national and local levels, one of which cut its teeth by mediating the NKK Kawasaki mill strike of 1946. The structure and function of these commissions in some respects parallels the National Labor Relations Board of the United States. But this law, too, was drafted by Japanese bureaucrats with prewar experience and detailed knowledge of continental European as well as Anglo-American labor relations. It obligated both parties to the labor relationship to "make special endeavors" to reach agreements without taking dispute actions, and it ordered the government to "assist the parties concerned with labor relations in order thereby to prevent to the utmost the occurrence of acts of dispute."[45] Although postwar German labor law imposes an even more stringent legal requirement that unions fully exhaust the possibility of a negotiated settlement before they can strike, the spirit of the Japanese law is similar.[46]

Through the postwar constitution and this system of labor laws, the Japanese state obeyed SCAP orders to guarantee workers the rights to organize, bargain collectively, and strike. But unlike its Anglo-American counterparts, and like those in continental Europe, it anchored the rights of labor in a state dispensation to society, rather than in the individual right of each worker to freely associate. This has left Japanese unions (and those in Europe) relatively susceptible to state intervention.[47] Over the past fifty years the legal system has often constrained Japan's unions, especially those with a radical agenda or a militant strategy. Legal expectations that unions negotiate in good faith and that the government do "the utmost" to head off disputes have not prevented thousands of strikes since 1945, but the law has had a constraining effect. Through labor commissions concerned to ensure social order in particular, Japanese law has generally bolstered cooperative unions and their corporate allies.

Workplaces in large private corporations eventually became citadels of Japan's corporate-centered society. The ascendance of the institutions of capitalism was common to many parts of the globe by the 1950s and 1960s, in particular Western Europe and North America, but in the long run, for better and for worse, the Japanese version has proved unusually total and durable. Because the international pressures of the Cold War were relatively constant across much of the globe and the social transformations of Japan's high-growth era were comparable to those elsewhere, the survival and growth of various capitalist systems worldwide have certain broad-stroke similarities. But such factors alone cannot explain the unusual staying power of Japan's capitalist hegemony.

Myriad threads of influence and interpretation affected Japanese labor relations, from American management practice and American foreign policy, through the Productivity Center and Nikkeiren, then onto the shop floors of individual factories. In various settings at national and local levels, workers and managers argued among themselves and against each other over what "labor-management consultation" or "industrial democracy" or "quality control" might mean in practice. In the course of these exchanges, ideas with a roughly American point of origin were transformed.[48]

At the same time, initiatives of the Japanese state in family and social welfare, education, and labor law unfolded in a distinctive mix of efforts to manage competition and potentially divisive social trends. These steps help explain the enduring authority of Japan's corporate-centered society. They were taken in part because the challenge to corporate hegemony at the grass roots of Japanese society was unusually serious and widespread in the 1950s. These were years of extraordinary polarization of left and right in national politics. They were also years of the street politics of the peace movement and the student movement. And the system came under attack at its very center. After a brief lull in 1950 and 1951, organized workers in some of the economy's most powerful strategic sites, from the sunset industry of coal mining to rising stars such as steel, turned to new forms of workplace activism, unusually threatening or promising depending on where one sat. For managers, this was a menace not found in the major economies of Europe or the United States, where the 1950s and early 1960s were a relatively quiet time. As they groped toward strategies to restore corporate prosperity and regain authority over the workforce, managers at NKK as elsewhere joined an intense struggle to define the relationship between democracy and capitalism in postwar Japan.

4   Reinventing the Steel Mill

Japanese managers in the 1950s built a foundation for the nation's remark-able postwar economic performance through far-reaching innovations in production and personnel management. At the same time, they began to nurture a workforce that would identify fully with the goals of the company, in large part by building an alliance with groups of organized workers will-ing to abandon the ambitious democratic agenda of the early postwar unions. With the false wisdom of hindsight, the social path from workplace struggle to cooperation was easily negotiated, and the economic road from devastation to "miraculous" growth appears to have been straight and wide. In fact, both cooperation and growth were reached with difficulty and at significant cost. Looking forward from 1950, one sees puzzling forks and division among actors at every turn.[1]

In the economic realm, the state could cling to a century-old fear of the foreign and encourage "self-sufficient" development. This would mean sub-sidizing domestic hydroelectric plants and coal mines to minimize reliance on foreign supplies. Or it could follow a bolder course toward long-run eco-nomic power and independence by promoting exports of finished goods and imports of raw materials. This would require allocating precious for-eign exchange dollars to import the cotton, the ore, or the oil that industry demanded. Recovery could perhaps be led by historically proven industries where Japan had a comparative advantage in cheap labor, such as textiles. Alternatively, the state could encourage investment in high-tech industries with high-value-added products. These held great promise but were plagued by high capital and material costs that outweighed the advantage of rela-tively low wages.

The misleading clarity of hindsight caused pundits in later years to label iron and steel the obvious "rice crops" of Japan's booming industrial economy. But in the late 1940s textile magnates boasted that "our cotton spinning firms will build the Japanese economy through exports; there is no need for the iron and steel industry."[2] This claim infuriated steel executives, but it seemed logical to many that resource-poor Japan import steel and revive the established star of textiles. Even Nagano Shigeo, the wartime director of the Iron and Steel Control Association who served after the war as president of Fuji Steel and then chairman of New Japan Steel, abandoned the rice of industry for that of agriculture on hearing the Emperor surrender. He invested his life savings in "two rice fields, a small starch factory, and a self-sufficient salt mill" in Hokkaidō.[3]

By the early 1950s, however, business leaders and economic bureaucrats decided Japan indeed must revive production of industrial "rice" in its iron and steel mills. Given this decision, however, the best strategy was far from obvious. Corporate executives had to weigh the merits of adopting expensive, unproven technology versus renovating old furnaces. Economic bureaucrats in the newly consolidated Ministry of International Trade and Industry (MITI) encouraged them to soldier on with patched-up old machines, objecting to major investment in new plants, especially by upstart entrants. Despite this guidance, the major steelmakers borrowed wherever they could and poured billions of yen into a bold investment drive. As they struggled to make profitable use of new furnaces, and rolling equipment to produce sheet steel (see Figure 2), they simultaneously launched a series of far-reaching, related innovations in managing work and workers. Unions vigorously opposed many of these steps. As managers set out to reinvent the Japanese steel mill, they believed themselves engaged in a battle with powerful international competitors and an increasingly antagonistic body of organized employees.

By 1950, NKK and the postwar Japanese steel industry as a whole had already weathered several profound crises. The Americans had abandoned plans to place a ceiling on Japan's steelmaking capacity and remove "excess equipment" as reparations. They had also abandoned the trust-busting program that would have divided NKK into several smaller firms. The industry had also begun to benefit from official support. To break a vicious cycle of coal shortages that inhibited the recovery of other industries, in turn keeping coal demand and productivity low, the state adopted the Priority Production program. Drawing on wartime experience, the economic bureaucrats allocated both coal and imported fuel on a preferential basis to steelmakers, which allowed them to revive production and feed steel back to the coal industry to rebuild the mining infrastructure and raise productivity. The Priority Production program succeeded in reviving both industries, and it placed an important official stamp of approval on investment in steel mills.

The government proved helpful in other ways as well. Until 1950, it continued a wartime practice by fixing steel prices well below production costs to help steel customers afford to operate. It made up the difference with gigantic subsidies to the mills. The state also used its control of foreign exchange to let the iron- and steelmakers import ore at bargain prices; it exchanged their yen for dollars at a special rate that more than doubled the overseas buying power of an ironmaker's yen compared to that of a cotton spinner.[4]

Nonetheless, prospects for the steel industry and the entire economy were bleak. Japanese iron and steel production in 1950 stood at just half of the prewar peak. Productivity was low by international standards, and costs were high. The state had made steel a priority industry to help the economy survive the unprecedented crisis of 1946–47, and industry leaders had regained confidence. But the draconian medicine of retrenchment prescribed by Joseph Dodge as economic advisor to SCAP in 1949 in order to subdue inflation threatened to kill the patient. The "Dodge plan" did halt inflation, but it stopped all state subsidies and loans.[5] Steelmakers lost their production cost subsidies and preferential exchange rates. Together with executives in virtually all basic industries, they found themselves starved for funds.

The mandarins of MITI in the early 1950s were convinced the steel industry was doomed without continued assistance of some sort, and they doubted it could succeed as a competitive export industry in any case. But the state was at least committed to facilitate the revival of a *domestic* steelmaking capacity, and top firms were determined to rebuild. From 1951 to 1961, the iron and steel industry embarked on two massive programs of investment and rationalization. The First Rationalization Plan of 1951 to 1955, and the second plan of 1956 to 1961, were drawn up by a cartel-like club of steel industrialists called the Japan Iron and Steel Federation (Nihon Tekkō Renmei) in close consultation with MITI bureaucrats. The first plan committed nearly $3 billion (at 360 yen per dollar) to purchase new rolling equipment and upgraded facilities for the integrated production of iron and steel.[6] This was a massive sum, representing about 15 percent of Japan's total investment in manufacturing in these years, and it transformed the industry. In 1950, Japan lagged far behind the United States and Europe in developing integrated iron- and steelmaking facilities; to make steel they relied heavily on expensive imported scrap iron. By 1960, every phase of production had been remade, with construction of large new blast furnaces for ironmaking, new basic oxygen furnaces for steelmaking, and new automated rolling mills, and the industry was internationally competitive.

A complicated combination of state orchestration, cartels and cooperation among firms in some areas, sharp competition in others, and plain luck marked this and many other episodes in the Japanese vault from devastation to world economic power in just two decades. Luck visited Japan in the form of the Korean War. Japanese leaders tastelessly exulted in what the prime minister called a "gift of the gods" and the 1952 NKK company history dubbed "blessed rain from heaven," export orders that came wrapped as American military procurements.[7] In the peak year of 1952, war procurements accounted for 63 percent of all Japan's exports.[8] The timing of this surge of demand was as fortunate as the amount, for it came quick on the heels of the deflationary shock of the Dodge plan. The steel industry lost the last of its government subsidies on July 1, 1950, one week after the Korean War began. Members of the Dodge mission, and some Japanese state officials, questioned the wisdom of continued investment in an industry where unsubsidized production costs exceeded the market price by 40 percent. But just three months later, soaring American demand for Japanese steel, and sharply higher iron and steel prices globally, allowed the Japanese against all expectations to sell their products at a profit without subsidy.[9]

The war boom was temporary. More significant in the long run was the ability to raise productivity and continue to operate profitably when the heavenly rain stopped falling. The Japanese state, MITI in particular, played an important role in helping this to happen. MITI worked with industry leaders to set levels and categories of investment in the First and Second Rationalization Plans. The government's newly created Japan Development Bank then helped fund these investments, directly by loaning 8 percent of the total in the first plan and indirectly by paving the way for "cooperative" loans by commercial banks to steelmaking and other targeted industries. MITI also took the lead in reducing the high shipping costs that plagued the industry. It drew together major iron- and steelmakers, shippers, and shipbuilders into an important project whereby a special joint-venture company purchased and operated huge new cargo ships. The Japan Iron and Steel Federation expected that these state-of-the-art vessels would reduce transport costs for imported ore by 20 percent.[10]

At the same time, competition and entrepreneurial initiatives contributed to the industry's remarkable performance. In 1950 an engineer named Nishiyama Yatarō convinced Kawasaki Heavy Industry to split off its steel division, which he headed, as a separate company. He then led this

Kawasaki Steel Corporation as it defied MITI by building two new blast furnaces and a huge integrated iron- and steelmaking facility on the coast of Chiba prefecture, across Tokyo Bay from the NKK complex.[11] MITI believed the high costs and uncertain demand made the project too risky, but despite its control over domestic capital allocation, it could not deter Nishiyama. He ended up borrowing much of the funds to finance the mill from the World Bank. The Chiba complex produced pig iron for immediate processing as steel, reducing the need to import expensive scrap. Its success pushed his competitors to build integrated mills as well.

For these established giants—Yahata, Fuji, and NKK—as much as for Nishiyama's new venture, building such mills required innovation and further tough decisions. To choose the best furnace to convert pig iron or scrap to steel, steelmakers had to assess the merits of at least seven alternatives. In the early 1950s, three long-established technologies existed to perform this task: Thomas converters, Bessemer converters, and the open hearth furnace. Each had its costs and its benefits, which depended on the range, the costs, and the qualities of the iron available for processing. The open hearth furnace was the most expensive to build and to operate, but it produced top-quality steel from the broadest range of materials. In much of the world, including Japan and the United States, it was the technology of choice.[12] In addition, in 1952 a small Austrian company had invented a fourth method, the basic oxygen furnace (BOF), and at least three other promising technologies were being developed in Europe and the United States. In the end, the BOF won the day. It polluted horribly, but in the 1950s this was an "external" cost not borne by the steelmaker. The BOF turned out to be cheaper to build and to operate than the open hearth furnace. It could produce high-quality steel from pig iron alone, or it could use scrap mixed with pig iron. But in the early 1950s the BOF had not yet been made to operate on a profitable commercial basis. Unsure of which way to go, most steelmakers around the world hedged their bets. They continued to build new open hearth furnaces throughout the decade, while they experimented with various new technologies.

Nippon Kōkan was the first in Japan, and one of the first in the world, to place some of its chips on the BOF by licensing the technology in 1955. This was followed by a rush of the top Japanese companies to make basic oxygen furnaces the core of their steelmaking system. The Japanese government made sure that this technology became available cheaply and diffused widely in a way that typifies its crucial role in promoting the postwar economic miracle.[13] A few details reveal a glimpse of the myriad ways that Japanese capitalists and bureaucrats violated the free market faith. When

NKK contracted for its BOF license, Yahata was also actively seeking its own separate deal, but MITI, working closely with the Japan Iron and Steel Federation, literally called the presidents of the two firms into a conference room and put an end to this wasteful competitive duplication of effort. MITI used its authority over foreign technology licensing to authorize a deal whereby NKK was the primary licensee, who would pass on BOF technology to its "competitors," designated sub-licensees. The participating firms organized a committee to pursue cooperative research and share the cost of royalty fees. In the end, Japanese steelmakers acquired BOF technology at a fraction of the price paid by the Americans.[14]

The decision to adopt BOF steelmaking technology and the concurrent decision of all the major players to build integrated iron- and steelmaking complexes were linked. The industrialists were responding to a common need to overcome high production costs that stemmed in large part from high material costs. In Japan at this time, imported iron ore was cheaper than imported scrap. Japanese firms built new blast furnaces because they would use imported ore to produce pig iron that would be cheaper to convert to steel than imported scrap would be. The basic oxygen furnace similarly was attractive to Japanese firms because it could make steel from pig iron mixed with little or no scrap at all. Investments in blast furnaces and oxygen furnaces thus reinforced each other. Then, as ever greater quantities of molten steel poured from the basic oxygen furnaces, a bottleneck loomed at the next stage, steel casting. The escalating logic of innovation pushed the Japanese to invest more quickly than their competitors in "continuous casting" machines because these more efficiently cast billets, slabs, and blooms directly from molten steel (see Figure 2).[15]

Japan's industrial investments in the 1950s were astonishing. The aggregate annual rates of gross capital formation have not been seen before or since in world economic history. The steel industry vastly expanded output and increased productivity (see Figure 3). It proved competitive in exporting to the recovering economies of Europe as early as 1955.[16] These achievements resulted from a process of orchestrated development in which industry cartels were as important as state guidance, and the combination of the two was crucial. The state facilitated and cajoled actors who competed with one hand and cooperated with the other. Ultimately these industrial investments paid great dividends to the economy as a whole and to the iron- and steelmakers in particular.

Huge investments in and of themselves did not guarantee prosperity. To make these pay, corporations in postwar Japan had to produce more efficiently. This meant controlling labor costs. As steel companies transformed their enterprises into integrated high-tech plants, they inevitably confronted the one production factor that talked back. For a time controlling the workers proved more difficult than building furnaces. Precisely for this reason, managers sought to extend their dominion over their employees' lives, on and off the job, to an unusual extent. Reinventing the steel mill meant both renovating the mill and remaking the system of labor administration.

The links between investing, managing production, and managing labor were direct when it came to restraining labor costs. As the 1950s began, the one advantage held by Japan's top steelmakers was their relatively low labor cost per ton. The obvious way to sustain this edge was to pay low wages, and the hard line of managers in annual wage bargaining certainly caused much of the confrontation between union and company in the 1950s. But labor costs involve more than wage levels, and in postwar Japan two other managerial strategies were equally crucial to contain them. First, if one could produce more with a constant or a shrinking workforce, wages per worker could rise while labor costs per ton of output fell. At NKK and throughout the steel industry, managers aggressively sought to streamline the workforce throughout the 1950s and 1960s, and this continually brought them into confrontation with unions. Second, whatever the gross wage bill may be, one can change the form in which it is distributed (output premium, seniority-based wage, merit-based salary) in hopes of motivating workers and linking pay closely to quality and quantity of output. To this end, NKK developed controversial new wage policies in the high-growth era.

One pioneer in NKK's endeavors to streamline both staffing and wages was Orii Hyūga. He was familiar with recent literature in American industrial sociology and determined to apply it in an "enlightened" way to control NKK's workforce. The programs developed by Orii and his colleagues undermined two assumptions currently made about Japanese management: that "permanent employment" is a time-honored custom; and that efforts to change this tradition and streamline the workforce began in earnest only with the recession of the 1970s. In fact, the protocols of so-called permanent employment are modern. They evolved as negotiated and legally regulated practices throughout the postwar era, as managers consistently fought unions and sometimes the courts for the freedom to control workforce size and to reassign or dismiss workers.

From 1948 to 1952, Orii Hyūga headed NKK's labor division at the Kawasaki mill. There he oversaw an exhaustive survey of the physical intensity of steelmaking. His staff determined machine operating rates, calories expended per task, break time, and idle time for every job in the mill. He recalled that with subsidies and favorable exchange rates abolished in 1950, and the First Rationalization Plan under way from 1951, "aggressive cost cutting was inevitable." Scientific standards to control staffing would be "powerful weapons" to this end.[17] True to his enlightened approach, Orii defined "scientific" to include respect for the physical needs of the workers, and he invited the union to participate in the survey. The Kawasaki mill's union sent just one man to join twenty labor division employees on the survey committee, a sign of indifference or perhaps hostility to a project that indeed resulted in a new set of standards, codified in a "Staffing Needs Assessment Manual" in 1952.[18] During and after this standard-setting process, the union bargained stubbornly to fight several proposed staffing cuts and oppose excessive overtime.

By effectively resisting staffing cuts, the union forced managers to seek a better strategy to control workforce size. In the mid-1950s, NKK embarked on a new program of "industrial engineering" (IE) to set job standards and "rationalize" workforce size. This initiative took nearly a decade to implement fully. It not only challenged the union; it also repudiated Orii's surveys, setting a newly formed IE section against Orii's labor division in a struggle for managerial turf.

The methods of IE came from the United States. In 1955 an NKK manager joined an industrial engineering study mission to the United States sponsored by the Japan Efficiency Association. The mission sparked steel companies and others throughout Japan to develop their own IE programs. NKK created an efficiency section in 1957, and in the three-way interaction of this section, the labor division, and the union, a crucial change took place. The labor division's existing system of job content analysis took the current work process as a given and assessed its staffing needs. The union likewise began with the work process then in place and argued over appropriate staffing. The advocates of industrial engineering differed fundamentally. They first questioned the mode of operation itself. They began by analyzing work design and then proposed changes that would "allow" reduced staffing.

For several years the young turks of IE were stymied. NKK had to win union approval for any changes in staffing levels, and the labor division represented the company in these negotiations. The efficiency section merely had authority to suggest changes. In the words of Morito Akio, one of the key young men in the engineering group, "from 1957 to 1960 or so, IE was an unwelcome, uninvited guest."[19] But in 1959–60 one Professor M. E. Mandel, an American industrial engineering expert, made fifty-one visits to

NKK as a consultant to the IE section during a thirteen-month stay in Japan. The company set up a large committee of employees from the labor division, the efficiency section, and other locations to work with Mandel, and gradually a more receptive mood developed.

Then in 1961 the IE section found its opening when the company began planning for a huge new mill in Fukuyama, a coastal site several hundred miles southwest of the Kawasaki plant. To start up this facility economically and efficiently, NKK wished to transfer to Fukuyama 3,000 veterans from the 15,000 Kawasaki workers, and it wanted to run the old mill without replacing these men. The company asked the IE section to devise a plan to cut staffing at the Kawasaki mill by 20 percent.[20] From this time forward, the work designs of industrial engineers drove staffing decisions. The labor division would be consulted and would implement these plans in further consultation with the union, but the initiative had shifted.

The embrace of industrial engineering followed the American model rather closely. But together with more distinctive innovations in wage policy, quality control, rotation of job assignments, and workplace supervision, it marked a breakthrough toward what has come to be called the "Japanese system" of labor and production control. In the steel industry, this breakthrough took place after the great strikes of 1957 and 1959 and a dramatic change in the union leadership. Only by remaking the union in a more cooperative mode could managers create a system that flexibly and totally mobilized the workforce to seek corporate objectives.

A program to reform NKK's wage structure unfolded in the 1950s parallel to the attack on staffing levels. As in so many other realms of corporate practice, managers seeking to regain flexibility in setting wages and controlling labor costs began by following an American model. An account of their efforts shatters a second pair of myths about Japanese labor and management: that seniority wages are traditional; and that only in recent decades, again spurred by the oil crisis, have managers aggressively introduced flexible wage systems reflecting the value added by productive labor.

Wages in the early 1950s indeed reflected a worker's seniority to a significant degree. But this was due in part to wartime state policy and was in part a result of the early postwar labor union offensive.[21] A man's base wage rose annually with very slight variation from person to person due to merit assessment. Even as this "seniority wage" system was taking root under state and then union pressure, managers resisted it as "evil egalitarianism." In the 1950s and early 1960s, managers in steel and throughout the economy began to remake this system.

Encouraged strongly by Nikkeiren, they drew on the American practice of "job wages." The idea was to pay a worker for the value of the particular type of labor, rather than simply reward him for putting in time at a factory. In practice, this job wage rarely came to account for more than a small fraction of a person's total wage, for neither managers, nor union leaders, nor rank-and-file workers found it to their liking. Veteran skilled workers in particular viewed age and seniority as the best standards for setting pay, while managers and younger workers liked the idea of paying in accord with an individual's latent or demonstrated ability. For their different reasons, all parties preferred pay that was based not on the characteristics of the job being done, but on characteristics of the particular worker.

Wage policy at Nippon Kōkan was typical. From the end of the war through the 1960s a base wage reflecting seniority, age, education, family size, and an annual merit rating was the most important of numerous components of a steelworker's pay.[22] Other major elements were two types of output pay called "efficiency" and "incentive" wages. In addition, NKK moved ahead of the pack by establishing a job wage in 1948 as part of Orii Hyūga's project to analyze job content scientifically. A job was assigned points, and thus a monetary value, based on the calories expended in performing it. Every man engaged in a broadly defined task such as "furnace work" would receive the same job wage, a feature criticized by veterans who received no credit for skill or seniority. It never accounted for more than 7 percent of an average man's pay, and in 1951 it was abolished.[23]

For the rest of the decade, despite a new plan in 1957 to introduce a "job factor" into the calculation of the output wage, labor managers were unable to implement a unified, companywide system of job wages. According to Orii, the union was the main obstacle. Many leading unionists had a major stake in both seniority and output pay, because senior skilled workers and those who received large shares of the output wage (direct producers, especially furnace workers) supported the existing system. Younger workers and those engaged in indirect, support roles (machine and electrical workers) were amenable to reform. Finally, from 1961 to 1963—as with the case of IE techniques, *after* the 1959 strike—the labor division and the union agreed to introduce a new, companywide job wage to account for a significant minority of each man's pay. A large portion of the old output pay was transferred to this category. Jobs were assessed in terms of their physical demands and skill levels, and wage rates were assigned to them. With the assumption that the higher the job rating, the more value added to the company, managers were trying to hold down labor costs by linking pay to productivity.

In these reforms of staffing and wages, the investment drive of the 1950s created direct pressure to produce more efficiently, which in turn sparked new programs to manage labor. In other realms, this causal chain was more circuitous. Japanese steelmakers in the 1950s were plagued by extremely high material costs, which nullified their labor cost advantage.[24] Not surprisingly, production managers tried all possible methods of cutting material costs. While the connection here to labor management was less direct, it was no less important.

More efficient use of raw materials was the greatest production challenge. While precise statistics are elusive, in the 1950s Japanese iron- and steelmakers imported nearly all needed raw materials, whether scrap iron, ore, coal, limestone, or oil. One analyst concluded that in the 1950s raw materials accounted for about 75 percent of the cost of iron and steel production in the integrated mills of the top six companies, far outweighing costs of labor and capital.[25] As late as 1957, a Japanese producer's cost in raw materials per ton of output was nearly more than double that for a typical American steelmaker.[26]

Japan's steel manufacturers eliminated this disadvantage in just over a decade. By 1970, their material costs per unit of output were roughly equivalent to those of American and European producers, and they had taken an important step toward becoming internationally competitive. The MITI-orchestrated transport project was part of this story. It helped lower import costs by developing economical large cargo ships. But the larger portion of cost savings came from producing more iron and steel with fewer and cheaper materials.

Such cost savings were achieved by innovations in production that linked the efficient use of labor to the success of the 1950s investment drive.[27] But the men dealing with material costs did not see themselves as labor managers, and they were not so designated. Only after the fact have observers connected these factors, arguing that by the early 1960s innovations in Japanese production and quality control (QC) techniques were pointing toward a distinctive system to organize work and mobilize workers.

A central figure in this story at NKK was Imaizumi Masumasa, son of NKK's founder. Imaizumi studied engineering and quality control at Tokyo University in the late 1940s with a great guru of this field in Japan, Ishikawa Kaoru, and he developed a fascination bordering on obsession with enhancing the efficiency and quality of industrial production in Japan. Both as a manager at NKK and as a leader in the Japan Union of Scientists and Engineers (JUSE), Imaizumi was a pioneer in the quality control movement.

When Imaizumi entered NKK in 1950, the company had no separate division of staff engineers to coordinate matters of quality and production management. Technical personnel were instead given line responsibilities, dispersed throughout the mill to work with shop supervisors and foremen. Their first responsibility was to manage production directly. In addition, they were to improve quality where possible. Imaizumi was assigned to the coke section. To make more efficient use of materials, he set out to devise a formal system to control quality in mixing coal with other ingredients and in running the coke ovens.[28] As he took on this challenge, Imaizumi found considerable support from his peers as well as top management. Even in 1950, before the American expert Edward Deming came to Japan and gave his now famous first lectures on this topic, a group of NKK technicians had formed a statistical quality control (SQC) study group. In 1951 NKK's competitors at Yahata and Fuji won the first annual Deming prize for their corporate quality control projects, and the next year NKK president Kawada issued a memorandum calling for "deeper understanding of statistical quality control among all employees." By October 1953 the SQC study group at the Kawaskai mill had become a committee headed by the mill director and staffed by the chief technical personnel from various divisions. This body coordinated a network of subcommittees at each production site. Experts on the central committee would visit the workplace groups and teach the detailed methods of SQC.[29]

This decentralized approach to managing production and quality was typical of Japanese manufacturers in the 1950s. Since well before the war, the division of responsibility between technical staff and line managers had been imprecise. As Japan began a feverish drive of catch-up industrialization in the nineteenth century, the pool of technical experts and skilled workers was shallow. This scarcity appears to have forced companies to throw all qualified personnel onto the front lines of production, leaving no room for the luxury of specialized quality control or production engineering staff. In Imaizumi's father's day at Yahata and NKK, a handful of veteran workers who had risen to the position of supervisory foreman had worked together with school-educated technicians to manage production at the various sites in the mill.[30] This interaction continued in most early postwar manufacturing industries.

Decades later, authorities on Japanese-style management began to praise these close ties between production workers, line supervisors, and technicians as key features of a flexible managerial style, better suited to meet the ever-changing technical demands of modern manufacturing than an American-style regime where engineers told workers and foremen what to do from the aloof and lofty perch of the production engineering staff. They called the close relationship between rank-and-file workers, their supervisors, and technical experts a secret of the world-beating Japanese system.[31]

But in the 1950s, NKK managers had no such pride. Determined to overcome what they considered the backward practices of the past, they looked to American industry for the secrets of success and decided that a specialized technical staff was a necessity and a strength, not a luxury or an obstacle. In 1954 NKK abandoned the dispersed committee approach to quality control by founding a new "control division" consisting of quality control, process control, and production control sections.[32] In the face of protests from line supervisors reluctant to lose their full-time technical assistants, the company pulled engineers, including Imaizumi, from their remote assignments on the shop floor to staff these units. The new QC section was charged to develop an expert overview of the entire production process, with the goal of planning and executing improvements from a central perspective. NKK was desperately seeking to Americanize its system of managing production.

Managers at industrial plants throughout Japan undertook similar initiatives, and they initially confronted American-style dilemmas as well. In the now classic story told and retold by QC experts such as Ishikawa and Imaizumi, after quality control was brought to Japan by the occupation forces in 1946, it remained the province of experts for over a decade. As in America, Japanese companies enthusiastically nurtured cadres of expert technicians trained in the obscure art of statistical quality control.[33] In addition, both Ishikawa and Imaizumi recall an American-style antagonism between such experts and experienced shop-floor leaders. The latter operated on the basis of experience and intuition. They complained that SQC was complex, esoteric, and useless knowledge imposed on them by experts who did not really understand production. Imaizumi recalls there was a "great social distance" between himself and the coke workers who distrusted him as an elite interloper.

Managerial programs that impose centralized expertise on workers are the essence of Taylorism, the system of scientific management first developed in the United States by Frederick Taylor in the early twentieth century, in which technical experts analyzed workers' jobs and told them how to perform more efficiently. The NKK decision to pull Imaizumi and his fellow engineers from production sites into a central quality control staff is emblematic of just such a Tayloristic approach in early postwar Japan.

But for some reason, numerous Japanese companies, NKK among them, tempered and then reversed this centralizing impulse in production and quality control. Ishikawa and Imaizumi both claim to have realized that rather than dictating to workers from afar, QC experts should work closely with the rank and file to draw on their expertise. In 1956 the company reported that

> we offer a one year general education program for blue-collar operatives expected to become leaders in the future, and as part of that we spend about 20 hours on the concepts and methods of quality control. By now, about 500 people have completed this course. Also, *in response to requests from each section,* we have dispatched quality control section staff to the shop floor to lead on-site short courses in QC, and in some places where the interest is very strong, have done this outside of working hours.[34]

Imaizumi recalls that foremen were the chief students in these mini-courses, which were designed to train them in the techniques of SQC and send them back to the shop floor to spread the word to others.[35] As a pioneer American advocate of quality control in Japan, Joseph M. Juran, noted sourly in 1954, "companies in Japan today are implementing QC through line supervisors . . . it is better to introduce QC by giving thorough training to a few groups."[36] These early activities mark the first stirrings of quality control as a system of widespread small-group activities, foreshadowing a shift in the meaning of the abbreviation QC from "quality control" to "quality circles." This was the start of a crucial breakthrough to "total quality control" (TQC) involving technicians, foremen, and the rank and file.

Three factors—the social legacy of late development, the impact of dramatic technological innovation on workplace society, and the need to respond to inroads made by militant unions—explain Japan's shift from centralized to companywide QC programs. These factors gave foremen, in particular, motive and opportunity to push for a participatory version of quality control. They had been interested in QC techniques before the QC section was set up.[37] Early shop-floor training in QC came "in response to requests from each section." NKK's supposed managerial innovation took place because the workplace leaders asked for it.

The legacy of late development that lay behind this turn was the absence of a sharp divide between line supervisors and technical staff. The practice of decentralized deployment of technicians—exemplified in Imaizumi's initial assignment to the coke section—meant that the line foremen were people who customarily worked *with* technical staff in making decisions about production and quality control. As Imaizumi enthusiastically tells the story, the early tension between this Tokyo University graduate and his foreman evaporated after several years on the job, on the day that he donated blood to a co-worker who suffered a serious injury.[38] Clearly a social gap existed between Imaizumi and the furnace workers, but it did not rule out cooperation among technicians, foremen, and unranked men.

As steelmaking and other technologies changed rapidly in the 1950s, foremen feared losing the prestige that derived from their mastery of old skills. They viewed quality control as a new tool with which to sustain their legitimacy as workplace leaders. Ishikawa reports that the foremen often came to technical experts and demanded to be taught these techniques in simple language.[39] Imaizumi similarly recalls that after initial reluctance, foremen embraced QC activity. Likewise, managers came to view QC as a way to boost morale and draw workers, especially foremen, away from union activism by mobilizing their energies in support of company goals.

Steel industry managers in the 1950s, committed to massive investment in new plant and equipment, thus began a multifaceted, ongoing drive to remake labor and production management. They sought to rationalize labor costs by streamlining the workforce with industrial engineering, introducing job wage systems, and better controlling quality and material costs. The results in all cases pointed toward some distinctive features of the Japanese workplace of later years: job security for core workers if they cooperated with industrial engineering and accepted the possibility of interplant (even long-distance) transfer; pay that reflected factors other than seniority; "voluntary" quality control activity with participation rates of nearly 100 percent.

At NKK and throughout the steel industry, these managerial initiatives of the 1950s were shaped and pushed forward partly in response to a renewed surge of union activism. In addition to new departures in managing wages, staffing, and production, all the major steelmakers addressed a crisis of workplace control by remaking the hierarchy of supervision. In the early 1950s at NKK, men in four supervisory levels were union members. They all began their working life at the bottom, typically working ten years before promotion to even the lowest of these ranks, twenty years or more before becoming a foreman.[40] Ranked workers were senior, skilled men with few formal managerial powers, but great informal authority. They advised staff on the performance of subordinates and on promotions and pay raises, and they monopolized the union local's elected offices. Policies of both company and union recognized that foremen were pivotal figures. The company sought their cooperation and that of their wives in its plans to rationalize staffing, wages, or family life and to improve quality control. The union sought to win their active support or, failing that, to constrain the ability of foremen to impose managerial decisions unilaterally upon the rank and file.

Konda Masaharu was the personnel manager charged with redesigning the job of foreman in the 1950s. He believed that labor relations at that time were "fractured" and strikes common because the attitudes of employees had changed under the impact of democratic ideas. Konda and his colleagues found the foremen to be ineffective managers because their position as leaders in the workplace had deteriorated. Beginning as early as 1951, NKK had made reform of the foreman system a major priority. The labor division carried out numerous surveys, deciding finally that the chain of command was confused, authority unclear, and promotions unbalanced. They wanted to define the foreman's role more clearly and shore up his authority over his subordinates as well as the company's control over him.[41]

But progress was slow. One major step, taken by the labor division in 1956, was to streamline the hierarchy from four levels to three, writing new job descriptions for each rank and re-assessing the qualifications of every supervisor. In the process, 685 men were promoted and 178 were demoted.[42] NKK continued to screen and educate foremen more carefully and clarify the chain of command. The insecurity generated among those thus scrutinized led some to support union activism through the 1950s and, as Konda notes, "despite this effort at reform, labor-management relations at NKK did not improve one bit."[43] To the contrary, NKK experienced the most intense strikes in its history in 1957 and 1959.

Through it all, the pace of technological innovation was furious. NKK actually lagged behind its competitors by several years in introducing a cutting-edge cold strip mill, but finally a new mill at Mizue, close by the main Kawasaki plant, started operations in 1960 (see Figure 4). At this point, after the great strikes, the company embarked on a second round of reform of the workplace hierarchy. Konda recalls: "At Mizue, from the standpoint of efficient use of modernized facilities, we adopted a centralized line/staff system, and we further simplified ranks from three levels to two levels." In this new "foreman system," the foreman's responsibilities were limited to supervision of day-to-day work operations, thus clarifying a division between line supervisors at the production site (foremen) and staff in the central office (technicians and white-collar managers). But in this more limited realm, the foreman's authority over the workers was increased. "As this was a state-of-the-art mill that involved a massive investment, we placed special effort into labor relations and used great energy and all kinds of 'tricks' to educate line supervisors about labor management."[44]

As Orii Hyūga recalled, innovation was far easier at the new Mizue mill where, unlike Kawasaki and Tsurumi, older social practices of diffuse supervision were not entrenched. Not until several years later, once the company felt confident that the new foreman system would work, did managers extend it to the older mills. Through these reforms, NKK was not simply trying to manage labor more efficiently. In the wake of bitter strikes, it was struggling to regain political control of the workplace.

NKK's program to "modernize" its labor management and control the workplace in the 1950s had a remarkably ambitious reach. The company sought not only to rationalize the productive activities of the men at the steel mill; it also implemented systematic programs to manage the leisure activities of workers and families and even the consuming and reproductive functions of their wives at home. One of NKK's most unusual and important extracurricular activities in these years was called the New Life Movement. Its object was not the male worker, but his wife.

This campaign, with prewar and wartime roots, began in the late 1940s as a set of loosely connected initiatives of local government offices and women's organizations that sought to "rationalize daily life," by which advocates meant improving morality, efficiency, and hygiene in the home through activities such as democratizing social relations, redesigning kitchens, and killing flies. In 1953, Nippon Kōkan became the first private corporation in Japan to join the movement. Later that same year, the Japan Industrial Club led the five major business federations to organize a New Life Movement Association, and two years later, the government declared its moral and financial support of a nationwide New Life Movement. The NKK program became a model for corporations around Japan, and by 1957 at least fifty major companies employing one million people had launched programs similar to that at NKK.[45]

The making of steel took place in a man's world. In 1952, just 6 percent of NKK's 26,391 workers were women, who mainly worked in offices at clerical tasks, with a handful serving as inspectors or lab assistants.[46] The male steelworkers viewed their jobs in gendered terms; union organizer Isobe Toshie spoke of his first days in the mill as "real man's work."[47] Such sentiments could help unions build solidarity on the basis of a common male culture of the workplace; but if technicians, foremen, and section heads were seen as part of the workplace group as well, Isobe's attitude could easily lead him to identify manliness with a company world as much as a union culture. Such gendered thinking provided a receptive environment for corporate calls for a male worker's wife to support her family by supporting his company.

Orii Hyūga's memoir neatly sums up the spirit animating the New Life Movement at NKK: "Workplace and home are intimately related parts of any person's life. Life in the family is the barometer for the next day's life. In principle, the housewife is in charge of family life, and we can say that the husband both takes his rest and builds his energy under her leadership. Thus, our goal was to elevate the housewives who played this role, and establish the foundation for a bright, cheerful home, a bright society, and beyond that, a bright, cheerful workplace."[48]

NKK, Toshiba, and Hitachi developed some of the best-known corporate New Life programs. They began with birth control, as managers joined with the Welfare Ministry and its Population Problem Research Center to discourage abortion and promote contraception. Over time, the movement broadened its mission and addressed matters of nutrition, shopping and cooking, keeping household accounts, child rearing, and use of leisure time. These companies set up a New Life Movement office in the welfare section of corporate headquarters and designated a personnel official in each plant to promote the movement. They assembled a staff of in-house employees and outside counselors to organize the wives of workers into hundreds of small groups.

By 1954, NKK had made 5,366 worker households the objects of New Life activity, dividing the city of Kawasaki into twenty districts of roughly 300 households, with a counseling center in each district. The centers dispatched counselors on home visits and organized the wives into small groups of about fifteen women each. These groups met monthly to discuss ways to improve hygiene, cook more nutritious meals, and better educate their children; they joined larger excursions to the theatre or the movies.[49] By 1963, 63 percent of NKK's 27,000 employee households were organized into New Life groups.

The movement appears to have been well received and influential as it reached out to the numerous full-time housewives of NKK workers and supported them in that role. An independent survey made in 1957 of 77 families in a working-class neighborhood in Kawasaki offers important evidence.[50] The men in this neighborhood were relatively skilled, senior workers; 21 worked at NKK, 7 at Toshiba, and 6 at Hitachi shipbuilding. There was at least one union member in 61 of the households. One can see the extraordinarily rigid gender division of labor in the fact that the husband and wife both worked outside the home in only 6 households. Most of the women in this survey had charge of household budgets; four fifths of the men reported handing over their wage envelope intact to their wives.

These women seem to have appreciated the company's offer to make their work more "modern," scientific, and respected. The 1957 survey found that all 21 NKK housewives who lived in the area were part of company New Life groups, with a group leader acting as liaison between the company counselor and the members. In addition to monthly meetings, they attended lectures on civic morality and classes on cooking, sewing, knitting, futon repair, or flower arranging, and they set off on shopping expeditions to learn to be frugal consumers. Counselors went from house to house to encourage contraception, and condoms were reported to be widely used. The survey concluded that the women were enthusiastic participants for a variety of reasons, including sociability; the monthly meetings were said to be an extension of "gossip by the well side."

The New Life Movement joined the contest between company and union for worker allegiance. Because of a new postwar sensitivity to avoid "undemocratic" intervention in people's lives, the movement's involvement was rarely made explicit. But it was certainly present, discernible in statements such as that by a Toshiba labor manager, who wrote in 1957 that the New Life Movement was a form of "service" to employees, a manifestation of goodwill and caring of company for employees that would "naturally" generate trust and intimacy between the employees and the company.[51] The 1957 survey of Kawasaki working-class families concluded by describing the different responses of worker's wives to the union newspaper and the New Life Movement newsletter: "Without question, these two family-oriented publications are sites of an ideological battle tied to union-company struggles."[52]

Organizing wives into support groups was also a common strategy of large unions in male-dominated workplaces in the 1950s. In the Miike coal mines, the wives' group was a source of great strength for one of Japan's most powerful unions. More than their husbands, these women were part of community networks that could build local support, and wives committed to the union cause would not pressure husbands to quit a prolonged strike. As managers at NKK reached out to the home with the New Life Movement in 1953, the union was launching competing efforts.

At the Tsurumi mill, the union began to build support among worker families, particularly those in company housing, when it purchased a movie projector in 1952 and began to sponsor several "family nights" each month.

In addition to entertainment, the gatherings offered a chance for leaders to hear complaints or requests from residents.[53] Both NKK unions then undertook to organize the wives of the steelworkers shortly after the company launched its New Life Movement. In 1953 the Tsurumi union designated one executive committee member as a full-time "family organizer."[54] Kamimura Hideji, one of the Kawasaki union founders in 1945 and later a full-time officer and union vice-president, helped organize that union's Housewives Discussion Society.[55] He later contended that the women's groups were an overlooked reason for the increased energy of both unions in the 1950s. The Kawasaki union extended the grassroots tactic of workplace struggle to this outreach program in December 1954 by systematically convening discussion sessions for wives.

Like the company's New Life Movement, the Housewives Discussion Society was organized into neighborhood units, the women chose officers from among their number, and they met to address shared problems. Group leaders became especially energetic supporters of the union, and during strikes the wives helped out with organizing tasks, as they had done informally in the past. The cover of the 1956 Tsurumi union history offered a powerful picture of worker and wife as a unit of action, a simple red line drawing of the steelworker, one hand clutching tongs, the other wiping his brow, with his helpmate at his side, gently touching his arm and gazing with care at his tired figure.[56]

In retrospect, this drive to mobilize wives behind the union was less effective than the company's New Life Movement at winning the hearts and minds of employees' homemakers. Ōshima Ai was a young woman hired in 1957 by the NKK welfare section as one of the six counselors who administered the New Life Movement. She maintained that the activities of the union groups were not as varied as those of the New Life Movement and did not generate the same enthusiasm, despite the small meal or transport allowance given to those who attended the union's sessions.[57] The official in charge of the union's Youth and Women's Section in 1957–58 similarly lamented that when NKK purposely scheduled New Life activities to coincide with union wives' discussions, women would choose the former due to peer pressure despite the train fare and free food they were given at the union meeting. The wives believed that actively participating in the New Life Movement would help their husbands advance at work.[58]

Although union activists and company managers defined the ideal workplace in conflicting ways, they held basically similar ideals regarding the home. Both wanted the wife to be a competent household manager who would nurture the husband to function effectively, whether at work or in the union. The vastly superior resources of the company put the union at a great disadvantage, and the New Life Movement was an important episode in the complementary histories of gender and work relations in postwar Japan. It involved major corporations directly in a campaign to reinforce the role of the modern homemaker as part of a broader corporate drive to "rationalize" society, raise productivity, and expand the economy. As the rationalization of the household proceeded parallel to that of the firm, the corporate-centered society became more firmly linked to a particular structure of gender roles. The movement worked to preempt the possibility that home and family might become sources of support for union values opposed to those of the enterprise.

Similar sharp divisions between a male-centered world of work, especially in industries such as steel or mining, and a female world at home were commonplace around the world at the time (and before and since). In the global history of industrial capitalism, many companies have directed personnel policies at reform of employees' family lives.[59] But the Japanese case is distinctive in some ways. The explicit and ambitious role of not only government agencies but also private corporations was unparalleled. The sociology department at the Ford Motor Company hired social workers to visit employee homes and help solve domestic "problems," as the company defined them, as early as 1915, and a few other major American firms followed suit.[60] A number of postwar German corporations offered social services to employee wives. But none of these efforts were as extensive and sustained as those of Japan's major corporations. Nowhere else did the business community with state encouragement organize a national campaign to orchestrate training for over one million wives of male industrial workers.

The Japanese case is without parallel as well in using small groups, or circles, to mobilize and educate housewives. The resemblance between the circles at the heart of the New Life Movement and quality control circles is uncanny. More than a decade after rural circles of the New Life Movement began to form in 1947, and about five years after the corporate version organized company wives into small groups, the quality circle movement took off throughout Japan. By the 1970s, millions of men, and a fair number of women, had joined small groups to solve the problems of daily work life, just as some women had done at home twenty years earlier. Workers in the 1960s and 1970s triumphantly reported reductions in cycle time and the like at company, then regional, then national conferences, as farm women and city housewives had done with kitchen redesign in the 1950s. Both movements reflect a distinctive pattern of social action and mobilization. At some level, latent or manifest, managers and workers must have been aware that their New Life endeavors informed their quality control projects. The organization of home and of work in recent Japanese history has been marked by the collective pursuit of efficiency, productivity, and rationality.

The union was the greatest obstacle facing Nippon Kōkan managers who tried to control the workforce and raise productivity by rationalizing operations. Union activists, with growing support from the rank and file, struggled for higher wages and also sought to control the workplace. They viewed this control as a step toward remaking the company hierarchy and, beyond that, the larger political order. It is no surprise that NKK labor managers took drastic, sometimes illegal, steps, including what Konda Masaharu called "tricks" of supervisor education, to change the union.

Among their most prominent legitimate initiatives, managers in steel took an extremely hard line in wage bargaining. They usually prevailed, but at the cost of increasingly bitter and prolonged strikes from 1953 through 1959. On the surface, wages were at issue, but the unbending managerial stand was grounded more profoundly in a growing determination to destroy or transform the union.

A second major above-board initiative of corporate Japan in the 1950s was a drive to remake management councils into building blocks of cooperative industrial relations. Thousands of collective bargaining agreements had been concluded in 1946 and 1947, usually for three-year terms. When these came up for renewal, executives insisted on revising them. At NKK managers wanted to repudiate contracts that had bound them to obtain union agreement for firings, transfers, and other personnel decisions and had created management councils with broad decision-making powers. Both the Kawasaki and Tsurumi mill unions resisted new contracts proposed in 1949 and 1950. When the old ones lapsed, company and union conducted their business for a time with no contractual framework to guide them. By 1952, with the unions demoralized and in disarray, new contracts were signed. These replaced the need for union "agreement" on personnel issues with a pledge to "consult" the union. They replaced the management council with a "labor-management discussion council" with a much-narrowed mission and limited powers.[61]

NKK thus anticipated a national campaign for joint consultation led by the Japan Productivity Center. Taking cues from European practice, but rejecting the German path of legally mandated works councils, from its founding in 1955 the Center promoted councils as institutions that company and union would create at the enterprise or plant level. In them, union or employee representatives would sit down with managers to exchange ideas in a context separate from collective bargaining. The councils were to be forums for consultation on issues where managers and employees were said to have interests in common: increasing productivity, improving safety, or operating employee welfare services. The Center in 1959 reported a remarkable pendulum swing over a decade. At their peak in 1947, management councils, often dominated by unions, had been established at 44 percent of all unionized workplaces in Japan. As labor laws were revised and contracts renegotiated, this fell to just 24 percent by 1950. In the early 1950s, both Nikkeiren and many managers were reluctant to replace these with more narrowly defined councils, fearing that unions would use them to seek managerial control. But this anxiety gradually receded, and by June 1958 the new breed of labor-management discussion council could be found in 37 percent of Japan's unionized workplaces.[62]

The Center had high hopes for these bodies, which it conveyed with the classic rhetoric of an American mode of business unionism. Joint consultation was expected to "solve new problems arising between labor and management in the course of technological innovation in a rational and peaceful way and build a system of positive cooperation between labor and capital." While "the first industrial revolution" was marked by "tragedy and confusion" and a fight to "divide the pie," in the new "second industrial revolution" technology would "expand the pie," and labor and capital would share it in a spirit of mutual respect.[63]

As NKK set up its new council in 1952, executives were determined "to stabilize the labor-management relationship on the basis of mutual trust" using "powerful PR," in Orii Hyūga's words, to "create a healthy labor-management relationship and protect the company."[64] Some steps were public and others were essentially covert. With the consent of the union, Professor Odaka Kunio conducted his first attitude survey at NKK in 1952, providing a social-scientific grounding for the company's effort. Odaka graded employee attitudes toward both union and company as negative, neutral, or positive. Both he and Orii expected that loyalties would be mutually exclusive. That is, they assumed most workers would be anti-company and pro-union, or the reverse. They dubbed these "con-pro" or "pro-con" workers. But the results at NKK and the other eight companies Odaka surveyed in the 1950s "confounded our expectations completely."[65] As in similar surveys in the United States, the "pro-pro" workers showing dual allegiance to company and union were the single most numerous type. Employees of divided allegiance were relatively rare (see Figure 5).[66]

Despite this welcome finding, Orii was troubled to find that the youngest workers were relatively pro-union and anti-company.[67] After five to seven years on the job, the "pro-pro" workers increased sharply in number, and veteran foremen were models of dual allegiance. In 1954 Orii concluded that personnel managers should direct their persuasive PR at younger workers above all and should carefully train supervisors in the art of nurturing loyalty among new recruits.[68] But before this was possible, he and his associates had to transform the union leadership so it could strengthen the allegiance of younger workers to the company.

To achieve this, managers at NKK and at virtually every major company in Japan took steps that systematically violated the letter of the law. Their most controversial practice was to nurture dissident factions within the union, called "informal groups" because they were not formally constituted in the union bylaws. Orii notes that "forces critical of the leftist tendency [in the union] began sprouting nationally around 1951." Using the passive voice, which avoids the question of agency, he reports that "in our company, as everywhere, the organization of these forces gradually progressed."[69]

Watanabe Tatsuo was a feisty labor division employee who entered the company in 1951, when a high school education still allowed one to enter a lower-level managerial track.[70] Watanabe began his career on the front lines of labor management, dispatched by the personnel office to tighten up the porous system of attendance and time recording at the scattered work sites around the mill. He soon became an able warrior in the battle to remake the union. "We identified a sympathetic group in the workplace, one that fortunately was just emerging on its own, and gave it all possible backing." Watanabe claims that such bodies typically started out as independent "study groups" but notes that company aid was critical to their growth. He and his colleagues embarked on a sustained project to build up these loyalist forces. Key institutions that greatly aided them included the merit evaluations used in the 1950s to determine annual pay increases and the expanded merit-based wages and promotions of the 1960s. The labor division made sure that merit evaluations favored the informal group members, who could argue with conviction to workmates that supporting the group was a wise career move.

Much of the activity to promote informal groups took place in a nighttime world of secret meetings in bars and restaurants. A labor division veteran of this demimonde, Kondo Haruhiko, recalls organizing meetings of his embattled allies in the smaller and more left-leaning Tsurumi mill union.[71] He would bring along leaders of an informal group at the Kawasaki mill to give the Tsurumi men a pep talk. As a university graduate Kondo saw his role as articulating the ideology of cooperative unionism. He would lecture workers on the dangers of communism or socialism as the road to destruction for the company and call for cooperation in making a bigger pie, so all could take home larger pieces. For Kondo, as for Watanabe and certainly for unionists on all sides, this activity was a mission more than a job: "I liked the work. I devoted myself to it. For years I hardly ever went home before midnight. I was addicted the way some people are to politics."

Secrecy was hard to maintain, and these efforts did not go unchallenged. Kondo recalls the union president at Tsurumi accusing him of violating the labor union law by meeting after hours with workers. Kondo retorted that "in spite of the union slogan that 'there is neither left nor right at Tsurumi,' the truth is that there's only a left, and the left group meets secretly anyway, doesn't it?! So what's wrong with organizing a right-wing group to restore the balance?"

In the Kawasaki mill alone, there were at least five informal groups within the union. The oldest and the most vigorous stronghold of company loyalists was the Labor Problems Research Group, allied to the right wing of the Japan Socialist Party. The father of NKK's Research Group was Kudō Shinpachi. Active in the union from its founding, Kudō had developed a visceral antipathy toward the Communist Party. In the 1950s, he joined with a number of like-minded workers around the mill to fight their enemy, and they eventually founded the Research Group. Kudō delights in the story of his visit to the famous anticommunist crusader (and former CP member) Mitamura Shirō. In the 1950s, Mitamura ran a private academy to train anticommunist activists. When Kudō showed up unannounced at his office, Mitamura was astonished: Kudō had come without financing or prompting from his company! "[Mitamura] told me I was the first such case in his experience," said Kudō, and Mitamura enrolled him with no tuition charge. Kudō finished his course, and he estimates that in subsequent years he sent about 500 young workers to the Mitamura school. They became the core of the Research Group.[72]

The group's members were almost exclusively production workers, with particular strength in Kudō's furnace section, but with support at every work site and thus every union local.[73] Members argued that the union's program to resist rationalization and promote workplace struggle was an absurd stance of opposition for its own sake. They stressed the need to cooperate with the company for the sake of both NKK and its workers. According to one of the few white-collar members of the group, Gotō Tatsuo, this simple idea gave the group its coherence. Its leaders were almost all ranked men with much prestige in the workplace. When negotiations took place between union and company, the Research Group would meet to map out a strategy to pressure nonmembers to support the company, and managers from the labor division, including the division chief, would sometimes attend.[74]

A second informal group emerged as an active force several years later. This was the Acorn Club (Shiinomi kai), centered on lower-level white-collar workers who were union members, especially men in the iron and coke sections. Its founders were mostly activists in the union's planning section who strongly opposed the union leadership. From 1954 to 1959, the Acorn Club evolved from a social club of like-minded union members to a faction with a coherent ideology and strategy. Members began meeting in 1954, and the group came into the open as a political force in 1959, when it circulated anti-strike petitions throughout the mill.[75]

These two informal groups continuously invoked the mantra of "cooperate with the company to share the growing pie." Other factions stood in uneasy alliance or in direct opposition to them. In the center, seeking to mediate the split between left and right in the name of working-class unity, was the "Third Group," founded by Isobe Toshie and named in the spirit of Nehru's concept of a third force of nonaligned nations during the Cold War.[76] To Isobe's left stood the largest faction on the union's executive committee in the 1950s, the group loyal to the left wing of the Japan Socialist Party. These socialist union leaders constituted an informal group called the Comrades Club (Dōshikai) at NKK and in unions throughout Japan. Their size invited tactical weakness. Because they could prevail in union elections in the 1950s though broad appeals to the entire workforce, they felt less need than their opponents to build a strong organization *within* the union, and the Comrades Club remained less cohesive than the above three factions until the 1960s. Only when they lost control of the union did the left-wing socialists' sense of crisis precipitate a belated drive to build a more formal "informal" group.

Finally, the Communist Party remained a significant minority force at NKK in the 1950s and 1960s. A few members had escaped the purge of 1950. Their strategy was to keep a low profile and organize from below as workplace activists rather than seek elected union office. They sought to revitalize the union at the production site on the model of the Miike mine union, joining nonparty workplace organizers such as Isobe.[77]

NKK sought to remake the union by nurturing the first two of these five groups, the Research Group and the Acorn Club. Eventually this strategy bore fruit, but the harvest was slow. Through the decade of the 1950s NKK's main crop seemed to be grapes of wrath. Not all managers supported the strategy of reliance on informal groups. Orii and Konda Masaharu, in particular, warned against the danger of becoming trapped by an informal group that could get out of hand, as in the notorious case of Nissan Motors. After it broke a bitter strike in 1953, the loyalist union at Nissan wielded powerful influence in personnel affairs for decades as the price of continued support.[78] To avoid the Nissan trap, Orii preferred to build loyalty to the company through training programs and PR aimed at the entire workforce rather than through secret support for union factions.[79]

Managers at NKK followed both Orii's strategy of generalized persuasion and Kondo's design for capturing the union via informal groups. In 1954, frantic maneuvering via foremen, supervisors, and informal groups allowed managers to convince the rank and file not to honor a planned strike. Kondo recalls, "I was not sure until the morning of the strike whether they would come to work or not," but Kudō's Research Group induced nearly 100 percent attendance among furnace workers, and the strike collapsed.[80] In 1955, however, the union's strike supporters held firm against such pressure and won a significant victory in a wage dispute. Despite their steady promotion of the loyalist factions, NKK managers seemed to be losing their grip in the face of the union offensive. New methods to control staffing and set wages were hotly contested. When they did prevail, advocates of the cooperative workplace relied to a great extent on coercion. The enterprise-dominated society had yet to make the leap from embattled ideology to hegemonic order.

5   *Forging an Activist Union*

As Japanese corporate managers remade the physical and social structure of the factory, they faced a heightened spirit of grassroots activism. Beginning in the early 1950s unionists in numerous major workplaces improvised a variety of shop-floor struggles. They revitalized unions that had been demoralized by the combined shocks of Dodge-plan deflation and the Red Purge, and more generally by the reverse course of the American occupiers and Japan's ruling elites. Famous early sites of shop-floor struggles in 1952 and 1953 included Nissan Motors, the Mitsui company's Miike mine, and the Hokuriku Railway Company.[1] Shop-floor activism then spread to ship-building, to chemical and paper pulp manufacturing, and to the iron and steel industry.[2] Unionists at NKK and the other major mills enthusiastically supported the tactic. The labor offensive of the 1950s broadened the scope of democratic institutions through which working people won some voice over decisions about the routines of their daily life as well as wages.

Other forms of activism flourished in these years. Millions of women and men joined politically oriented "cultural circles" as well as student and citizen movements against nuclear weapons, the United States–Japan Security Treaty, and efforts of the Liberal Democratic Party (LDP) to curtail civil liberties and revise what it condemned as the "MacArthur constitution." As progressives outside the factory and labor activists within began to work together for these causes and win significant popular and media support, a sense of crisis deepened among superintendents of order in the LDP, the bureaucracy, and the business elite. Common phrases of the time referred to an impending "total confrontation of labor and capital." Credible prognosticators spoke not of enduring conservative or corporate hegemony, but of its collapse.[3] For sober observers on all sides, the future appeared to be up for grabs.

At NKK, the Red Purge of 1950 brought the firing of 144 workers and generated a strong fear that speaking up might "cost us our jobs, and even the chance to work for any company." But beginning in late 1952 and coinciding with the start of the company's rationalization program, the unions at both mills began to revive.[4] The Tsurumi union bought a "radio car" (a car with a speaker on the roof to broadcast mobile messages) and movie projector to use for worker education, increased the strike fund levy per worker, redesigned union publications to reflect rank-and-file voices more directly, and put more energy into mutual aid activities.

The most important new initiative was a two-pronged organizing strategy to stimulate members to raise complaints and negotiate them forcefully.[5] Each mill's union began to hold regular workplace discussion meetings at which members were encouraged to voice their grievances. The unions also implemented an ingenious "organizer" *(orugu)* system to facilitate such meetings and to address the issues they raised. Organizers and assemblies were the critical tools that brought a new measure of democratic vitality to these and other unions.

Problems stemming from the dual role of foremen as supervisors and union members provoked these reforms. At NKK and in most Japanese companies at the time, each work site (the coke furnace, the number 1 blast furnace, the pipe rolling section, and so forth) was constituted as a union local with anywhere from 50 to 500 members. Foremen or crew bosses were usually elected as president and other officers, in part because they had the flexible schedules needed to serve in these unpaid positions. An unranked worker often feared asking a local union officer, who was also his supervisor, to press a complaint about work conditions.

The plant-level executive committees of both the Tsurumi and Kawasaki unions designated several full-time officials to serve as organizers precisely to offer such men an alternative route of appeal. They assigned each organizer to patrol a handful of locals. Their decisive innovation was to have the organizer report directly to the executive committee, bypassing the local officers. He was to patrol his "beat" regularly, get to know the workers and their complaints, and relay these to union headquarters in weekly reports. The executive committee would decide what action, if any, would be taken. In addition, the organizer, rather than the head of the union local, would run the workplace discussion meetings.

Matsuda Takezō and Isobe Toshie offer rich accounts of the organizer system at the Kawasaki mill. Among the union's founders in 1945, Matsuda had been elected to a variety of full-time posts since 1948. In 1954 he was chosen to head the newly created organizing division. Isobe was hired as a furnace worker in one of the rolling mills in 1947, and he quickly became active in the union local. In 1952 he was elected to a full-time union office. Two years later, he was one of three union officers, all unranked workers in their early thirties, assigned to work under Matsuda. Inspired by the activism and militant tactics of workplace organizers in the Ube Chemical and Nissan Motors unions, the organizers raised the banner of workplace struggle.

As Matsuda recalls, their goal was to revitalize the union by replacing organizing from above with the self-generated activity of the rank and file. This meant moving away from a notion of organizing as an activity focused on mobilizing for strikes to organizing around day-to-day problems in the workplace. Their mission was to "dig up" problems in the workplace, bring the union leadership into closer contact with the mass of the workers, and end the domination of the union by foremen and, through them, by managers. Not surprisingly, Matsuda reports that managers such as Konda Masaharu were shocked. But they could not prevent the organizers from going to work. Full-time union officers had been restricted from entering workshops freely, but in 1954 the union won a major victory when it negotiated permission for the organizers to wear a special armband that signified their right to go into any workplace and talk to anyone.[6]

The idea of dispatching organizers from headquarters to generate local self-activity has its contradictory aspect. The 1956 history of the Tsurumi mill union reported much initial confusion about the organizer's mission. He was supposed to spend at least twelve hours per week walking around his assigned areas, talking to workers, reporting all problems to union headquarters, and bringing back answers as soon as possible. But many officers of the union local were suspicious and critical of the organizers, whom they correctly viewed as a threat. Rank-and-file workers feared retribution if they so much as talked to an organizer.[7]

At both Kawasaki and Tsurumi, this initial hesitation gradually subsided. People began warming up to the organizers and bringing complaints ranging from low staffing to long hours to restricted bathing time. The Tsurumi history claims that after about a year, workers sought out the organizers on their own and came to expect union support on a number of issues.[8] As organizers built a trusting relationship with the local rank and file, the latter offered new support for the union's central leaders. Over time, confrontations with supervisors increased in intensity.[9] Perhaps most ominous for managers, although still unusual, was an almost anarchic turn: the organizers would sometimes negotiate with supervisors and win concessions on the spot, without taking the matter back to union headquarters.

But success raised new problems. The union headquarters lacked the time, personnel, and power to resolve the many issues raised by organizers and workplace meetings. Some problems could only be resolved locally, some went beyond the bounds of the firm, and some set union members against each other. The organizers had succeeded in getting workers to speak out, but in raising the expectation level they sparked a new complaint: the union listened but could not act. The NKK unions responded by negotiating with the company to set up various expert committees of management and union representatives to settle issues raised by organizers and workers in discussion meetings. They in large measure overcame what critics had called the union's "absence" at the local level and "began to build a new order of workplace labor-management relations."[10] Workers at NKK were beginning to link formal union structures and activity with informal, semi-autonomous workplace customs. They were making heard a formal laborer's voice on issues previously settled unilaterally by supervisors. A democratic spirit of grassroots activism was taking hold.

Similar excitement echoed through workplaces nationwide, as dozens of unions improvised their versions of the shop-floor struggle. But the NKK union was unusual in at least one respect. Perhaps no other group of workers was so closely studied by so many. The Kawasaki and Tsurumi mill unions published detailed histories in their tenth birthday year of 1956.[11] The Communist Party cell at the Kawasaki mill published an equally detailed report ("From the Furnace") that same year.[12] Then, almost as if they were publishing a set of follow-up studies, from 1956 to 1958 three eminent labor economists at Tokyo University led a team of graduate students in a field study of unions at several major companies, including both NKK mills.[13] In addition, numerous short reports by freelance journalists provide supplementary insights.

Sifting through this archive of the daily routine and its tensions at the NKK mills, what Orii Hyūga would later recall as the "unimaginable" atmosphere of this era can be retrieved. As the shop-floor struggle gained momentum, first dozens and then hundreds of workplace assemblies were convened each year. Organizers presided over lively debate, negotiating some matters on the spot and taking up others in plant-level bargaining.

The Tsurumi union's history lists eighty-five demands generated by assemblies in that mill's twelve principal workplaces in the spring and summer of 1954.[14] This is a remarkable record of grassroots response to the organizers, complex in its logistics and both exhilarating and exhausting for the workers. Many of these shops ran on three shifts. To ratify a demand, at least two meetings were needed. A representative of the night shift, for example, would caucus his group and report to an assembly held in mid-afternoon, when men from both morning and afternoon shifts were at the mill.

Money and time, safety and staffing: the organizers and the workplace meetings addressed fundamental issues. Each of these covered a wide range, although the matter of money may have been the most complex. Two issues were of particular concern to the plant union and the locals: the distribution to individuals of centrally negotiated "average" wage increases and the calculation of output wages. The vigorous activism of union members sought to influence both the level and the structure of pay. This impeded NKK's flexibility in its drive to rationalize production and won a new bottom-up voice over some of the most significant decisions in the workplace.

Managers in the 1950s were anxious to regain their discretionary power to set individual wages, which had greatly eroded in the wartime and early postwar years. Only by rewarding some men more than others, managers believed, could they motivate employees to be loyal and productive. They clashed with the union on several details of their wage authority. What was an acceptable range around an "average" increase in the base wage? If the overall NKK union federation agreed with management on a companywide average raise of 7 percent, could the labor division at the Kawasaki mill give some workers 15 percent and others 2 percent or even zero? And in the system of merit rating that would accompany such differentiation, what were the standards? In particular, how much weight would subjective judgments of attitude or diligence carry? By the mid-1950s, the Tsurumi union was typical of many others in vigorously challenging individual merit ratings in public meetings, setting up monitoring committees, and forcing occasional corrections.[15] Such activities were unprecedented.

Managers also sought greater discretion to link pay to production with systems of output-based pay, and here too the union locals and plant headquarters began to exercise a portentous new power. At workplace discussions, men often demanded that output wages be reduced in importance. They complained that output-linked pay differed across workshops, a charge likely to be true by the very nature of the beast. In one instance, the men in a union local objected to their shop's relatively meager output pay.

They forced the union headquarters to take up the complaint in a new production subcommittee of the plant's management discussion council and won a 20 percent increase.[16]

Distributing output pay to individuals was even more controversial. NKK assigned workers "achievement points" plus points for rank and attendance and allocated individual shares in proportion to the point total. Supervisors held much discretion in setting points based on their view of a worker's diligence, cooperation, and sense of responsibility. At dozens of workplace discussions, recent NKK hirees expressed outrage at low output pay and its unfair allocation: "Abolish the point system," they would say; "The ranked men get too many points"; "Make the output ratings public."[17] On occasion, a section chief would recalculate points in response to complaints raised in union discussions and pressed by the organizer. At Tsurumi, union pressure forced the company at least to record a worker's point total on his pay envelope.[18]

At the same time, since NKK set a companywide budget for output pay, one group's gain was another's loss. Only bargaining at corporate headquarters could work out a balanced and predictable system of output premiums, and a predictable monthly premium would hardly serve managers who wanted to dangle an incentive before the workers.[19] Although shop-floor agitation did not transform the system on the spot, it was one factor that led NKK managers to eliminate output wages in the late 1950s and replace them with job wages and, later, merit wages. As the angry chorus of shop-floor complaint pushed managers to improvise more acceptable ways to set pay, democratic initiatives on the shop floor were bearing fruit.

With time, as with money, the union organizers and the rank and file spoke up energetically. In their complaints one glimpses a workplace society defined by customary expectations about appropriate routines. Efforts to protect these routines were sometimes informal and had nothing to do with the union. At other times, the union tried to institutionalize the unwritten rules of the workplace or defend certain favorable rules codified in earlier struggles. All these activities set workers against supervisors. The corporation had not yet snugly integrated the body of workers into a hierarchy of control; its hegemony was incomplete and contested.

The struggle over work discipline evokes images of a schoolteacher barely in control of the class. When Watanabe Tatsuo joined the labor section fresh out of a vocational high school in 1951 his first job was "attendance monitor." Each morning he made the rounds of the various gates to the mill, where employees "punched in" by turning over name tags that were hanging on a large board. He tried to catch those who played hooky and had friends turn their tags. He was similarly charged to look for discrepancies between workplace and personnel office overtime records. These are scenes of three-way suspicion: the labor section did not trust workplace bosses to enforce discipline, the foremen resented Watanabe's intrusion, and the workers protected each other. Not until the 1960s, he recalls, when the union had been transformed, did labor managers create a workplace order where they could comfortably delegate authority to local supervisors without constantly peeking over their shoulders.[20]

Watanabe and his colleagues imposed stricter time discipline as part of the broader push to rationalize operations. When foremen followed their lead and tightened the screws, workers tried to defend or expand existing margins of respite. In one episode from late 1953, an assistant section head (the highest ranked employee who was a union member) ordered his subordinates to obey the letter of the company's law, which specified a thirty-five-minute lunch break. Customary practice had been a full hour's rest, allowing time for a precious quick bath. Several hundred furious workers, including some crew bosses and foremen, reacted with a wildcat refusal to work overtime.[21]

In later years workers turned to the union in similar situations. In one case, men on the morning shift throughout the Kawasaki mill began to complain about pressure from foremen to show up fifteen minutes ahead of the official 6:30 A.M. starting time. This overlap with the night shift would allow a smooth changeover, and it was actually not new. Years before, the union had negotiated a "shift-change allowance" to compensate the morning workers for this extra quarter hour. But the allowance had not been raised since 1950. At workplace discussions in 1957 and 1958 at the Kawasaki mill, union members demanded a higher allowance, and their leaders made some gains in plantwide negotiations.[22] Shop-floor struggles also addressed vacation days, and organizers and discussion groups offered a new means for workers to restrain petty abuse of authority in the granting or denying of time off. Young unranked workers spoke out bitterly against supervisors who ordered sudden, unauthorized changes, and these complaints occasionally led the union to convene special workplace assemblies.[23] The men in one rolling workshop won an unusual agreement through the discussion group for a self-governing system to rotate vacation days, which removed authority from the foreman's hands.[24]

Workers similarly tried to regulate overtime from the grass roots, but their own ambivalence got in the way: they disliked long hours, but they needed the money.[25] Sometimes unranked men called for higher staffing to reduce pressure for overtime. More often, they protested to organizers not so much about the gross amount of overtime as about foremen who imposed it arbitrarily or allocated it unfairly. In workplace discussions they criticized foremen who gave poor merit ratings to men who refused overtime. In one extremely complicated episode of uneven overtime allocations at five different steel bar worksites in 1957, the union leaders gathered local opinions via organizers and discussion meetings, and they negotiated an agreement that guaranteed a "full" overtime income even to work groups with short allocations.[26] Here NKK was unable to impose its will on the workforce.

The flip side of the overtime coin was short staffing, and the NKK unions took this issue up with great energy, reflecting and nurturing a democratic spirit in the workplace. The company had tried to regulate manpower more tightly in the early 1950s with its staffing surveys. The labor division's staffing section judged appropriate crew size by consulting a committee of section chiefs and foremen. The union generally kept its distance from this committee, but union organizers simultaneously solicited rank-and-file opinions on appropriate staffing levels, using workplace discussions to distill a bargaining position.[27] In some cases the foremen would accept such locally derived opinions and push their superiors for more generous staffing. But when foremen wore the company hat and pressured subordinates to accept smaller crew sizes than they wanted, the organizers would submit complaints to plant-level negotiations.[28]

Of the various issues dug up by the organizers, this matter of "appropriate staffing" *(tekisei yōin)* posed the greatest actual and potential challenge to the rationalization program. In April 1954 there was a dispute in the Kawasaki mill's transport section, which had an authorized workforce of 276 but was short 29 people.[29] Despite the shortfall, the company replied belligerently to union demands for more staffing by reassigning five transport workers to another site. The employees responded with a series of informal meetings held at lunch and after hours, where they sharply criticized the reassignment. They circulated petitions and collected signatures; the transport local held an executive committee meeting and then a full assembly on April 17. In the meantime, the company imposed the reassignment order, effective April 16. The assembly on the 17th voted its "absolute opposition," and on April 20, against a background of plantwide postering and leafleting, the union took the case up in the plant-level management discussion council, composed of equal numbers of union and company representatives. The union carried out a survey of work hours in the transport section, finding that most workers had taken only three days off in March. In the face of this resistance, NKK rescinded the reassignments.[30]

NKK's workers protested understaffing and overwork throughout the 1950s. As the organizers built rapport in the workplace, the union came to involve the rank and file in extensive debate and action concerning job assignments and appropriate staffing levels. They did not always prevail, but even when the company got its way, it might do so only after continual workplace discussions had preoccupied several hundred workers over a two-week period, giving many a first experience of speaking out in mass meetings dealing with such crucial issues.[31] Sometimes the union made a significant difference. In the fall of 1954 the Tsurumi union carried on an unprecedented "struggle for more people," collecting local opinions on short staffing, presenting them to the management discussion council, and winning a net increase of 75 positions.[32] These efforts continued, and the 1958 platform adopted by the Kawasaki mill union at its annual assembly called for a renewed push to influence staffing levels. The union announced it would carry out a staffing needs survey through workplace discussion meetings, seeking a goal of "the number of people needed to complete work in regular hours, allowing for full use of vacation days."[33]

The labor division thus met ongoing resistance as it enforced tight staffing in the name of rationalization. From 1953 through the end of the decade, staffing at NKK was established through negotiations when company judgments clashed with views generated from the workplace.[34] But for the union to define comprehensive staffing quotas and negotiate to enforce these was extremely difficult. Workers themselves were torn between the desire for a reasonable pace and more money; a demand for more co-workers could often be satisfied with higher overtime or output pay. In addition, defining a "reasonable" workload required more time and technical expertise than the union could easily muster.

In 1949–50 at the age of twenty-four, Nakao Yasuji, later to become a full-time union official and then a prefectural assemblyman from the Japan Socialist Party, was a union officer responsible for staffing negotiations in the benzol processing section, one stronghold of shop-floor struggle in the Kawasaki mill.[35] He recalled that his co-workers had a "feeling or sense of what was enough, what was too much to ask, or how many people were enough. But there was no effective term to articulate this. A term like 'appropriate staffing' was used, but this was the company's term, not the workers' own."[36] Viewing matters from the perspective of the industrial engineering staff, and speaking of experiences of about ten years later,

Morito Akio made the same point: "The union people did have a sense of work norms, of a fair day's work, of what was a busy shop and what was a loose one, but they had no analytic vocabulary to express this. They had a sense developed through intuition and experience."[37] Nakao claimed the union failed to define its own standards for appropriate staffing levels, and he considered this a major cause of the union's ultimate failure to oppose rationalization effectively.[38]

Even before the union began to promote shop-floor struggle, workers who conspired to deceive the attendance monitor or refused overtime in wildcat actions retained a sense of standards and interests separate from, and often opposed to, those of the company. Sometimes their foremen acted as captains of this separate but hierarchical body. At other times, the foremen pushed their subordinates to quietly serve the company and themselves, so that lines of opposition set unranked workers against foremen and company. The NKK steelworkers constituted a self-conscious class, but one whose boundaries were shifting and permeable.

Generating the spirit and the practices of shop-floor activism from this base was a halting process of trial and error. Each incident involved many people in risky decisions about how much they could ask for, through what means. On one hand, workers might damage their long-run prospect to make foreman if they protested too much. On the other hand, they could ruin a relationship with co-workers if they resisted a call to refuse overtime. For any group of working people to make of their union a body that might codify and enforce imprecise customary expectations is time-consuming and difficult.

Measured against this difficulty, the voice of unionized employees in matters of workplace daily life and long-range planning grew substantially under the system of organizers and discussions. The union set up an internal system of committees and subcommittees in 1954 to coordinate the demands bubbling up from below.[39] It confirmed the fears of many managers when it began using the company's structure of joint consultation committees as forums for pushing these demands rather than as sites for building consensus. Late in 1954, some Tsurumi union locals founded their own weekly workshop newspapers, and the plantwide *Tsurutetsu Labor News* expanded from a two-page sheet to four pages, the additional space devoted to reports from the shop floor.[40] From the fall of 1954 through the winter of 1955 both the Kawasaki and the Tsurumi unions undertook major grassroots campaigns, the former a "concentrated struggle" to win workplace-generated demands, the latter a "contract-enforcement struggle" to implement fully the protections of the collective agreement. This activism reached a peak from 1957 to 1959, when the fourteen locals at Tsurumi convened an average of forty-six shop-floor meetings per local per month.[41] The NKK unions had energized their members.

NKK unions were also taking this vitality outside the workplace, both reaching out to the home and engaging the grand political issues of the day. Japan's politics in the 1950s, like its labor-management relations, were contentious and explosive. As part of a grassroots movement for peace and democracy, NKK activists opposed both the presence of American troops and repressive domestic political reforms such as a revised police law.[42] They joined hundreds of other unions in sending members to demonstrations supported by Sōhyō.

Several NKK workers, including Nakamura Kōgō and Matsuda Takezō, were arrested for their prominent role in two rowdy demonstrations. One opposed expanding the American military complex at Sunakawa in 1957. Another confronted President Eisenhower's envoy, James Hagerty, sent in 1960 to plan a presidential visit that was ultimately canceled when authorities decided they could not guarantee his security. NKK fired its arrested employees for violating a controversial work rule forbidding "conduct that dishonors the company." The union resisted bitterly, taking the company to court and charging that the dismissals were unjustified. After ten years of courtroom battle, they won their case.[43]

Such struggles absorbed tremendous amounts of the union's time, energy, and funds. This was not necessarily a wise use of scarce resources. On one hand, these struggles galvanized support among a portion of the rank and file, and to this extent political engagement strengthed the union. It created vivid, immediate links between workers, families, political parties, and the broader public. It surely helped the men who had been fired. But on balance such activities probably diverted energy away from issues of more immediate concern to most workers.

One can see this indirectly by scanning the pages of Gotō Tatsuo's remarkable memo book.[44] Gotō was a leader of the loyalist Research Group who served as full-time union officer from 1956 to 1970. Although hired as a blue-collar worker in 1951, he had graduated a vocational high school and taught elementary school for a year before entering the mill. A meticulous record-keeper, his job was to monitor production and quality data. In 1956, a veteran boss in the Research Group recruited him to run for union office. "I stayed in a full-time union position for nearly twenty years, rather than going back to the workplace, because of the difficult struggle among the union factions. I supported the [cooperative] labor unionists in the [anti-communist] democratization movement, and I couldn't leave the position before things settled down."[45] Five thousand pages from his dozens of memo books from 1957 to 1963 detail his day-to-day activity, including notes on all the union meetings he attended. His diary shows that in the aftermath of the Sunakawa and Hagerty incidents, times that were critical in the evolution of workplace activism at NKK, union leaders were preoccupied by continual discussions of how to raise funds for those fired, how to demonstrate in their defense, how to argue their cases in court. This political activity was not the top concern of most members. At a time when about 70 percent of union members at the NKK mills typically voted in favor of strikes over wages, only a bare majority, if that, would approve strikes on issues such as opposition to a new police law or the renewal of the security treaty.[46]

The politics of the Cold War both energized and divided the union movement. Of course, the ultimate failure of Japanese unions to sustain the activism of the shop-floor struggle of these same years must take account of numerous factors, especially a disagreement among workers on the wisdom of the tactic in and of itself. But in a way that sets the Japanese case apart from several European ones, the Cold War drove one more wedge between unionists who were already at odds. Leaders on the right wing of the union movement argued that the workplace struggle tactics of the union's militant leaders were hurting the company. They complained as well that political campaigns were diverting the union from central economic issues of production and wages. To combat the union's left wing, they sought an even closer alliance with management.

As the contest for the workplace spilled over into the home in sparring between the New Life Movement and the union's Housewives Association, and as it spread to the streets in demonstrations and to the courts in their aftermath, it also permeated the world of leisure. Efforts to organize workers' cultural activities raised complex questions of the proper relationship between political parties, the union, company managers, the burgeoning mass culture industry, and the private lives of ordinary workers.

Company-run recreation had deep roots. It first appeared early in the twentieth century in textile mills where paternalistic owners recruited young rural women by promising to educate and cultivate them in place of their parents.[47] During and after World War I, employers of male workers developed similar programs to slow turnover and oust labor unions by nurturing worker loyalty. In the 1930s and early 1940s, corporate-sponsored recreation proliferated dramatically under pressure from the state to bolster morale for war mobilization. By 1942 NKK offered workers at each mill access to eighteen different sports clubs, from judo and archery to basketball and boating, and a dozen or more cultural activities, from a photo club to Japanese chess. The offer to participate was hard to refuse. The company's official history of 1942 noted: "[The welfare office] works to make sure each employee participates in one club or another."[48]

This impressive array of company recreation continued after the war in most companies, and the list of clubs in NKK's 1952 history was slightly longer than a decade before.[49] But the company was no longer the only significant provider of structured recreation, and its coercive powers were weakened. Throughout the nation, the immediate postwar years witnessed a great burst of enthusiasm for "circle" activities independent of corporate control. As a term meaning "a small group carrying out cultural activities," the word "circle" (pronounced *saakuru*) had entered Japan in 1931. Its original meaning was political: a circle was a vanguard group producing literature, theatre, or paintings aimed at spreading revolutionary ideas among the populace.[50] In the postwar era, the word expanded dramatically in its range. It came to denote any small group engaged in cultural activities, as well as the housewives of the New Life Movement and even the small groups of the quality control movement.

In the immediate postwar years, the city of Kawasaki was a particularly active center of cultural circles. In 1947 the Keihin Alliance for Labor Culture claimed thirty-two member unions in Kawasaki and Tsurumi with 35,000 members in various circles. Toshiba was famous for its brass band, and NKK for its theater.[51] In the heavily politicized language of the early postwar period, these were "autonomous" activities. Autonomous here meant independent of corporate control but not independent of other affiliation. In fact, political parties of the left, especially the Japan Communist Party, were the most active and effective organizers of these circles. A number of so-called independent circles formed separately from—and opposed to—the JCP, but their organizers were usually no less committed to mobilizing on behalf of a class-conscious political movement.[52] The contest for the workplace spilled over onto cultural terrain, where companies, unions, and political parties sought the after-hours commitment of workers and their families.

The Red Purge dealt a sharp setback to the CP network of workplace-centered "autonomous" cultural groups, but in tandem with the labor offensive of the 1950s, new groups for classical music appreciation, singing, poetry writing and more—with varied political ties—proliferated fantastically. In 1955, the Sōhyō federation founded a national body to support workplace circles, and the mid- to late 1950s was a golden age for circles of all types.[53] In this pre-*karaoke* era, choral groups were among the most popular activities. So-called Singing Voice *(utagoe)* circles first appeared soon after the war, especially in unions with JCP leadership, although virtually every union had its songs and a chorus. Sōhyō entered the songfest in 1953, sponsoring regional and national choral festivals in cooperation with the national Singing Voice organization and setting up networks to promote choruses in each industry. One 1957 survey listed thirty choral networks organized by industry and affiliated with Sōhyō, including one for iron and steel.[54]

In 1956, the NKK chorus drew the attention of one of many publications of the circle movement. The forty young, male members of the Kawatetsu Singers met Saturday and Wednesday nights at the union hall. When the group was founded in 1953, some workers and union leaders viewed it with suspicion as a "leftist cultural action" and tried to suppress it.[55] Indeed, some of the founders envisioned the chorus as a politicized vanguard that would attack the union leadership. But the latter gradually decided that co-opting the widespread enthusiasm for circles would be wiser than trying to suppress it.[56] In a series of negotiations with the Singing Voices leaders, the union offered the organization recognition as a union activity in exchange for a promise to soft-pedal ideology. The seriously political youths migrated to reading and study circles, and "those who really liked singing remained." At lively evening choral sessions the Kawatetsu men might be joined by young women bus-fare collectors from a nearby union. Monthly folk dances for workers from half a dozen nearby plants as well as regional and national Singing Voice festivals bolstered solidarity with workers locally and around the nation. Managers feared the chorus, denounced the singers as a bunch of "reds," and had supervisors advise workers that joining it would harm their careers, reportedly to no avail.[57]

A basic contradiction persisted between three roles for the circles. They were to be groups simply for recreation and self-cultivation, agents that might independently nurture a democratic citizenry at the grass roots of society, and building blocks of a national political movement. Local union leaders often viewed the circles with justifiable fear. The most enthusiastic members tended to be young, single workers who had time to gather for poetry writing or singing during evenings or holidays. The groups often did become sites for dissident critiques of insufficiently combative, older union leaders, activity that would alienate members who just wanted to sing or listen to music.

Despite such internal tensions, over the course of the 1950s a mutually reinforcing relationship developed between unions and circles. The circles were nurturing union activists of the future, and the union was protecting circle leaders from discriminatory treatment by managers. By 1955, in addition to the Singing Voices, union-supported circles at the Kawasaki mill included music appreciation, movies, reading, and sports groups.[58] In the late 1950s, Japan's business elite responded to the circle movement with alarm, organizing their own cultural federations and distributing detailed manuals on how to control "workplace recreation." As in so many other realms, NKK eventually emerged as a leader in the esoteric field of "recreation policy" intended to extend corporate hegemony over the workers, but in the 1950s it and other corporations had limited control over employees after hours.[59] In these years of growing enthusiasm for shop-floor activism, groups of music lovers or folk dancers served as parallel, sometimes related sites of employee activity independent from and opposed to the company.

As they generated this labor offensive at the production site and outside it, unions in the steel industry sought to forge stronger national links. From 1946 to 1951, separate mill-based labor unions had affiliated with the competing federations, Sanbetsu or Sōdōmei, but the collapse of Sanbetsu after the Red Purge generated momentum for national unity. In 1951, unions at five major producers (Yahata, NKK, Fuji, Sumitomo, and Kobe Steel) joined to found Tekkō Rōren (Japan Iron and Steel Industry Labor Union Federation, or Nihon Tekkō Sangyō Rōdō Kumiai Rengōkai). In late 1952 Tekkō Rōren in turn affiliated with Sōhyō.

The officers at federation headquarters, who were elected and forwarded from the member unions, faced a tension between their roles as representatives of plant unions and as executives of a national organization. In Tekkō Rōren's first two years the links among constituent unions were especially weak. The federation struggled to coordinate what it called "joint" action in fundamentally independent wage bargaining by member unions. From 1953 through 1957 the federation then made strides toward its major goal of consolidating authority to pursue industrywide wage bargaining.

They sought this goal by shifting power from local unions to Tekkō Rōren headquarters. The basic local units of the federation were not companywide federations of plant unions, such as the NKK labor union federation, but the unions at individual mills within a company. During each round of wage bargaining, Tekkō Rōren's executive committee replaced itself with an "expanded central struggle committee" (ECSC) consisting of the fourteen executive committee members plus thirty-one other delegates representing both major and smaller mills. This hybrid body, both a representative and an executive entity, was intended to mobilize broad knowledge of the situation throughout the industry. Its size imparted expanded legitimacy, but it was unwieldy. Multiple delegates from major unions imported their factional politics into federation headquarters.[60]

When the federation was founded each plant-level member union had the power to approve or refuse to join strikes called by the ECSC. Tekkō Rōren leaders desperately wanted the authority to call a strike from the center and make the decision stick. In 1953, they moved in this direction by implementing a two-step process by which each plant union's membership would vote to authorize its executive committee to call a strike or cancel one and then take a second vote to transfer this authority to Tekkō Rōren's ECSC. These "transfer votes" gave the ECSC power to lead concerted actions, but they theoretically left each constituent the option of voting to reconsider its first decision, rendering the second vote meaningless.[61]

Armed with this new power, Tekkō Rōren gradually bolstered its authority. It led the steel unions in a series of increasingly coordinated annual wage offensives. Reinforcing this national progress was the growing enthusiasm in many workplaces for grassroots activism, coupled with frustration among workers that inflation was eroding their buying power while steel company sales and profits soared.

In the spring wage bargaining of 1953, Tekkō Rōren for the first time convinced all the major unions but Yahata to transfer strike authority to the ECSC, although Fuji Steel's unions reneged the night before the strike was to begin, telling Tekkō Rōren they could not enforce a strike order to their members. The unified strike immediately collapsed amidst great recrimination. The Yahata union in particular was reluctant to strike, angry that in the previous year it had been left out on a limb as the only union to carry out threats of a work stoppage.[62] Clearly company and factory patriotism remained powerful. Nonetheless, in the face of inflation and the Korean War boom, each individual union was able to win a modest "base-up."[63] This term is a useful Japanese shorthand for a cost-of-living increase in a worker's base wage that comes on top of the seniority- and merit-based raise given to each worker each year.

The 1954 bargaining took place in a daunting economic environment.

The Korean War had ended, drying up the "heavenly rain" of procurement orders. Once more all the major unions except Yahata voted the two-step transfer of strike authority to Tekkō Rōren, and the Fuji, Sumitomo, Kobe, and NKK unions indeed carried out a single twenty-four-hour strike together on June 17. But industry executives argued fiercely that the recession ruled out any overall base-up whatsoever, beyond small individual merit raises. On the eve of a second joint strike, set to last forty-eight hours, Sumitomo and Fuji's unions dropped out. They accepted the "zero reply" leavened with an increased summer bonus.

Workers at the NKK mills were outraged at both the "zero reply" and the quick collapse of joint action.[64] In the Kawasaki union, activists in the machine, steel bar, and transport locals called for further action by NKK alone, as a step toward a stronger movement in the future. The Kawasaki union executive committee hesitated. A strong minority warned against a hopeless strike just to make a point. But the NKK unions did carry out a second strike, this time for forty-eight hours, on June 24. They also agreed to a "third wave" strike of seventy-two hours on July 1–3 if they failed to receive a satisfactory reply.

At this point the company further divided the already uncertain work force by offering a larger summer bonus than usual. In addition, as Kondo Haruhiko recalls, the labor division launched a frantic effort to force the union to back down, several days of maneuvering through foremen to convince the rank and file not to honor a further call to strike. In particular, supervisors argued that a three-day shutdown would damage the blast furnace beyond easy repair. Workers at Kawasaki were unwilling to take this risk.[65] As the union debated the merits of a third action, the executive committee canceled round three at the eleventh hour, and a tumultuous union assembly of local delegates voted 381 to 258 to call off the strike.[66]

NKK managers could not repeat this anti-strike campaign the following year. The union offensives in the workplace and in wage bargaining in 1955 bore fruit.[67] As talks began this was not immediately apparent, for Yahata still held back from transferring strike authority to the federation. But Tekkō Rōren then achieved two breakthroughs. First, management at Fuji Steel broke ranks and offered its union a 950-yen base-up on September 3, three days before the first scheduled industrywide strike. If precedent had ruled, Fuji's union would have accepted the offer and dropped out, but the federation and the other unions convinced Fuji to stay the course. Second, on September 6, as the first joint strike took place, the union at the Yahata mill voted strike authority over to the federation for the first time ever. The unions at most of the major mills carried out five joint day-long strikes. Yahata joined from the third action and Fuji kept pace even after managers increased their offer to 1,440 yen on September 10. On September 9, in a heavy rain, and again on the 14th, the NKK Kawasaki union held huge assemblies attended by 7,000 members, who took off on spirited demonstrations snaking from the mill to the train station, "completely washing away the dirty charge of ten years' standing that Kawatetsu demonstrations were like funeral marches."[68] On September 17, at the twelfth formal bargaining session of the dispute, NKK managers finally offered an 800-yen increase, or 5 percent for an average worker.[69]

At this point, every company had given its unions a cost-of-living increase. After intense debate in the ECSC, Tekkō Rōren declared victory and called off the joint struggle. But workers at Tsurumi and Kawasaki were not finished. The Kawasaki union assembly voted to continue its strike by a comfortable margin of 345 to 205. Both mills shut down for twenty-four hours on September 22. Ten thousand workers held a joint rally at the Kawasaki mill's baseball field, and the unions sent 300 men in a bus caravan to corporate headquarters in the heart of the Tokyo business district.[70] Executives reportedly panicked, deciding that "if the strike goes on any longer, we're in trouble. For the sake of building healthy labor-capital relations, we need to end it."[71] They added 300 yen to the base wage offer (now 1,100), and 200 yen more to the output wage. To satisfy union calls to distribute the average to favor low-paid younger workers, they agreed that 550 yen of the raise would be given as a fixed increment across the board, with the rest allocated in proportion to each worker's base wage.[72] Given the prospect that expanding output would bring much new hiring, this decision favoring young workers was a significant concession.

In a poll of Kawasaki union members immediately after this settlement, 91 percent rated their satisfaction as "high." In addition to the new solidarity with the other major mill unions, they were pleased that many workers had refused to obey work orders issued by supervisors on strike days.[73] These were of dubious legality, but they had effectively cowed some employees in the past. For the union, the strike imparted a new confidence. It stood as a model of what was possible and helped inspire the militant actions of the next four years. For managers at NKK and across the industry, the events of September 1955 were a cautionary tale of the dangers of breaking ranks. Steel unions were threatening to go the way of coal: union control at the shop-floor level and aggressive industrywide wage bargaining.

The authority of the corporation was shaky, perhaps even crumbling, in the steel mills of the 1950s, and steel was by no means the home of the most vigorous movement of workplace struggle. Workplace activism was weaker in processing industries such as pulp and steel than in auto plants, mines, and railroads.[74] If the intense, chronic conflicts between steel companies and unions mark a relatively tame case, the dimensions of the overall challenge to corporate hegemony in large private firms were clear. Managers presented the interests of the company and of workers in a world of new technology and increased productivity as one and the same. For this common good, they promoted more "rational" systems of industrially engineered job design and job- or merit-based wages.

Union activists and many members rejected this view of harmonious interests. They suspected that new technology and rationalization would make their work lives less secure. They feared that managers would impose tighter staffing and harsher work conditions, unwanted transfers, and less secure or predictable wages. They saw the union in the workplace and throughout the industry as a tool to oppose such changes. This was a vision of the desirable workplace order sharply at odds with that of management.

As the union offensive built on their activism, the Kawasaki and Tsurumi unions came to constrain the NKK labor division's ability to enforce tight staffing, and the company faced the prospect that such restraints would become even more forceful. Wage settlements in 1955 and 1956 set steel industry labor costs on an ominous trajectory for managers (see Figure 6). If unions continued both to constrain rationalization and win substantial wage increases, the Japanese steel industry could not have built its impressive cost advantage. To the extent that it was prevailing, the workers' movement was diminishing corporate prosperity and probably slowing economic growth, but it was also giving members a measure of democratic control over their lives at work. The stage was set for a showdown.

6 *Breaking the Impasse*

More than thirty years later, the men who led the great steel strikes of 1957 and 1959 and those who opposed them agreed on one point. These were extraordinary times. Normal routines were forgotten; spare cots and mattresses were in great demand. Konda Masaharu, who spoke of the 1959 strike as "the tensest days of my life," slept at his office at the Kawasaki mill for two weeks. Inoue Jutoku, head of the labor division at corporate headquarters, "basically lived at the company during the strike, sleeping in a dorm [near the Kawasaki mill.] My wife was not pleased." And Isobe Toshie, workplace organizer and founder of the Third Group faction, camped at union headquarters in Kawasaki for forty-one days. When he finally went home, his commuter pass had expired, and he was apprehended for riding without a valid ticket. "But when I explained what had happened, the ticket checker [himself a member of a union] was happy to let me pass."[1] Participants justly remember these events as turning points in their lives and the history of postwar Japan.

The 1950s was the decade of the knock-down-drag-out strike. The point is not that strikes were frequent. What distinguishes this era, what makes it a watershed, is the intensity of each incident and the shared underlying issue of control over rationalization. The years from 1957 through 1961 saw the greatest number of workdays lost to strikes of any time since the immediate postwar explosion of the labor movement and the exceptional year of 1952 (see Figure 7). Both the number of workdays lost per dispute and the number of days missed per striking worker peaked in these years and declined sharply thereafter. The numerous strikes in Japan from the 1960s through the present have almost all been short and hardly newsworthy, an hour or a day of muscle flexing to accompany ritualistic wage bargaining, but the actions of the 1950s drew widespread media attention and were marked for posterity by their length: the 100-day Nissan strike of 1953, the 145-day Ōji paper strike of 1958, the 49-day steel strike of 1959. The granddaddy of them all was the strike at Mitsui's Miike mine in 1960. It lasted for a full year and rallied an unprecedented network of supporters who journeyed to Kyūshū to join the picket lines.

The steel strikes were not simply typical. More than the other landmark strikes of the 1950s, they pointed the way to a new labor-management relationship that would ultimately take on global importance. The course of the battle itself changed the balance of forces at NKK and in steel, and it catalyzed a new social order at work, with ripples extending far beyond. At stake was the scope and quality of democracy, and the shape and pace of economic growth.

The Course of the Strikes

The wage struggle of 1956 was a prelude to these battles. Its result suggested that managers were learning how to avoid repeated failure as quickly as the unions were learning to build on past success.[2] Tekkō Rōren did lead four rounds of concerted strike actions, and it managed to get Yahata on board for the third round, but the companies stuck firmly to their positions. When Yahata refused to join a fourth round unless it were delayed, and Fuji's Hirobatake union and two of Kobe Steel's mill unions accepted company offers, joint action collapsed. All the unions settled for the initial offer of a 700-yen base-pay raise. Observers called this a meager result at the peak of the spectacular "Jimmu boom" of 1956, dubbed the greatest boom since the time of the mythical emperor Jimmu.[3]

Local company patriotism thus remained intractable, although local enthusiasm for the union was also great. The NKK unions had supported the strikes with votes of 90 percent or more in favor.[4] Yahata's leaders had sharply criticized the other unions for striking too soon and too often, before bargaining backed by a *threatened* strike could have an impact. By allowing the other unions to strike, and threatening to join their actions down the road, Yahata's huge union won a free ride buoyed by external pressures even as it undermined its erstwhile allies. To make such defections more difficult, Tekkō Rōren prepared for the 1957 wage round by firming up its authority to call strikes. Its members agreed to new bylaws setting forth a more tightly binding procedure for strike votes. First, delegates to a national union assembly would vote to authorize a strike and grant the central strike committee power to call it. Local unions would then be asked to ratify this decision. As before, this was a two-step process; but the initiative came from the center, and the federation leaders believed that local unions would find it harder to renege on a commitment to honor a decision of the national assembly.[5] Thus, in the fall of 1957 the steelworkers' unions were poised for their strongest industrial action ever.

Tekkō Rōren led a succession of eleven industrywide, one- or two-day walkouts known as the "eleven-wave strike." The plant unions and enterprise federations at the five major steel companies put forward a common demand for a 3,000-yen monthly raise. The wave of strikes to enforce this began on October 8. This was an unprecedented display of unity, but the unity of industry executives was equally unprecedented. They started with a "zero reply," refusing any increase in base wages at all, and the Big Three of Yahata, Fuji Steel, and NKK sustained a tactic of "one-shot" bargaining, refusing to make any adjustment whatever to their initial offer. On December 10, Tekkō Rōren called off the strike.

The 1959 struggle repeated this result with a different cast and plot. The five major unions put forward a common demand for a 2,000-yen base-up, met by a common offer of an 800-yen increase in the average output premium. Unions at Sumitomo and Kobe refused to join a Tekkō Rōren–led strike, and the supposedly tighter central strike control failed to prevent Yahata from dropping out after two days. All three accepted the initial offer. Determined to "escape from Yahata dependence," the unions at Fuji Steel and NKK carried on alone. They completely shut down their rolling mills for seven weeks, an action inscribed in local legend as "the forty-nine-day strike." But on April 21, with the unions torn by internal dissension, they accepted the original offer of 800 yen in output pay and returned to work.[6]

During both strikes, a profound conflict of interests and ideologies issued in unusually grand calls for sacrifice and harsh charges of bad faith. When NKK made its formal "zero reply" in 1957, it stressed that steel paid higher wages than most industries and concluded, "The present is a time of excess for you workers, but a time of great hardship for the company. What is more, in the midst of this time of troubles, the company must bear any burden to complete the second rationalization plan. The future progress of Japan's economy depends on this, the greatest endeavor in a century for our company."[7]

Perhaps aware that NKK was only forty-five years old, the unions were not moved by such grand appeals:

For the past four years the company has not once responded in good faith to our wage demands. If times are bad they slap us in the face with "this isn't the time for a pay raise," but during a frenzy such as the Jimmu boom, they pound us with "rationalization comes first." They preach company patriotism whenever they open their mouths and exalt rationalization as the "greatest endeavor in a century," telling us our wages are high . . . and completely ignoring the reality of our lives as workers. Trumpeting managerial paternalism, they suppress our wages and expose the essence of capitalism.[8]

Although the company was correct to claim that pay for steelworkers was relatively high, theirs were among the most dangerous and grueling industrial jobs of that time. Despite a downturn in demand in 1957, steelmakers were still reporting some profits that fall, and they were making record gains in 1959. Cash flow and profits sufficed to offer the small settlements that would have avoided a strike.[9] Konda Masaharu admitted: "Of course even though times were slow during one of the strikes, a few-hundred-yen raise wouldn't have broken the company."[10]

Only on the surface were these struggles over relatively modest union demands for higher base and retirement pay. More profound issues account for the stubborn refusal to grant any raise at all, and the willingness of unions to risk an all-out strike. Managers believed the ability to *afford* and also to *enforce* the entire rationalization program was at stake, so they were willing to play a dangerous game of chicken with their expensive new furnaces. At every turn they spoke publicly and loudly of the "great hardship" of the industry's relatively high wages and the need to "bear any burden" to afford rationalization plans. To retire their vast debt, it was crucial that revenues and profits grow sharply.[11] Their solution in the short term was to hold the line on base wages with zero replies and make any unavoidable small increases contingent upon larger gains in output. For the long run, the goal was to establish the precedent of one-shot bargaining. The companies would nurture an understanding cadre of union leaders and make only one "reasonable" offer that it could afford and that the union would know it could not refuse.

The union's leaders easily recognized the connection between the strikes and rationalization. The Kawasaki platform in 1958 noted that the managers were united by their great fear that the union might become "a second Tanrō" (coal miners union), a true industrial union with a class-conscious agenda. Some members not only saw this connection but agreed it was valid. The Tsurumi platform lamented that corporate talk of the need to hold down wages to afford to invest had some pull with workers.[12]

Unionists as well as managers understood that enforcing rationalization was a fundamental issue. They knew that shop-floor activism over work conditions, staffing, and wage decisions compromised NKK's ability to operate the new equipment to maximum effect.[13] They realized that determination to put an end to this sort of activism undergirded managerial intransigence in a strike that on the surface was simply about wages. They were launching an all-out push to solidify the achievements of several years of workplace activism, transcend interfirm divisions, and establish industrial bargaining. In the end, their dual commitment to the union and the company undermined this drive.

The run-up to the 1957 strike began in April. To overcome the divisions that had compromised the 1956 round, Tekkō Rōren convened numerous strategy meetings, including several special meetings of officials from the Big Five unions. Each mill union held parallel sessions to rally local support. By midsummer the federation and the mill unions had worked out a detailed tactical program, addressing the controversial problem of protecting the equipment while shutting it down: employees would bank the fires at some blast furnaces, run others at 30 percent capacity, and completely halt electric furnaces.[14]

Preparations moved forward with both enthusiasm and serious concern. In a survey of Tsurumi union members, a strong 86 percent supported a wage demand of at least 3,000 yen, the level eventually sought.[15] But federation and local leaders were well aware that a strong minority of members doubted the ability of the union to sustain an industrywide action and the wisdom of trying.[16] In the balloting of late September, two of Kobe Steel's unions refused to ratify the national assembly's strike decision, and in almost every union support fell short of the previous year, in part because of the forbidding economic climate. Demand for steel had fallen from a 1956 peak, inventories were high, and some members concluded that only an impossibly long strike could cause the companies sufficient pain to win concessions.

On September 19 and 20, each of the Big Five steelmakers replied the same way to the identical demands of their unions: no raise at all in the base wage or retirement pay.[17] On October 8, the unions at Yahata, Fuji, NKK, and Sumitomo joined together for the first of eleven "waves" of twenty-four- or forty-eight-hour actions, a total of nineteen days of strikes spread out over nearly eight weeks. The unions planned to use the intervals between waves to bargain, backed by the credible threat of further strikes.

Although the demands and the strikes were coordinated by Tekkō Rōren, actual bargaining as always took place at separate companies. At NKK, the enterprise-wide Council of Plant Unions held only two bargaining sessions with management between the first and last waves, and these two were unproductive. By early November doubting voices were raised by union members at all levels, from workshop to federation, with increasing force. The union, these men said, must escalate its tactics or quit, and they deemed the former impractical. Others countered that rising external attention brought increased pressure upon management to compromise from its intransigent zero reply: the strike had been discussed in the Diet, and on November 18 the respected chair of the Central Labor Relations Commission called on both parties to negotiate in good faith, as did numerous newspaper editorials.[18] In the face of the zero reply of the steelmakers, these observers were implicitly calling on the companies to compromise.

The union optimists glimpsed a ray of hope when Sumitomo Metal broke ranks with the zero-reply stance to offer its union a 500-yen boost in output wages, although no hike in base pay. Sumitomo's union eagerly accepted this offer, and the ninth wave went forward on November 19 as a forty-eight-hour strike of unions at the Big Three only: Yahata, Fuji, and NKK.[19] But the companies simply restated their zero replies.

Just prior to this, NKK management made an emergency request that the Kawasaki union allow operations to resume at several furnaces. Managers claimed that the blast furnaces were at risk and the basic oxygen converter, NKK's proud new technology and source of future advantage, was beginning to crack. The NKK strike leaders later admitted that "fear paralyzed the union" at this request.[20] In its 1958 platform, the Kawasaki union looked back and lamented that too few members had the appropriately detached attitude that "care of machinery was the company's responsibility."[21] After extensive debate, the Kawasaki union accepted the company's request and forwarded it to the expanded central struggle committee (ECSC), which granted an exemption for the furnaces in question. Yahata representatives objected sharply that they had resisted identical pressure from their company.[22] The threatened crack in the furnace had severely fractured the solidarity of the unions.

In early December all the unions gained relatively strong year-end bonuses in separate negotiations, which further deflated pressures to continue. Union leaders realized they would be unable to pull off the scheduled twelfth wave of seventy-two hours set for December 11. On the 10th, Tekkō Rōren called off all further strikes.

In "self-criticism" published immediately after the event, most unions tried to find something positive to say: this was by far the most sustained display of unity ever among the major unions, including Yahata. Most of the medium-sized steelmakers had granted raises, as did the smaller two of the top five, Kobe (without a strike) and Sumitomo. NKK Kawasaki reported progress in winning cooperation from subcontractors and temporary workers, and important support from the Housewives Association.[23] But none could deny the failure of the Big Three unions "to crack the wall of the zero reply," and all three sustained severe internal bruises.[24]

This disastrous experience cast a long shadow. The leaders of Tekkō Rōren and most member unions remained committed to the workplace activism and aggressive wage demands of the previous five years, but they were wary of rushing back into battle. The federation decided to wait out the 1958 wage round and rally its forces for a strong push in the spring of 1959, this time in concert with a growing number of industrial federations that since 1955 had been organizing a loosely coordinated "spring wage offensive."

The 1959 drive began with several encouraging signs. The economy was booming once more. Steel output and profits had never been higher. Steel federation leaders believed they were poised to win a significant base-up for the first time since 1955, and the major unions prepared demands for a 2,000-yen average raise. The NKK union strike funds had been replenished over the previous eighteen months. Kamimura Hideji remembers that "most workplaces strongly supported the strike" in this "historic time," and Isobe Toshie describes 1959 as "the peak era in union history. Discussions in the workplace were active and there was tremendous vitality."[25] Within the community, according to Gotō Tatsuo (who opposed the strike), "there was much support especially at the outset, since merchants were so dependent on the patronage of NKK workers. But subcontractors wanted to see a quick end to it, since they were losing business."[26] When it came time to ratify the strike vote of the Tekkō Rōren assembly in mid-February, workers at the two NKK mills and three Fuji Steel plants produced fairly strong majorities in favor of a strike.

The optimism was misplaced. Yahata ratified the strike by the barest of majorities, less than in 1957, and most of the plant unions at Sumitomo Metal and Kobe Steel denied strike authority to the federation. The unions at NKK and Fuji were determined to carry on in any case, and with a reluctant Yahata joining forces, they began what turned out to be a forty-nine-day shutdown of their rolling mills on March 4, in advance of the management reply to their demands. On March 7 all three companies offered an 800-yen average raise in output pay. At a long meeting of the ECSC, Yahata's union argued for accepting this offer and then dropped out. At this point, the Fuji and NKK unions raised the banner of "escaping Yahata dependence." They held to a reasonable hope that executives afraid of losing customers to rivals would sweeten the pot to get the rollers moving. In addition, according to Nakamura Kōgō, pride was a powerful motivation: "When the other unions dropped out because their right-left balances were different from NKK, our initial calculations no longer held up. Then it was no longer a matter of rational calculation but of emotion. We couldn't be the first to blink. We had to stick it out or lose all our credibility."[27]

Remarkably, the Fuji and NKK unions sustained the 1959 strike for seven weeks. They alternated brief millwide strikes with prolonged "focused strikes" in the rolling shops. This had the advantage of minimizing the risk to the furnaces while preventing the company from shipping finished goods. But it divided the workforce into striking and nonstriking groups. Many of the latter grew resentful of their idle co-workers who drew strike pay from a common pot. As the strike dragged on into April and the company simply repeated its initial offer at angry bargaining sessions, opposition to the strike intensified, especially at the furnace sites. On April 20, the NKK and Fuji union assemblies voted to end their strikes and accept the original wage offer of seven weeks earlier.[28] For the third time in a row, the companies had sustained one-shot wage bargaining.

The base of the NKK unions eroded dramatically during these tumultuous weeks, as it had in 1957. The sight of iron and steel bars piling up in the baseball field next to the rolling mills tore at some employees, and a widely held fear of damaging the company immobilized the union. One man recalled, "I cannot describe how [badly] I felt watching the unfinished ingots keep piling up in the ball field." Such a vision would become a core theme in the legend of the folly of 1959 as told by the anti-strike factions at all the steel companies to later generations of union members.[29] As the ingots mounted, reports circulated that Sumitomo had snatched away major NKK contracts to supply pipe to Tokyo Gas and the telephone monopoly. At the same time, contradictory rumors circulated that Yahata Steel was filling customer orders on behalf of NKK, putting the NKK mark on Yahata products in a powerful gesture of corporate solidarity. The former reports would convince loyalist factions that a prolonged strike would destroy both company and union; the latter suggested to strike supporters that the company could outlast them.[30]

The depth of employee concern for company equipment set the Japanese steel unionists apart from those in other nations. Although completely shutting down a blast furnace indeed would cause the lining to crack, and relining the furnace would be time consuming and costly, it was possible to bank the fires against the furnace wall, sustaining the heat and preventing major damage. In the 116-day steel strike in the United States in 1959, and in many others, union members banked furnaces without hesitation.[31] The NKK workers knew of such precedents, but they lacked confidence in their ability to bank the blast furnaces properly, so they ran them at 30 percent capacity instead. Managers argued that even this was risky.[32] The Japanese steel unions sought technical advice from the U.S. steelworkers' union, which sent a delegation to Japan in 1959, but their encouragement could not overcome the reluctance to bank the furnaces.[33] Thus, the NKK and Fuji unions turned to the internally divisive choice of the "focused" strike limited to the rolling mill. In such decisions, union members revealed a widespread sense of responsibility for "their" steel mill, in part surely produced by the traumatic endeavors of postwar survival and rebuilding. Such attitudes made it extremely difficult to sustain a shutdown.

Managers displayed—indeed flaunted—a different sense of responsibility. During the 1959 strike NKK president Kawada Jun reportedly said, "This is a fight to destroy the union even if we wreck the machines."[34] This bold claim may be apocryphal; the only surviving oral or written testimony is secondhand. But word of Kawada's supposed statement was circulating among workers during the strike, and they had much immediate evidence that their bosses were following the spirit and even the letter of this claim. Konda Masaharu confessed that "the union people had a technical problem. They couldn't stop the furnace completely, or they thought they couldn't, and we encouraged them to think this."[35] Isobe Toshie "was not sure how feasible it really was to bank the furnace, but I think we were duped by supervisors into believing it was impossible. I don't remember Kawada's comment, but supervisors were always saying things like that to intimidate people."[36] And even in 1991 Nakao Yasuji pounded the table and raised his voice when he told the story of one section chief, Hayashi, who was in charge of the basic oxygen furnace during the 1959 strike. The furnace was supposed to remain in operation during the strike, but Hayashi took over the controls and threatened to cause a malfunction, wreck the kettle, and pin the blame on the union.[37]

Different assessments of responsibility for NKK's equipment and future prosperity nearly caused the union to split in two. During the weeks of the shutdown, strike supporters held numerous assemblies and outdoor rallies, which Isobe says the company did its all to obstruct.[38] Kitazume Shun, co-founder of the Acorn Club, tells of pro-strike demonstrators camped outside his home and his constant fear of a beating. The Kawasaki union's executive committee held several open all-night meetings, with large numbers of rank-and-file members looking on. These gatherings, as well as workshop meetings of union locals, produced bitter mutual denunciation: "Red! Strike-crazed adventurist!" and "Traitor! Company pimp!"[39]

The informal groups were in continual session. Kudō Shinpachi's longtime mentor, anticommunist agitator Mitamura Shirō, set up a temporary office near Kawasaki station.[40] Both labor managers and the anti-strike informal groups began plans to launch a second union. This was a common endgame in many all-out struggles in the 1950s. The company would join hands with a minority of loyalists who would raise the banner of a second union, win immediate recognition, and return to work. A combination of inducements and coercion would then lead most of the first union members to switch sides over the following months or years.[41] Inoue Jutoku claims that the leading advocates of a second union were the managers in the labor sections at each mill, anxious to build a more open alliance with the informal groups. They put together a detailed plan with estimates of expected members from each work site.

Both labor managers, such as Inoue, Orii Hyūga, and Konda Masaharu, and informal group leaders, such as Gotō Tatsuo, Kitazume, and Kudō, ultimately rejected this course. The parties to this aborted second-union conspiracy concluded that a formal split would raise more problems than it would solve. It would leave an intolerably bitter aftermath—in Gotō's words, "children, wives, and workers throughout the town divided, literally fighting each other as I saw in Muroran" (after a steel union split there). It would also force the labor section to deal with the second union as well as the remnants of the first union indefinitely.[42] Managers instead continued their drive to transform the existing union by supporting the informal groups at every turn in their drive to win control of the union.

Parallel to this grueling struggle over wages, a second dispute over the transfer of employees to a nearby new plant took place at the Tsurumi mill, of equal if not greater import to the contestants. In 1959 NKK was in the process of building a new cold strip mill in the Mizue district adjacent to the Kawasaki plant, and managers planned to transfer 16 percent of the Tsurumi workforce to help staff it (see Figure 4). The Tsurumi union initially pressed NKK to build the new facility at Tsurumi, and when the decision for

Mizue was announced in January 1957 the union declared "a state of emergency," something it had done only once before, after the Red Purge in 1950.[43]

If the wage strikes were about affording rationalization plans, the Mizue transfer fight was about the terms of enforcing them. Union activists wanted the greatest possible voice in both the conditions of the transfer—wage and rank guarantees, training programs at full pay—and the choice of transferees. Potentially their voice over such matters could obstruct smooth operations at Mizue. As negotiations took place over the next two years, union members recognized that "winning the wage struggle will help us win favorable conditions for the Mizue transfer."[44]

NKK's labor managers, on the other hand, wanted the freest hand possible, particularly in choosing men for reassignment. They believed many veteran workers would not be able to adjust to the new jobs, so they insisted on discretion to transfer only those they judged adaptable.[45] It was also an open secret that (in Isobe Toshie's words) they "transferred the loyal, quiet workers" to Mizue and left a disproportionate number of militant union activists at Kawasaki and Tsurumi.[46] The managers' goal was to create a "strike-proof" mill that would serve as companywide strike insurance. Each mill's union took its own strike vote, and taking heart from the precedents of Kobe Steel in 1957 and Sumitomo in 1959, managers were confident that the Kawasaki and Tsurumi unions would not push for a strike unless all three mill unions were in favor. Mizue's union would be NKK's foolproof strike veto.[47]

From March 1958 through August 1959, the plate rolling local at Tsurumi most directly affected by the impending transfers convened no fewer than 217 meetings, an average of three each week.[48] Union members used the workplace discussions to demand information, as much choice as possible, and job security and wage guarantees. The prospect of moving to Mizue held promise of safer and lighter physical labor, but it also threatened to disrupt familiar routines, eliminate jobs, and cut wages as output premiums were reassessed. Crew bosses and foremen stood to lose the advantage of their jealously hoarded skills, and younger men feared that experience accumulated through slow apprenticeship might be nullified in the move. This issue could draw young workers and foremen together in opposition to the company, but it turned out that NKK was able to divide and conquer through strategically placed promises to protect informal group leaders and members.

As the union negotiated over the transfer terms, a deep fault line broke to the surface. Activists on the executive committee and younger unranked workers held the highest hopes for a strong union voice in transfer decisions. But despite the several years of efforts by organizers and the executive committee to create an activist union at the grass roots, the veteran foremen who dominated the union's workplace locals emerged as the controlling figures of a Mizue policy committee, created by the union in December 1958. Over the following months "the company chose the transferees and reported [the names] to the union." The policy committee was unwilling to support individual complaints about the transfer orders, which would have called its authority into question. Its role was essentially to enforce the company decisions, and this generated much bitter criticism.[49] The strike vote for the 1959 wage bargaining was taken just at this time, and the balance of forces was similar. Rank-and-file workers upset over the handling of the Mizue transfers strongly supported the strike against the reservations of senior workplace leaders.

The aftermath of the 1959 strike was extraordinarily bitter at both Tsurumi and Kawasaki. Kitazume recalls the assembly at Kawasaki that voted to end the strike, from his perspective a victory, as "an awful, intense experience."[50] The Kawatetsu strike leaders published an anguished self-criticism soon after the event, desperately seeking to restore unity and support for their stewardship of the union: "We are painfully aware that in the wake of this defeat, intense criticism of the leadership is being raised in the workplace," they wrote, and pleaded for reconciliation between strike supporters and opponents and "courage and effort to overcome our weaknesses."[51]

Many of their readers, it turned out, were either unwilling or afraid to give them another chance. In the union election that followed, in the autumn of 1959, the forty-nine-day strike was the main issue, and candidates of the informal groups who had opposed it won several key posts, in particular the two offices of vice-chairman.[52] The Research Group and the Acorn Club were gradually taking control of the Kawasaki union's executive committee, and similar forces were making gains at Tsurumi. Over the following years they never looked back. By 1970, these groups plus Isobe's Third Group had merged into a new companywide "informal organization," the Sōyūkai. The 1959 actions were the last strikes of any consequence at NKK or any major steel corporation in Japan, and managers have sustained the practice of one-shot wage bargaining to this day.

Explaining the Outcome: United Capital, Divided Labor

That managers at the major companies displayed greater solidarity than organized workers is superficially puzzling. Capitalists are in theory

competitors, while the essence of a union is the solidarity of all wage workers. In the steel strikes, this conventional wisdom was turned on its head.
The workers at NKK worried about interfirm competition at least as much
as their bosses. Common sense suggests that because capitalists own
machinery and workers simply operate it, the "owners" have the greater
stake in preserving it. However, many NKK workers were more upset than
managers at the prospect of damaging valuable furnaces. The Tsurumi
union's self-criticism after the 1957 strike made the point with the following
pithy note: "Managers are far more class conscious than we realize."[53]

Yet hindsight renders the failure of the unions to win any base-pay raise
in 1957 or more than a paltry incentive pay hike in 1959 all too predictable.
Looking back, it is easy to dismiss these strikes as doomed efforts. But to
imagine the experience of this historical moment, one must put this false
certainty aside. Behind their facade of hard-line unity, steel executives faced
a crisis and were not sure they would prevail. Newspaper accounts at the
time give the impression of a nation whose workers were up in arms. In
October and November of 1957, almost every day a front-page story told of
the strikes in steel or of others in coal, shipbuilding, and both private and
public railways. Steel industry sources told the press that top companies
would face severe shortages of operating funds if the strike continued too
long.[54] Only in retrospect was it clear that the union could not hold out long
enough to force the major producers to make concessions.[55]

The contrast between capitalists in agreement and unionists in disarray is
exaggerated in part by their contrasting modes of operation. Unions took
strike votes and published the results in bulletins and newspapers, so disagreements were public. Corporate in-fighting was usually hidden behind
closed doors; but if their internal conflicts were not public, they were sharp.
The solidarity within and among steel companies was not inevitable, and its
sources are not obvious. At least three major fault lines threatened to
destroy their common front.

Starting closest to the workplace one finds a variety of conflicts among
labor managers themselves. Unlike their colleagues at the main office, the
men in the labor sections at each mill were in daily contact with workers.
They felt the pressure of union activism directly, and they tended to push
for quick solutions.[56] But the practice of rotating managers through assignments in the labor section in the mills and the labor division at corporate
headquarters prevented this inclination from producing an entrenched
"peace faction" of field officers.

The wisdom of relying on informal groups and intervening closely in union politics had been controversial for years. A high-road group identified with Orii Hyūga preferred to win the general allegiance of workers through companywide programs of enlightened human relations, while a conspiracy faction, particularly strong among those with long experience at the larger Kawasaki mill, was certain that hands-on manipulation through informal groups was the only viable approach.[57] More immediately relevant to the surface cause of the strike, a group of younger people in the labor sections objected to the tactic of the one-shot reply. This practice, also termed Boulware-ism after its notorious practitioner at General Electric, Lemuel Boulware, was an import from the United States. Men like Okuda Kenji viewed it as a denial of the commitment to good-faith bargaining. They favored making some concession, however slight, in the interests of promoting "healthy labor relations."[58]

Another set of conflicts set the functional divisions of the company against each other. The most consistent voices for moderation, even peace at any price, were the salespeople. Takemura Tatsuo was the NKK director charged with labor affairs in the late 1950s, and he recalls "intense internal fights" at board meetings. "The salespeople were opposed to taking on a strike, were opposed to an all-out push to establish one-shot bargaining. They feared losing sales. It was very hard to achieve unity."[59] Takemura's direct subordinate in 1959 was Inoue Jutoku, chief of the labor division at corporate headquarters. Inoue was an arrogant hard-liner who shared Takemura's antipathy for unions. He was known among his friends and many foes as "Emperor Inoue." He notes that "of course salespeople prepared for the strike by building up inventory, but this was not enough for a long strike, and it was soon exhausted. Sales executives like Yoshiwara and Yasuda reported that rivals were stealing their customers, and they fiercely, hysterically pleaded with the company to settle. I told them, 'No way on earth.'"[60]

In addition to salespeople, two function-based interests were the finance group and the internally divided labor managers. When times were good, Takemura recalls, the finance executives, like those from sales, infuriated him with requests to share the wealth and avoid an even more costly strike. But more often, they supported a hard line to keep down wage costs.[61] The labor managers, especially Orii with his stress on enlightened programs to build positive human relations, were scorned by the finance people as "socialists" when they sought funds to improve work conditions or raise pay. The labor managers conveyed their sense of isolation by calling themselves "special villagers," a euphemism for Japan's caste of outcasts who continued to experience widespread discrimination and prejudice.[62] But the isolation of the labor managers, especially after the strikes, came from the anger of colleagues who blamed them for not somehow preventing the strike more than from specific criticism for softness or socialism. Indeed, after several years of dealing with the increasingly activist and militant unions at Kawasaki and Tsurumi, the senior labor managers at NKK spoke to those outside the division with one voice, especially in 1959. As Inoue Jutoku put it, they were determined "to destroy the union" as it then existed.[63]

At the time of the steel strikes, the contest inside NKK set sales executives urging moderation against labor managers and finance managers urging a hard line. With a career labor man as company president, the hard-line forces expected to prevail. But this would not necessarily happen at every company, and a third set of tensions played out among the various steel-makers. At a time of expanding markets and intense sales competition, any company could be tempted to concede and settle quickly to get a jump on its rivals. In 1957 both Fuji and Yahata managers were rumored to favor slight wage increases. NKK's Inoue Jutoku, who had attended the same elementary school as Fuji Steel's president Nagano Shigeo, took advantage of the old-school tie to visit Nagano and urge him to stay the course.[64]

One axis of interfirm competition was especially powerful. It produced the only public crack in the unified managerial position behind the zero-reply and one-shot wage bargaining. This was a tension colloquially presented in regional terms as Tokyo versus Osaka (or Kantō against Kansai), but better understood as a difference in scale and type of company. It set the Big Three (Yahata, Fuji, NKK), all integrated iron- and steelmakers head-quartered in Toyko, against the smaller two of the Big Five (Sumitomo Metal and Kobe Steel), primarily steel-bar and -plate producers headquartered in the Kansai region. Inoue blasted the "merchant-like . . . abacus mentality" of the Kansai firms, always willing to compromise and "hand over a *furoshiki*" (a neatly wrapped package of cash) in order to return to work.[65] Indeed, after the eighth-wave strike in 1957 Sumitomo did abandon the zero-reply, one-shot approach by offering a 500-yen output pay raise. This alignment also helps explain why Yahata would protect NKK's customer base in 1959 while Sumitomo took advantage of the strike to encroach on it.

Ultimately such divisions were contained. At the industry level, cross-company consultation had cemented enduring alliances. Starting in the late 1940s, Takemura Tatsuo met frequently with his opposite numbers from Yahata, Fuji, Sumitomo, Kobe, and even Kawasaki Steel to exchange information and coordinate their relative wage levels. They met in Tokyo, in Osaka, even at Yahata in Kyūshū. Sometimes they stayed up all night until they were certain none would back down from a common position.[66] Takemura's protégé Inoue tells a similar tale. Beginning in 1953, he began meeting regularly with similarly placed labor division chiefs of the other top firms for drinks, for mahjong, and above all for golf, "best because there were no telephone interruptions and plenty of time to talk as we walked down the fairway." They would agree on standard wages for "Jack Sumitomo" and "John NKK," taking into account the varied composition of their workforces. They dubbed themselves the "Club to Enforce our Will" (considerably more euphonious in Japanese).[67]

Both Oogi Shinichi and Konda Masaharu recount their version of this story for the 1950s and 1960s, when they took their turns atop the labor division and gathered regularly with their counterparts. Oogi claims that he and the other Big Three managers were not happy to share plans with Sumitomo, because of its past betrayal of corporate unity, and Konda notes that in the 1960s the "Kantō Three" would meet once or twice a week over drinks after hours in Tokyo, while Sumitomo and Kobe consulted in Kansai. The former would usually inform the latter of their decisions only after the fact.[68] In this fashion, the unity of the steelmakers rested on a structure of collaboration, especially among the top three, constructed by generations of labor managers who continued to meet for decades as they climbed the corporate ladder from section to division chief to labor director.

Another factor reinforcing corporate solidarity, both within each firm and among them, was the commitment of the top man at each company to confront and transform the unions. While Yahata was the largest company by far, NKK's president in the 1950s, Kawada Jun, spoke with particular authority on labor issues. He was a major force on the labor committee of the Japan Iron and Steel Federation and was widely considered one of corporate Japan's most important voices on labor policy.[69] By all accounts, Kawada was strong-willed. His experience in dealing with the labor movement reached back to the production control dispute of 1946, when he suffered a broken nose in a fight with union demonstrators. In order to hold down wages and remake the union over the long haul, he supported his labor managers in their clash with sales executives, and he urged his counterparts at Fuji and Yahata especially to make this their common cause.[70]

In the end, managers put disagreements and competition aside. They exchanged valuable internal information about wage costs. With one exception they stuck to their initial zero reply in 1957. Yahata even protected

NKK's customers. Inoue Jutoku spoke of the need for companies to join together on grounds of "principle" and scorned the "mercenary" attributes of the Kansai companies (that in theory, of course, were *supposed* to be mercenary). When push came to shove, the steel companies chose "principled" unity over short-term profit seeking.

The political structure of the economy is an important part of the explanation for this choice. The contestants for the workplace did not play on a level field; the state defined its mission as helping steel industrialists sustain unity. On the eve of the 1957 strike, the chairman of Yahata steel was named to an industrial policy working group formed by MITI to address a perceived tightening of corporate credit sources. One month later, at the height of the strike, this seems to have borne fruit. MITI and the Ministry of Finance announced that iron and steel would be among four priority sectors receiving government investment loans in the coming fiscal year. Nikkeiren was a powerful body that threw its weight behind the zero reply of the Big Three.[71] Most important, MITI and major banks quietly arranged a 5.9 billion yen ($16 million) loan of "strike funds" to the top steelmakers.[72]

To note this support, however, begs a further question about Inoue Jutoku's "principle" that led him and his colleagues to risk two costly strikes. A government will not always help industrialists sweat out a strike when the latter can afford to offer a raise. Bureaucrats arguably value order above all, and one can imagine them jawboning executives for short-term concessions to bring social peace and not anger the unions further. After all, the steel companies were making strong profits in these years.

What finally ruled out this conciliatory course and reinforced the unity among Japanese bureaucratic and business elites was their shared understanding of the long-term political and economic threat of the unions in steel and coal. In a 1967 essay in a trade publication for labor managers, Konda explained it clearly:

> The union was very leftist and radical, and at this moment the company felt it had to confront it and defend management authority. A sense of crisis pervaded the company. We had to prevent [the steel unions] from becoming a second Tanrō [coal miners' union]. Our labor policies were not just the concern of labor managers but of the entire company and of top management.[73]

Konda had visited the Miike mine in Kyūshū and mines in Hokkaidō with other NKK section heads. He had a specific sense of the coal union menace. Those unions, he said, would accept new machinery that would raise output, and thus output wages, but they would not accept a revised structure of output wages. Pay thus rose in a straight line with output. Workers took home all the increment; the company saw no benefit. Steel could not afford this. It had to control wage costs as output rose.[74]

In other words, the union as it existed made it impossible to afford rationalization. Even more disturbing, it did not allow managers to enforce the rationalization program fully. This was the two-part principle upon which industrialists and the state closed ranks.

This principle also convinced just enough company-focused employees to render the union's dual pursuit of shop-floor activism and aggressive wage bargaining impossible. It is important to understand that the forces were well balanced; militant and cooperative unionists both had strong ideological and social roots in the workplace. The very process of defeat and its aftermath solidified the base of the cooperative forces and made their triumph seem inevitable.

Workplace activists of all stripes articulated their appeals with passion and growing sophistication over sake and beers in the bars lining the streets outside the mill. At the heart of the appeal of the mainstream union leaders (the Comrades Club) at both Kawasaki and Tsurumi were basic commitments to a participatory vision of grassroots democratization and to a firm belief that the interests of workers and capitalists stood in fundamental opposition. The Tsurumi union's 1958 platform justified the program of shop-floor struggle in this way: "What we mean by the democratization of management is to force managers and capitalists to recognize the social nature of production . . . and to this end create *institutions to ensure worker opinions will be reflected in management.*" In late 1959, after two failed strikes, these same leaders presented what would turn out to be a last-gasp defense of the unionism of the 1950s: "Democratizing the workplace, democratizing management—these are difficult tasks. They can't be achieved by a single union in piecemeal fashion, because in the present social structure, *the demands of the managerial organization of the company and those of ourselves, the workers, are always opposed.*"[75]

"Democratization" was also the byword of the loyalist informal factions from their earliest days, but grassroots activism was not at all what they meant. For them, a democratic union was one that repudiated the Japan Communist Party absolutely and, according to some, maintained no permanent ties to any political party. At the same time, a democratic union in this sense could be, and in later years invariably came to be, tightly controlled by its senior leadership. Some of these unionists, especially those inheriting the social democratic tradition of the Sōdōmei (then Dōmei) federation, agreed with the left-leaning mainstream that the interests of management and labor conflicted. They believed in maintaining a strong organization that would credibly threaten to strike as a last resort in any given bargaining situation. To this extent, the rhetoric and ideology of cooperative unionism in Japan was essentially the same as the "free and democratic" labor unionism of postwar Western Europe and North America. In the unions of the AFL-CIO in the United States, the DGB in Germany, the CISL and UIL streams in Italy, and elsewhere, "free and democratic" was a code phrase for anticommunist, and professional union leaders headed well-disciplined, centrally controlled unions that accepted the basic system of a capitalist economy and bargained, sometimes with militance, to defend the interests of working people in that system.

The informal groups such as Kudō's at NKK or Miyata Yoshiji's at Yahata transformed this cooperative ideology in a fundamental way. Miyata in particular was the strategist who marshaled these forces. He argued with deep conviction that "what I oppose is political party activism. I differ with Dōmei, with its tie to the Democratic Socialists, since Dōmei to some extent does oppose capitalism, does have an affirmative view of a kind of socialism . . . I don't see any structural opposition between the interests of labor and capital. The issue is only one of trust. So long as the two sides trust each other, there is no basic conflict."[76] The process of mutation toward ultra-cooperative unionism was gradual, and had just begun during the 1950s.

Social divisions among workers underlay these opposed political visions. In 1958 the Tsurumi mill union published a valuable poll of attitudes toward going on strike for higher wages among workers at five steel mills. It showed that enthusiasm for shop-floor struggle, political action, and cultural circles came mainly from the young. In a neatly descending line, the great majority of workers in their twenties "vigorously favored" striking, while only a minority of older men did so.[77]

In the 1950s these discontented young men proved able to place enough of their numbers into union offices to build a relatively young and militant majority on the executive committee at each mill, which in turn supported local activism. Although foremen attempted to dominate the union locals as in the past, they could no longer suppress rank-and-file opinions. Each local would elect members to a plantwide union assembly at the ratio of one delegate per sixty local members, and these men in turn chose candidates for the executive committee.[78] The assemblymen tended to be unranked, younger workers, as were the executive committee members.[79] At Tsurumi in 1958 the average age of the executive officers was thirty-three, which was exactly the average age of Tsurumi's unranked workers (crew bosses and foremen averaged forty-one and forty-seven years of age).[80] At the Kawasaki mill in the 1957 and '58 elections relatively young men in their early thirties with about a decade of work experience, "who had the skills to do high-level work but whose wages and status were relatively low," led numerous successful, bitterly contested election campaigns against senior local bosses.[81]

The activism of the thirty- and twenty-somethings of the 1950s stemmed from frustration at hierarchy in the workplace. In sharp contrast to the well-known "Japanese-style" practice of later years, most work sites in the 1950s were closed societies. Jobs did not rotate and transfers to other work groups were rare. Instead, members climbed a ladder of increasingly skilled jobs and ranks at an excruciating pace measured in years, even decades.

In Kudō Shinpachi's open hearth furnace, for example:

> a crew boss ran each eight-man crew, and senior, experienced workers did the more skilled tasks, such as checking furnace temperature, making sure molten metal was the right consistency. We assumed it took a new recruit three years to learn enough to be a full-fledged worker. At that point the crew boss recommended to the foreman that the new man be recognized as such, and this was passed up to the assistant section chief, a university graduate. He would almost always go along.[82]

In one rolling shop at the Kawasaki mill the machinery dated back to the 1920s. The Tokyo University researchers visited this shop.[83] They reported that the oil supply post required little experience and was given to beginners. Transfers from roller to roller were not mechanized at every point, and the heavy and demanding labor of catching the steel bars as they came hurtling off roller number 5 and quickly shifting them to number 6 was a "starring role" requiring at least three years' experience. At the helm of the finishing process stood crew bosses with at least ten years' experience, gripping the roller handle that controlled the dimensions of the finished pipe. "Adjusting the handle was critical. But there was no gauge or other indicator. It all depended on the skill and intuition of the operator." Individual technique differed to such a degree that the unfinished work of one crew could not be left to an incoming crew! The crew bosses were said to be protective of their skills and passed them on with reluctance, and the younger workers often felt ready to advance to more skilled jobs well before they were allowed. Work was artisanal and hierarchy rigid.

Most of the "young" NKK workers whose discontents energized the union from below had been hired before 1952, at which point the company's rationalization drive to streamline the workforce and raise productivity imposed a seven-year freeze on all regular hiring of new middle-school graduates or young adults. The youngest of these recruits brought their new democratic postwar education to the workplace, while those slightly older had experienced the wartime devastation and postwar democratizing moment as impressionable teenagers. These men were willing to challenge authority. They saw in the union a means to demand higher pay and protest the slow pace of advance within the workplace. In their eyes, the bosses included old-line foremen within the union as well as corporate managers. Their support for workplace activism, and that of the executive committee, reflected anger at dual pressures from the foremen's long-standing, heavy-handed control and new managerial controls over time, wages, and staffing.

The impact of advanced age and rank upon worker allegiance reversed that of youth. In the late 1950s crew bosses and foremen were typically men in their late thirties, forties, and fifties with fifteen to thirty years' tenure. These men dominated the offices of the union locals, either by serving themselves or appointing trusted protégés.[84] They were a bulwark of dual loyalty to company and union. Odaka's surveys found that 54 percent of NKK foremen were both pro-company and pro-union, and the 1956 survey discovered that dual allegiance was stronger among former union officials, who were mainly ranked men, than among other workers.[85] As long as their control of the workplace was secure, the ranked workers could reconcile their dual loyalties without trouble, sometimes representing their charges in pushing managers for better conditions, other times enforcing the company's wishes on subordinates. A foreman sympathetic to a union demand for more staffing would cover for a man off on union business by turning his tag for him. At other times, when strikes were imminent, he might follow labor division orders to pressure subordinates to vote against the strike.[86]

When young activists at NKK challenged entrenched practices whereby these supervisors dominated the union and colluded with managers, the balancing act was no longer so easy.[87] Suddenly these men felt a squeeze from below and above. They were aghast at the impudence of their subordinates. They feared that new production technologies were about to demolish old work sites and render their monopoly on hard-won skills obsolete. They saw that new management policies to streamline the line hierarchy and retrain old bosses as modern foremen were cramping their style and edging out those who could not adapt. The company wanted more reliable supervisors, the union executive committee wanted consistently militant leaders, and the Tokyo University survey team concluded that "for both the union and the managers, right now [1957–58] the greatest problem is how to control the shop-floor organization."[88]

Many foremen responded by joining hands in the informal groups with quiet help from the company to protect themselves and recapture the union. One of the few white-collar members of the Labor Problems Research Group, Gotō Tatsuo, recalled that "the leaders were almost all ranked workers who exerted formidable influence in the workplace. When major issues were up for negotiation, the group would meet to map out a strategy to pressure nonmembers to support it." On occasion labor division personnel, including the division chief, would attend these meetings.[89] Watanabe Tatsuo, for one, was busier than ever nurturing the informal groups, working mainly through the new foremen and crew bosses.[90]

Where older technology remained in place the workplace hierarchy was relatively unshaken and activist challenges more easily contained.[91] Kudō's open hearth furnace was one stronghold of the Labor Problems Research Group, so secure that Watanabe Tatsuo occasionally would send him promising young workers who had turned to the left, with a mandate to wean them from the Communist Party.[92] It also appears that the sites of direct production—blast furnace, open hearth, and rolling shops—were more firmly controlled by loyalist informal groups than sites of support processes—electric power, raw material storage and processing—or machine maintenance. The latter four shops contributed a disproportionate share of militant activists. They rarely ran night shifts, and even the younger unranked workers had considerable freedom in the use of their time.[93]

These divided orientations toward confronting managers and the company played themselves out in the growing visibility of the informal groups in the years leading up to and during the strikes. Of the five factions at the Kawasaki mill, two strongly supported the union's activist turn, two opposed it, and one wavered in between. Four of these factions crystallized for the first time as active informal groups in the process of reacting to the militant initiatives of the 1950s or defending them. Only the Communist Party cells had maintained a consistent presence as a politically conscious body since the 1940s. The other groups evolved from inchoate tendencies to cohesive factions. With tacit and direct support from managers and outside consultants, both the Acorn Club and Kudō Shimpachi's Labor Problems Research Group defined themselves in more explicitly political terms, as did the union mainstream in the Comrades Club (Dōshikai, supporting the Socialist Party), and the Third Group seeking in the name of unity to bridge the sharp chasm opening up between the others.

Similar informal groups were found in every major steel mill, and every major industry, and like-minded bodies sought each other out. Both the rising force of shop-floor struggle and then the bitter strikes of 1957 and 1959 accelerated the creation of the factions themselves and their coalescence into larger clusters and, ultimately, visible, nationwide networks.[94] As early as 1952, Kudō Shinpachi made the acquaintance of anticommunist organizers from the Yahata mill after the second annual Tekkō Rōren convention and discussed "doing something about the nest of leftists at NKK."[95] With the opening of a Tokyo office of the International Metalworkers Federation in 1957, the IMF also began to work as national and international broker of this incipient alliance, sending interested union leaders on trips abroad and introducing them to each other.[96]

Within the mill, annual elections of union officers and votes to authorize or call off strikes propelled these factions to organize themselves more tightly and rendered them visible. This process gathered steam at Kawasaki in 1956 when the union executive committee moved to a more democratic system of contested elections. This replaced the existing procedure, where members voted to approve or reject a single slate chosen by the executive committee.[97] For the rest of the decade and into the 1960s, union elections were hotly contested.[98] Kudō Shinpachi "had to campaign for our candidates after hours, so I never got home before 10 P.M. at election time," while his foe, Nakao Yasuji of the Comrades Club, "made home visits to workers and sometimes stayed out all night."[99] The elections were nominally nonpartisan, and factional allegiances were not listed on ballots. While most workers knew who stood where, Kudō and other leaders would meet group members in each workplace to make sure every one knew which candidates were theirs. Managers joined the fray too, however illegal it was. Watanabe Tatsuo of the labor division would gather loyalist foremen and sub-foremen and make sure "each of them had at least half of his subordinates lined up firmly behind the company-supported candidates." Much of this precinct politicking took place in bars, and since "I didn't have an expense account for this, I had to arrange to falsify a foreman's overtime record, and we would drink on that money."[100]

Despite such opposing efforts, until the strike of 1959 the factions of the left usually elected majorities at both Kawasaki and Tsurumi, and most other major steel mills as well.[101] A majority of NKK workers supported the strikes and the union leadership enthusiastically in 1957 and 1959, but a strong minority of about 500 active members in the Research Group and the Acorn Club opposed the 1957 and 1959 actions from the start. They won further support during the strikes. Gradually Isobe's Third Group pulled closer to them; it rejected the belief that struggle itself would teach the importance of solidarity in favor of the idea that unity must be achieved prior to any strike action. Young workers supported shop-floor activism and the adamant wage demands, and maintenance and machine workers were a particular stronghold of support for militant activism, but furnace workers had long been the key source of support for the Research Group. Their opposition to militant unionism grew ever stronger and louder, especially during the partial strike of 1959, which had them at work most of the time. By the end of that strike, the Acorn Club, the Research Group, the Third Group at Kawasaki, and similar factions at Tsurumi were working more closely than ever with managers to obstruct their union's leaders.[102] Across the steel industry, a growing minority, then a majority, of employees rejected calls for unified industrial action and gave priority to the local interest of their employers. At NKK, a majority came to reject the union's call to stay the course of the strikes.

The local patriotism of steelworkers trumped industrial solidarity in part for reasons common to unions in general: they are relatively open and democratic bodies by definition, and this makes them subject to manipulation in a way that a company is not. Imagine, for example, that NKK's labor division distributed minutes of its meetings to all employees, or that meetings of the board of directors of NKK or of Japan Iron and Steel Federation were matters of public record, and that decisions were taken by votes. This would have replicated the situation of the executive committee of NKK's plant unions, the companywide union federation, or Tekkō Rōren's expanded central struggle committee. How much easier it would have been for the union at every level to reach into the company, seek allies, and draw unity and strength from its awareness of the division among executives, as managers did with workers.

Yet union procedures in all countries are more open than those of top management, and unions elsewhere facing similar divisions have sustained industrial unity—and been willing to bank furnaces. Management claims that the strike would ultimately hurt the company by costing sales or destroying machines drew particular force from the fact that the workplace and factory had historically been natural units of organization and identification for unionists of all persuasions. Craft guilds of early modern artisans in Japan had played little role in the training and credentialing of workers, and they exercised little control over the supply of labor. Like workers in Korea, another country where unions have been organized by factory and company but have often been militant, industrial workers in Japan from the Meiji era onward had no trade-based organizing tradition to inform their decisions.[103] In such a context, the most logical base for organizing and for action was the familiar workplace, the site of a person's most significant group of peers outside the family.

The company was also the place where a person acquired the skills and the identity of "steelworker." In sharp contrast to Germany, for example, industrial Japan developed no state-supervised system to train and certify workers independent of the employers. NKK workers learned their skills on the job or in company-run schools. After the 1920s, it became increasingly difficult for workers to make lateral moves from one major producer to another. In the mills of the 1950s, the closed hierarchies of workplace society encouraged an identity as an "NKK steel man," not as a generic "steelworker." This identification with the firm flowed from a long context of weak trade organization and segmented skill formation.

The cooperative inclination was reinforced in some industries more than others. Industrial unions *were* effective in some cases, most notably coal mining. What distinguished such cases of durable horizontal organizing was relatively strong state regulation of demand or prices that dampened the consciousness of competition between companies. In less regulated industries where some degree of interfirm competition took place, such as steel in contrast to coal or railways, industrial solidarity was particularly difficult to sustain.[104]

The process by which postwar Japanese unions were created added further pressure to repudiate actions that appeared to harm the company. In the immediate crisis after 1945, union activists across the political spectrum were committed to help companies survive and recover. They demanded to be active participants and at least co–decision-makers to this end. In the 1950s union rhetoric on the left vowed to "oppose rationalization absolutely," but in practice this did not lead workers to reject new technology. Even the most ardent workplace activists focused rather on controlling the impact of new machines, placing limits or conditions on their introduction and use. The majority of the workers remained in the "pro-pro" camp: pro-union in its effort to improve their work conditions and wages, and pro-company in its effort to recover and grow. NKK workers held back from tactics that would have increased the cost of their strike to managers because many believed themselves responsible for the equipment and the enterprises upon which their livelihood depended, a belief rooted in the workplace focus of their struggles to survive since the war.

Despite all these pressures to cooperate with management, several years of shop-floor activism, the energetic efforts of the organizers, and the hundreds of discussion meetings had excited the majority of the workers about the potential for the union to offer them a voice in matters of everyday work life and to improve their wages. One should understand these historical and structural factors as a set of weights that just barely tipped the balance at a critical moment when workplace activism and wage militance had not taken durable institutional form. Only in retrospect, after managers followed up on the strikes to build stronger alliances with cooperative factions, reorganize the workforce, and enhance their own control, do these forces favoring cooperative labor relations appear as an iron cage that predetermined the outcome.

Labor division chief Inoue Jutoku was reassigned soon after the 1959 strike, in a clear rebuke to his abrasive leadership. Other managers blamed him for prolonging or even causing the conflict. Decades later, Inoue gleefully admitted he took the fall for the company. "I was delighted at the outcome of the 1959 strike, even though I was transferred. It was the greatest effort of my career, and I was happy to take responsibility."[105]

His successors continued to differ over the relative wisdom of hands-on manipulation of union factions versus more generalized efforts to win the loyalty of employees, but their initiatives were effective. The union's leadership gradually fell into the hands of the loyalist informal groups, and union policies shifted accordingly. A "state of the union" document prepared in late 1959 by the newly elected executive committee at the Kawasaki mill union offered signs of this change.[106]

This statement began by nodding in the direction of the few remaining stalwarts of the union's left wing, including Nakamura Kōgō. It acknowledged that "in the past several years our movement has become significantly more energetic and the fighting strength of our union has increased to allow ever larger struggles."[107] Nonetheless, it said, trust between the rank and file and union leadership was deteriorating. Rising absenteeism from local meetings was a sign of a decline in union democracy. The only way to restore trust in the leaders was to win a dispute, but the only way to win was to rebuild the organization. How to break this vicious circle? The union had few answers. The leaders offered a plaintive reminder that "the proper behavior in an organization is to follow the decisions of the union, no matter what party or faction one belongs to."[108] They begged for tolerance toward foremen torn between roles as company servant and union leader: "we shouldn't immediately call them company pimps or reactionaries."[109] They ended by calling for a renewed focus on shop-floor "activities" to address local issues of safety as one way to restore trust, but the tone of these remarks was far softer than the strident rhetoric of previous years. Indeed, the decision to use the word "activities" and not "struggles" clearly signaled a new approach.

In the steel industry in the following years, companies like NKK began to harvest the fruits of previous investments. They could afford to raise pay more rapidly than in the past, and they offered more generous pay hikes than before, which helped cooperative unions gain hegemony in the workplace. These unions came to abandon the strike as a weapon, even of last resort. They turned from "bargaining" to "consultation" as the preferred mode of dealing with the company. By the 1970s, the pattern of cooperative unionism had sunk such strong roots, both in organizations and in people's minds as an expression of a uniquely Japanese "culture" that the intense divisions and conflicts of the 1950s were dismissed as unwise or described as unimaginable.

The democratic vision of leaders and members atrophied as unions became bureaucratic entities, powerful vis-à-vis their members, but meek toward the company, key pieces of the hegemonic structure of power in Japan. The militant tone, the assumption that the interests of workers and company were opposed in substantial ways, and the aspiration to build a new society by energizing an egalitarian, participatory spirit in the workplace gradually vanished as managers and their union allies established a new order in the workplace.

In later years unions continued to address issues raised by the activists of the 1950s. Companies and unions in steel mills worked out a basic understanding and a set of rules about wage distribution, staffing levels, and transfers that offered some protection to workers, although less than that sought in the 1950s. The unions of the 1950s had sought these protections by pushing for participation from the base of the workplace. They tried to define standards for the well-being of members independent from the business demands of the firm. The triumph of managers and cooperative unionists opened the way to the economic miracle as it retreated from such democratic goals.

7 Fabricating the Politics of Cooperation

From the 1960s through the 1980s the unions that had sought a voice in decision-making rooted in shop-floor activism became marginal actors in Japan. The idea that employees were best served by devoting themselves wholeheartedly to company goals became a widespread article of faith, and the hegemony of corporate values took hold in workplaces and the wider society.

The concept of "hegemony" has no simple or universally accepted definition. It reaches back to the writings of Antonio Gramsci, but he made only scattered and partially developed reference to the term. Drawing on the interpretations of various readers of Gramsci, I understand hegemony to be a state in which common-sense assumptions of how things are and ought to be are so pervasive that people can barely conceive of any other meaningful arrangement of their lives.[1] In this, hegemony is distinguished from an ideology, which can be one of several alternative understandings. To the extent that capitalism becomes so entrenched that it excludes alternatives as foolish or unthinkable, it has become a hegemonic system that transcends particular ideologies.[2]

The story of NKK and of steel since the 1950s has been both an emblem and a powerful motor of changes that reinforced such a hegemonic order in Japanese workplaces. Steelmakers were pioneers in developing internationally noted programs of participation for quality control. Managers were leaders in the drive to streamline industrial labor forces, rotate jobs and deploy workers flexibly, and link pay to ability as they assessed it. Newly cooperative unions and managers worked out a system of "one-shot" wage bargaining that set standards or ceilings for the rest of the economy and led the way toward a broadly based national decline in strikes.[3]

From 1960 to the present day, no strikes of significance have taken place at any major steel company in Japan; none whatsoever—not even one-day symbolic protests—have occurred since 1965. Although brief work stoppages remained common for a time during wage negotiations in other industries, both the number and the intensity of union actions everywhere followed a similar downward trend (see Figure 7). Marked by the traumas of the past, the politics of the Japanese workplace shifted profoundly. Steel retained its emblematic and strategic place in the history of work in Japan, but the theme of the story changed completely, from turbulence to order, from contest to control, from polarization barely contained to cooperation carefully orchestrated. There were aftershocks to the upheavals of the 1950s, but the very intensity of their experience taught managers to be always vigilant in the political task of containing dissent and directing the workforce.

This cooperative order was not achieved easily, and one must admire the adroitness of the managers. Their hegemony cannot be understood simply as based on the hyper-exploitation of workers. Managers put costly effort into socializing the workers to make corporate goals their own, and they proved willing to make significant concessions to co-opt potential opponents; but they exacted a political price in sharing economic fruits with labor. Employees gained affluence and a measure of protection by accepting the close, often coercive, embrace of the company; but they had to sharply narrow their concept of democracy in the workplace and surrender personal autonomy.

The core ideas of the cooperative gospel that enabled corporations and unions to consolidate hegemony were simple. Their proponents always put them forward in negative and positive terms, ever fearful of the prospect of a revival of class struggle ideology. The goal of unions was not to transform capitalism, but to improve it. Unions and workers should participate in the workplace not through activism that challenged management and assumed conflict of interest, but by working flexibly to accept new technology and offering suggestions for improvement through quality control programs. The result would be an expanding pie of production and profits. Unions existed to ensure that workers were not sacrificed on the altar of rationalization but received their fair share of the bounty of productivity gains in the form of higher pay or shorter hours.

Through the 1970s and 1980s, the steel unions led the nation in preaching that in this limited role as watchdogs, organized workers should follow a doctrine of restraint, not assertion. Unions need not bargain to defend workers who cooperated in rationalization; they could simply consult with managers in good faith, taking into account the situation of the firm and the national economy, restraining current wage demands to keep inflation low and ensure future investments and long-run benefits. Advocates dubbed this stance "correct" labor unionism, and they claimed for the politics of friendly consultation among elected union officials and like-minded corporate leaders the label of industrial democracy. In the glowing language of an informal group at the Toshiba corporation, this was a world in which "the development of the enterprise" and the "happiness" of the workers were "indivisible."[4]

Managers welcomed these sentiments and helped refine the message. A 1970 textbook on labor management relations used to train supervisors at NKK began by giving positive industrial relations credit for the nation's great economic performance. It stressed that such relations were achieved through long, difficult experience and offered a pithy summation of the philosophy of the corporate-centered society: "Our labor, livelihood, and social contributions only exist via the organization called a corporation." Unions exist to raise the economic level of workers by cooperating to increase corporate income and then to discuss the distribution of profits. In an era of great transformations, corporation, union, and employees must all be flexible as they respond to changing industrial structures and technology.[5]

To hear managers train foremen with this message is neither surprising nor peculiar to Japan. Executives everywhere have argued that industrial relations are not a zero-sum contest and that workers should accept new technologies that increase productivity in exchange for a share of the gain. Many unions throughout the capitalist world since 1945 have agreed. But compared to cooperative unionists elsewhere, the mainstream of Japanese labor leaders became extremists in the cause of moderation. The 1968 platform of the Iron and Steel Liaison Congress, an industrywide network of informal groups, claimed without reservation that labor-management relations were "based on trust," not conflict. Unions should strike "only when their interests are harmed *and* trust is betrayed." This platform could be read as admitting that harm to workers is not cause for action unless it takes place through a betrayal of trust. Similarly, unions should cooperate to rationalize operations because "prosperity of the enterprise makes possible improved livelihoods for workers, and rationalization makes corporate prosperity possible." Unions should merely seek to "reduce sacrifice by the workers to the smallest amount possible in advance."[6] With this claim, the Liaison Congress, whose leaders included NKK stalwarts Kudō Shinpachi, Gotō Tatsuo, and Kitazume Shun, agreed that rationalization might well require sacrifice by workers, and it has.

The leaders of this congress, above all Miyata Yoshiji, acted through the 1970s and 1980s as masterminds of a process by which nearly two thirds of organized workers were unified in a single national federation, called Rengō. Their guiding beliefs made them extraordinary in their willingness to accept "sacrifice" and in the degree to which they repressed any thought that collective action might be needed to make sure workers took home their fair share. As they defined themselves in these terms, it no longer made sense to talk of labor and management as opposed interests, or to understand the labor movement to be a project aimed at transforming society.

Yet the cooperative labor unionists in their ascendance retained an important sense of mission. What united them among themselves and with the company and sustained the fervor of the informal groups for decades was summed up in the 1983 platform of NKK's new companywide informal group. The members were indeed part of a "movement," but one that aimed "to protect workers as human beings and banish all elements that would injure or alienate this [humanity]"—that is, a movement to "banish all parties and policies" of the left from labor unions.[7]

In pursuing this mission, the purported lessons of history were powerful tools. Isobe Toshie recalls that for years after 1959, "the company and right-wing union people brandished the forty-nine-day strike" as an object lesson in the folly of class-struggle activism. In 1980 Kondo Haruhiko contributed his telling of the 1959 morality play in an essay for the PR magazine of an NKK subsidiary where supporters of the Japan Socialist Party had been gaining strength and making noise about a possible strike. In constant rounds of study groups and seminars, new generations of recruits to the informal groups acquired what they were fond of calling "ideological armor," a combination of tactical training in union politics (how to win elections, how to convert young workers from the Communist Party), history classes on the bad old days, and philosophy lessons on the flaws in Marxist thought.[8]

As they refined the ideology of cooperation, corporate managers and union leaders extended their hegemony not only through straightforward persuasion but through bruising political machination. Informal group members never accounted for a majority of employees or union members at NKK or any company. If Leninism is the strategy by which a politicized vanguard leads the masses to a socialist revolution, postwar Japan was home to a sort of Leninism-through-the-looking-glass. Informal groups acted as a vanguard intent on leading the masses in the politically correct opposite direction.

In the bitter aftermath of 1959, a considerable corps of old-style activists remained at the national headquarters of Tekkō Rōren and its local units, pressing for a political strike to oppose renewal of the United States–Japan security treaty in 1960 or calling for joint support for the Japan Socialist and Japan Communist parties. The newly confident advocates of cooperative unionism in steel, led by Miyata Yoshiji, responded by leap-frogging the industrial federation, first pulling together like-minded unionists elsewhere into a national front and then absorbing Tekkō Rōren. Miyata joined with informal group union leaders in automobile and electronics manufacturing and shipbuilding to found the Japan Council of the International Metalworkers Federation (the IMF-JC) in 1964.

The effort took place amid accelerating international and American activities directed at Japanese labor, in part reflecting the strategy of Ambassador Edwin O. Reischauer (1960–1966). The Reischauer line sought to reach out to the Japanese left, intellectuals, and politicians as well as unionists, and win their support for the United States–Japan military alliance and American foreign policy more generally. Robert Kennedy's 1962 visit to Japan, for example, included several meetings with Japanese labor leaders.[9] The formation of the Japan Council (JC) of the International Metal Federation (IMF) in 1964 was the most important of these endeavors for the steel industry, and over the next two decades the IMF-JC, with the steel union federation in the forefront, would push the entire Japanese labor movement toward ever more cooperative policies and philosophy.[10]

The founding of the IMF-JC was a slow and contentious process. In the late 1950s, officials of the IMF, a federation with substantial European as well as American membership, began their efforts to induce Japanese union federations in the iron and steel, nonferrous metal, electronics, automobile, machine, and shipbuilding industries from both Sōhyō and Dōmei (formerly Sōdōmei) to join the organization. But IMF officials refused to allow individual Japanese unions to join directly, in the justifiable fear that such moves would lead to splits in Japan's industrial federations and national centers. Instead, they encouraged Japanese industrial unions to come together in a supra-partisan "Japan Council" of metal industry unions that would join the IMF as a single body. It took seven years of delicate and not-so-subtle maneuvering to achieve this end. Key figures included American officials in the IMF, notorious union cold warriors with CIA ties.[11]

In its coverage the IMF-JC corresponded roughly to West Germany's IG Metall, a sprawling federation of unions in heavy industries ranging from automobiles to electronics to shipbuilding and iron and steel, although the IMF-JC had no centralized control over its constituents at all comparable to that of IG Metall. The council sought a "free and democratic" union movement, in essence a less confrontational relationship with management than that advocated by the left wing of Sōhyō. As secretary of the steelworkers' federation, Miyata Yoshiji frankly claimed that "the IMF is so powerful that we may be shut out of world steel markets if we do not join."[12]

Tekkō Rōren did not join the IMF-JC until 1966 and did so only by a 12 to 11 vote after a dramatic all-night meeting of the executive committee. Miyata won this ballot by promising that the Japan Council would act only as a "window" for international contacts and not as a domestic political force. His opponents correctly feared the Japan Council would be a wedge for the cooperative forces to capture the union movement at home, repudiating its antiwar, pro-socialist politics, its workplace activism, and its wage militance.[13]

Almost immediately, the council showed its true intent, emerging in 1967 and 1968 as a voice for restraint in the spring wage negotiations and organizing its own "wage offensive council." The year 1968 also saw the complete takeover of Tekkō Rōren by a beefed-up Liaison Council of informal groups. Over the next twenty years, the Liaison Council and the IMF-JC reached out to other industrial union federations through numerous alliances and networks. Through false starts and complicated, rocky negotiations, this drive for unity finally issued in the formation of the All-Japan Private Sector Labor Union Federation in 1987, which then enveloped public sector unions as well to become the Japan Labor Union General Federation, or simply Rengō, in 1989.[14]

As the ultracooperative forces at the national level won the day within the union movement, they simultaneously cultivated newly intimate ties to the state. In the early 1970s Miyata argued vigorously that unions should take the lead in restraining wage demands to break the spiral of wage-price inflation, and as president of the IMF-JC he opened a private "hot line" to communicate with Fukuda Takeo, later prime minister and at the time deputy prime minister and director of the Economic Planning Agency.[15] To the delight of the government, the IMF-JC in 1975 agreed to accept wage increases nearly 50 percent lower than those of the previous year, placing an effective ceiling on the wage demands of other unions as well. In 1976 these labor unionists pioneered a Japanese-style income policy through consultation among the four major JC federations. Their goal was to coordinate wage decisions in line with national economic trends.[16] Although business leaders in the past had preferred local wage negotiations to bargaining with militant industrial unions, they were willing to consult at a national, cross-industry level with these understanding partners.

The ubiquitous entities that have enforced the politics of cooperation at the grass roots are the informal groups. Some of these are publicly advertised bodies formally separate from the union, organized by a company's personnel section and open to all qualified comers—for example, a "Cheerful Dorm Association" or a "foreman's club." These draw on a portion of the workforce holding some trait in common and serve to mobilize a company-oriented group spirit toward corporate goals. Toyota Motors is famous for its numerous bodies of this sort.

More sinister have been groups also built from the ground up by a company personnel office, but in secret, usually with help from professional "labor consultants." These bodies have acted as cells within a union, intending to take it over or split off to found an opposing second union. Famous groups brought to light through court challenges by unhappy members or outside investigators have been active at Sansui Electronics, Japan Nestles Chocolate, the Yukijurushi food processing company, and Toshiba. The Ōgi Kai (Fan Club) at Toshiba was founded in 1973 and by 1985 enrolled 3,000 of the electronic giant's 70,000 employees. As such groups were and are of dubious legality, their extent is unknown, but certainly they have been important at dozens of major companies.[17]

Probably the most common sort of informal group is the sort that emerged at NKK and throughout the steel industry in the 1950s and flourished thereafter. In the 1960s, as many as six separate groups at NKK were active at the Kawasaki, Tsurumi, and Mizue mills. In 1970 the company consolidated these three adjacent plants into a single Keihin Steel Works, shifting most operations to the newly developed landfill island of Ōgishima that linked the three mills. The unions at each mill merged into a single Keihin Labor Union, and the informal groups combined into a single body called the Sōyūkai. Compared to Toshiba's secret society, the Sōyūkai was less covert. It emerged from relatively autonomous factions within the union, although the company personnel section and outside consultants offered ongoing help.

The fact that virtually all unionized workplaces in Japan from the 1950s to the present, and many non-union sites, have been home to informal groups of one of these types, often for decades, testifies eloquently to the continuous political challenge of sustaining the solidarity and control of cooperative unions.[18] Once ascendant after 1959, a potential Achilles heel of the newly cooperative order in steel mills was the prospect of renewed challenge from below. At NKK as elsewhere, the authority of informal group unionists and labor managers was uneasy at first. In the early 1960s, Acorn Club and Research Group members recall fear of physical attack, "nasty graffiti all over." They wrote of denunciations reminiscent of a [Chinese communist] "people's court" at meetings where they argued against a strike in 1965.[19] One primary goal of labor managers was to make and keep the new Mizue mill strike-proof, and despite their best efforts at transferring only "people ready to build a movement in the opposite direction from the labor movement," the company inadvertently assigned a few hidden CP members to Mizue. In short order these workers had organized a cell, and shop-floor activists of the left briefly held sway in several workplace locals.[20]

But the company was able to suppress these challenges. Kondo Haruhiko recalls that the labor division kept in touch with informal group leaders, "foremen, white-collar, and technicians, generally union local chiefs, and relied on them to recruit the rest."[21] The Sōyūkai grew from 940 members in 1971 to 3,500 in 1982 (35 percent of the total union membership). New recruits would be sent to evening courses at private training centers—Mitamura Shirō's Labor Studies Center, the Fuji Political University, or the Japan Political Economy Research Center founded by apostate CP leader Sano Manabu. Watanabe Tatsuo attests that "when they returned to the workplace they were an effective and increasingly powerful informal group, and the company determined to cooperate and further bolster them, giving them preferential treatment in promotions, for example. The whole endeavor bore great fruit."[22] Because the foremen who controlled the informal groups and the union locals prepared the increasingly important annual merit evaluations of rank-and-file employees, most workers had a powerful pragmatic reason to support the union leadership.

By the mid-1960s, in fact, the informal groups were so well entrenched that some managers worried they had succeeded too well. The second union at Nissan Motors was well known for its ability to demand favors as the price of peace, and one NKK manager recalled that "however close management was to the informal groups, we were always concerned that they could get out of hand, as at Nissan, where the union began to intervene in personnel decisions." For this reason, Konda Masaharu consistently opposed reliance on the groups, but he notes that NKK was fortunate to have several separate informal groups in the first decade of their ascendance. "If one got uppity and pressed for some special treatment in exchange for cooperation, we could always turn to the others."[23]

If a runaway informal group was one danger of success, decay from within lurked as another. As the union abandoned both strikes and workplace activism, it had fewer achievements to boast of. Managers began to fear that without some old-style union assertiveness, disillusioned workers might turn back to the remaining advocates of workplace activism and wage militance. When these old-guard forces at the three major steel companies raised a strong campaign in 1965 to break the one-shot bargaining system, Konda's colleagues at Fuji Steel and Yahata argued that "we should allow, even encourage, the union to strike this once for the sake of its organization. Without some show of energy, the union will lose legitimacy, and this will hurt the company in the long run."[24] In fact, unions at Sumitomo, Fuji, and Yahata did walk out in twenty-four-hour "protest strikes," perhaps with the quiet blessing of management, but Konda saw this as a "foolish" idea. At NKK, the efforts of the Acorn Club ensured there would be no strike.

The two regular tests of the new regime of union-company control were biannual union elections and yearly wage bargaining. Once the Research Group, the Acorn Club, and allied groups at Tsurumi and Mizue gained the upper hand, they rewrote the election rules to help them control union offices. In 1965 NKK's unions retreated from the system of contested elections introduced at the height of grassroots activism in 1957. They moved to a two-stage process that eroded union democracy and impeded insurgent challenges. Members first chose candidates in workplace primaries that were relatively easy for supervisors to monitor and then held a millwide, up-or-down ballot on a single slate. Yahata similarly moved to a "recommendation system" that allowed the top officials to hand-pick the one slate on the ballot. The nuts and bolts of voting were equally forbidding to dissenters. Balloting often took place in full view of local union officers, who were usually supervisors. Ballots were typically counted in secret, and candidates had no right to have representatives present.[25]

Both old left unionists of the Japan Communist Party (JCP) or the Japan Socialist Party (JSP) and New Left advocates supporting non-partisan local activism bitterly complained of formal and secret manipulation. Informal group leaders would meet with managers on company time to discuss election strategies. At morning meetings of a work crew, foremen would give election speeches, and after hours they would lobby subordinates to support the proper candidates. Nakao Yasuji told of a case where an old-guard activist managed to win a local election by three votes, but was then defeated by three votes when the union ordered a revote due to a reported violation of procedure.[26] By the 1980s, corrupt, power-hungry, sex-crazed union bosses were stock characters in the hugely popular genre of business comic books and business novels, and the image of big company unions as immoral and boss-ridden was a tenet of Japanese mass culture.[27]

Despite popular cynicism, the electoral grip of the informal groups remained firm. In July 1960 three of the top four posts at NKK's Kawasaki union fell into Research Group / Acorn Club hands, although old-guard activists held a number of executive committee seats. By the 1970s, at most one or two activists from the left sat on the twenty-person executive committees of the unions at each NKK mill and the enterprise federation. Through the 1960s dissenting workplace activists typically won 25 to 40 percent of the votes in contested elections at most major steel mills, and similar totals rejected the official slates. The proportion of dissenting voters fell to roughly 15 percent in the 1970s. By the 1980s, managers and informal group leaders had made 90 percent of the votes their measure of victory. Occasional insurgencies even to the extent of a 20 or 30 percent ballot for a JCP candidate set off loud alarm bells, with personnel managers scrambling to found new informal groups.[28]

The dominion of the company and informal groups was tested and affirmed annually in the spring wage offensive. For a time considerable sentiment in favor of wage militance survived at most of the major mills. In the 1960s NKK union members usually voted to authorize the steel federation to call a strike at its discretion in response to company wage offers. In 1961, 1963, and 1965 unions at all major producers except NKK indeed walked out on twenty-four-hour strikes to protest company wage offers. But more sustained actions that might have forced higher offers proved impossible, in large part because newly installed union leaders at the Mizue mill in 1961 and at all the NKK mills thereafter essentially repudiated the strike votes of their own members. They plausibly argued two points in meetings of the Tekkō Rōren central strike committee: only a prolonged, industrywide strike could force the corporations to improve their initial wage offers; and (precisely because of their own presence) the federation lacked the solidarity to conduct such actions. Condemning brief protest strikes as meaningless, they refused to join the twenty-four-hour industrywide actions of 1963 and 1965. Their actions clearly violated the spirit and probably the letter of their members' strike votes, which had delegated strike authority not to the mill union but to Tekkō Rōren.[29]

Over time, the rhetoric of spring wage "struggles" and "demands" took on the quality of anachronistic cliché. Between 1966 and 1972, the strike votes at each mill produced gradually smaller numbers of "yes" votes and more frequent refusals to authorize a strike. Few leaders believed it possible or desirable to carry out lengthy industrywide actions, and union leaders at other mills now joined those at NKK in rejecting brief protest strikes as well. In 1972, they took the next logical step by ending the twenty-year practice of local voting at the start of a bargaining round to authorize a strike if negotiations stalled. In the new "after-the-offer" system, each union would wait until its leaders had reached a tentative wage agreement with the company and then vote on whether to accept it or reopen bargaining and possibly strike. No union at any of the top five companies has called a strike under this system.

The year 1959 was thus the last time the unions made a serious try to force the major steel companies to raise their initial public wage offer, and 1955 was the last time that a strike in fact succeeded in forcing concessions. The system of one-shot wage bargaining was first imposed in 1956. It was sustained with great trauma in 1957 and 1959, and perfected from 1960 through 1972.

To maintain this system in the face of a rank and file that often wanted to take further collective action, managers and unions in the steel industry improvised a complex array of springtime procedures. Managers at the top firms began by consulting extensively among themselves. NKK's labor executives, division chiefs, and section heads would meet weekly with their counterparts at other firms from winter through early spring to decide on their wage offer and coordinate bargaining activity.[30] As Konda Masaharu put it in 1967: "the steel companies compete fiercely for sales, but they act in perfect concert in labor management."[31] The trick in these meetings was to decide on a pay increase that all the steelmakers could afford, yet one not so low as to discredit the cooperative union leaders and provoke insurgency. In these calculations, the specter of a revival of 1950s unionism was a shadowy presence that kept managers honest in their wage offers despite the absence of overt pushing and shoving by the union.

After several initial rounds of private, unofficial talks with union leaders to ascertain their expectations, the labor managers of the top firms would come together and decide on their offer. They would present this to the union leaders, again in a private, informal context, and they would later sit down for a dozen or more formal "negotiating sessions" with union leaders and numerous informal discussions with former unionists now in supervisory posts.[32] Unions continued to use fighting words in these meetings and in public, proclaiming in 1980, for example, that "we absolutely refuse to accept [this wage offer] that lowers our real wages." But such assertions had long been ritual incantation.[33] As one anonymous manager claimed as early as 1967: "We don't [meet] to hear union opinions on how much of a raise they want. We have confidence in what we are ready to offer, and we are meeting with union leaders to tell them that 'we are going with such and such a raise' and to ask them to take responsibility for taking care of the matter [by getting members' consent]."[34] In this man's confident vision, union and company were partners imposing a decision on the rank and file.

The two sides indeed acted together to sell each year's wage agreement to a sometimes dubious body of employees. The union would convene occasionally heated workplace discussions during the wage offensive, where local leaders argued to the rank and file for accepting the offer as the best deal possible under that year's circumstances.[35] Managers also reached out directly to employees. They wrote in company PR publications of the need for restraint in a lean year or the need to invest profits for the long run in a fat year. They also lobbied through informal group leaders who were workplace supervisors, prompting these men to make the case for a given wage settlement in face-to-face meetings of each work team.[36]

On occasion, workers at a particular mill would challenge this pattern of negotiations that scarcely whispered a strike threat. At NKK's Kawasaki mill in 1965, even though only 51 percent of the workers voted to authorize a strike, the pot nearly boiled over. Junior workers represented by the union's youth division made an enthusiastic push for a strike, and the mill's central committee was set to join the federation's scheduled stoppage until peace petitions from numerous union locals forced the committee to reverse its stand. The Acorn Club's assessment of the spring offensive expressed pride in the club's "reconfirming the true value of our group" in leading the drive to stop the strike.[37]

But more often, especially in the 1970s and after, the hold of foremen and crew bosses made it nearly impossible for dissenters to push the union anywhere close to the brink.[38] Managers came to fear the silent erosion of the cooperative union's legitimacy more than a noisy rebellion. Although he rejected his colleagues' proposal to allow a show strike to prop up the union, Konda Masaharu was among the publicly fretful voices. In 1967 he wrote that continued one-shot wage settlements might dangerously weaken rank-and-file support for union leaders.[39] At least one opinion survey conducted by the NKK union in 1967 revealed widespread discontent with the modesty of wage increases relative to both inflation and the huge economic expansion. But workers no longer possessed the political means to organize such grumbling into broad-based, open resistance.[40]

In addition to making aggressive wage demands, the steel unions in their activist incarnation had built a movement from the ground up through organizers, local discussion sessions, and workplace struggle. They had sought control over hours and vacations, a voice in the allocation of bonuses and individual merit ratings and raises, and authority over the crucial matter of staffing levels. In the new politics of workplace cooperation, the union continued to address these issues. But just as an orderly system of one-shot bargaining replaced the unpredictable wage struggles of the 1950s, a system of consultation in meetings of union leaders with company executives replaced bargaining over demands generated from the workplace.

The move to consultation was a national trend with international backing. The Japan Productivity Center had been a strong advocate of labor-management consultation since its founding in 1955, and in 1960 it launched a new series of publications and seminars to promote discussion councils as forums where employees and managers could exchange information and reach decisions about work conditions in a cooperative atmosphere. Through the 1960s and 1970s, virtually every unionized company in Japan put in place a system of union-company consultation that either operated in tandem with collective bargaining or in place of it.[41]

In steel as elsewhere, labor-management consultation became increasingly elaborate. Although the union and the company were equally entitled to bring an issue to the conference room, the most common practice was for the company to introduce important business plans that affected employees and seek union understanding and support, perhaps for the shutdown of a facility and the transfer or voluntary retirement of workers. In the early years, talks often began at the last minute and unions complained that this was notification, not consultation. They sought more frequent meetings with longer lead time between the first presentation of any major change and its implementation. As companies became more confident of the cooperative commitment of their partners, they agreed. At New Japan Steel, the world's largest steelmaker (created in 1970 through the merger of Yahata and Fuji), union and company representatives in the 1970s began meeting for several months of prior consultations before formal consultations took place over key issues. Through this mechanism, the union sought to protect workers as steel plants were continually streamlined.[42] At NKK as well, labor-management councils at corporate and plant levels frequently discussed staffing cuts. Managers would propose to reduce staffing as new equipment was set to come on line. The union would ask its local officers to evaluate the plans and report back to the council. In some cases, an initial proposal would be modified to accommodate union concerns.[43]

To the extent that the details of these transfer plans or staffing cuts could sometimes be changed, so-called consultation actually included an element of bargaining. At first glance, the give-and-take over these issues resembled the process of the 1950s, when workplace organizers raised concerns over staffing and forced these on the attention of union headquarters. Until the early 1970s, the NKK union continued to send men with the title of organizer to sample workplace opinion on key issues and report back to the leadership. But in the 1960s and 1970s the organizers were no longer charged to dig up local grievances and aggressively press them. Instead of being a resource for local activism, they were to serve as relatively passive communicators from union leaders to members and a means for the union heads to monitor the base.[44] In sharp contrast to the earlier philosophy of workplace struggle, the premise of the new order of consultation was that a peaceful agreement would be reached. The threat of either wildcat or authorized protest was scarcely present.

In a parallel shift, the center of gravity and authority in the system of union-company and union-worker relations moved upward. In the politics of workplace struggle, the center of gravity had been low; individual plants and sometimes even the workshop had been the site of key negotiations. In the politics of labor cooperation, executives at corporate headquarters met with union leaders of the companywide federation to make key decisions. Workshop locals and plant-based unions lost their autonomy as they were integrated more tightly into enterprise-wide union federations. A critical symbol of this change in steel came in 1975 when the enterprise federations at the top companies took over from individual mills the right to maintain membership in the Tekkō Rōren federation.

The enduring hegemony of cooperative unionism set Japan apart from both Western Europe and North America, where the late 1960s and 1970s witnessed extensive labor protests at the grass roots and a profound polarization of labor-management relations. In Japan, the politics of cooperation survived and proved its worth to corporations, but its value to the employees was limited.

Beyond higher pay, the activist unions of the 1950s had sought control over the work pace, staffing and job assignments, better safety, more predictable vacation schedules, and more objective, openly defined wage systems. In this effort, they pursued a participatory politics of workplace activism. Unions that embraced cooperative unionism in the 1960s did not abandon these concerns, but they turned to a top-down mode of politics to address them. They turned away from workplace organizing, relied less on collective bargaining, and stressed trust, exchange of information, and closed-door consultation between top managers and union leaders. For employees, the specific settlements resulting from this new labor politics were mixed, and the withering of unions as sites of democratic self-determination was itself a major loss.

Iron- and steelmaking in the 1950s had been arduous and risky. Employees worked six days a week. Eight-hour days plus two hours of overtime were standard. To make this regime bearable, the workers had carved out precious spaces of respite between bouts of heavy labor. The young Nakao Yasuji mastered the game of *go* during idle stretches in the benzol workshop.[45] Imaizumi Masumasa recalls that night-shift workers at the coke furnace in 1955 usually slept for one third of their nine-hour stint.[46] Okuda Kenji grimly corroborates Imaizumi's memory: one morning in his early days at NKK, he discovered that a sleeping worker had died from inhaling gas fumes during a night-shift nap.

Most men woke to tell the story, but night work was a constant burden for Japanese workers. A 1975 survey found that 58 percent of manufacturing employees and 42 percent of all wage workers were periodically assigned to night shifts, while one in six manufacturing employees was actually working a night shift at any given time. Shift work was most common in processing industries—petrochemicals, pulp, and metals—where the technology of production demanded constant operation. In steel mills in the 1950s and 1960s, about 60 percent of the workforce labored in shifts. The men at a shift worksite were divided into three crews working eight-hour shifts, with an additional fifteen minutes' paid overlap time to allow a smooth changeover. Each crew worked every day, so it was overstaffed by about 30 percent to allow each man to take one day off per week and provide for holidays, vacations, and illness or injury.[47]

The unions had pushed for shorter hours since the 1950s. They zeroed in on the shift issue in the late 1960s and called for a new system of four crews working three shifts. Their goal was to increase the number of days off and eliminate the grueling double shift required when the night crew changed over to a day shift.[48] Eventually, pressure from the labor market more than the union led managers to make the change. By the mid-1960s the extraordinary pace of economic growth had created a labor shortage. Orii Hyūga and his colleagues at other firms concluded that to attract new recruits, the steel mills would have to change their reputation for long hours and difficult work.[49] But the same labor shortage made the companies loathe to undertake reforms that would increase staffing needs. In May 1968, the big three steelmakers simultaneously informed their unions that "unless the economic situation changes dramatically, we will implement a four-crew, three-shift system on April 1, 1970," and in 1969 NKK held the first of twelve bargaining sessions with the union.[50] Through similar processes, the major mills adopted basically identical systems. Both unions and companies proclaimed the result a rich fruit of the cooperative order.

The company added a fourth crew to all sites of shift work. At first glance, this expands the workforce by one third, but since each crew in a four-crew arrangement can rest as a group, there is no need for extra staffing on a crew to allow for days off. Even so, simply adding a fourth crew while eliminating the relief men on existing crews would have increased overall staffing by 14 percent.[51] But the tight job market made companies loathe to hire more people, and managers were determined to tighten the work pace and impose leaner staffing.

The union's negotiating goal was to win ninety-eight hours—roughly two weeks—less work per employee per year. Under the new rotation eventually settled upon, regular days off for each worker indeed increased by more than two weeks annually, from sixty-eight to eighty-three, and an additional eight paid holidays were built into each man's work schedule.[52] The union appears to have done very well. But in practice, the reform granted only a forty-one-hour annual reduction per employee. The devil was in the details.

The steelmakers reduced total break time, including meals, from one hour to forty-five minutes per shift (a 3 percent increase in real time worked per shift). They saved another quarter hour of labor costs by cutting out pay for the fifteen minutes of overlap time added to each shift. The union complained bitterly about this unpaid overtime, but accepted it in exchange for one extra day off per year. In addition, and most important in the long run, the steelmakers accompanied the change to four crews with far-reaching reassessments of staffing. In some cases, standard crew size was reduced because new equipment required fewer workers. In other instances, companies cut staffing by expanding the scope of a multiskilled worker's responsibility. They eliminated some supervisory slots by giving oversight responsibilities to regular workers. They also recalculated standard work loads using peak operation as the normal rate. Drawing on the idiom of Tokugawa-period peasants who had concealed rice paddies from tax collectors, steel managers searched out the "hidden rice fields" of customary work practice.[53]

The unions balked at these changes but ultimately agreed. To implement the four-crew regime, NKK mills in the end increased staffing just 4.5 percent, and Yahata made no new hires.[54] In Orii Hyūga's words, "if we were to reduce hours to international standards, we had to increase the intensity of labor to international levels."[55] Under the old system, two or three men on a crew would take their forty-five-minute meal breaks together, in three or four turns per shift. On the new, lean crews, employees wolfed down their meals alone in twenty-five- or thirty-minute lunch breaks, up to eight turns per shift stretched out over four hours. Anticipating a 1990s lament for vanished community in a civil society where Americans went "bowling alone," Japanese critics mourned the fracture of workplace solidarity brought on by eating alone.[56]

Ideally, the union would have protected some of its hidden fields inside the mill, surrendered others in exchange for more time off, and forced managers to hire more people on the reasonable grounds that new technology had raised productivity enough to afford this. The NKK union's "fundamental stance" toward rationalization adopted in 1966 stated a first goal of "maintaining existing working conditions and eliminating sacrifice by workers."[57] In practice, the union traded long-standing customs of respite and community for a net gain of five days off per year. The companies, on the other hand, achieved close to an ideal result. They ended up with a leaner, more productive work regime.[58] Critics on the left blasted this result as a loss for the workers, while pragmatic new unionists called it a fair trade. One is hard pressed to call it a union triumph.

Statistics on leisure time and safety at NKK bolstered the case of the critics. When *employers* in major industrial centers including Kawasaki were surveyed about working hours, they reported a decline in the 1960s. But anticipating the much-noted phenomenon of unpaid overtime imposed by Japanese employers in the 1980s and 1990s, studies that directly questioned *employees* in large urban factories in Japan found that men actually worked longer hours in 1970 than 1960, with married older men showing the greatest increase (5 percent). These men also reported fewer hours of sleep, less time in conversations at home, and less time for leisure.[59]

Accident rates in the steel industry improved dramatically between 1950 and 1970. When Orii Hyūga headed the insurance section in the NKK labor division in 1950, the safety record was "horrible." He credits the cooperative efforts of unions and managers with dramatically improving matters. But the company's own statistics reveal that the real gain in workplace safety came precisely during the years of greatest labor-management confrontation and workplace activism in the late 1950s. Between 1951 and 1955, 72 men died in accidents at work, while over the next five years, 43 NKK workers died. Further improvements were slow to come. The death toll for 1961–1965 was 40, and from 1966 to 1970, 37 NKK workers died in work accidents (see Figure 8).[60]

The overall accident rate also plummeted through the 1950s, but scarcely improved after 1962. The gains of the 1950s were probably due to newer, safer production facilities as well as the efforts of workplace activists to enforce protective rules. In addition, critics from the 1950s through the 1970s charged that supervisors under pressure to run safe workplaces would lean on subordinates not to report accidents, and take sick days rather than request injury compensation.[61] The cooperative unionists in the 1960s fared no better, and perhaps fared worse, than the activists of the previous decade in protecting their members' lives.

The verdict on wages is mixed as well. Virtually all Japanese working people prospered to some extent in the 1960s and early 1970s, and the steelworkers rose with the national tide. The nominal incomes of Japanese wage earners increased 12 percent per year in the 1960s. Consumer prices rose 6 percent, so the average worker gained substantial real earning power throughout this decade of the "economic miracle."[62] Labor-management cooperation was part of a system that delivered unprecedented access to a middle-class life of clothing off the rack, home appliances, high school or college education for children, color television, travel, and the chance to own a car or a home. More Japanese people than ever before, including the men in the steel mills and their families, came to enjoy these rewards.

But direct returns to the pioneers of labor-management accord in the steel industry were not impressive. In 1960, after a decade of militant unionism, steelworkers in the Tekkō Rōren federation enjoyed the highest wages of any group of organized workers. The unions dominated by their informal groups then spread the gospel of short-run wage restraint for the sake of long-run security of income and job. By 1970, after a decade of strike-free wage deals, the steelworkers had lost their advantage. Union members in electronics firms had taken over the top spot, and pay for steelworkers was roughly comparable to that of workers in other major unions.[63] If the industry as a whole had been failing, one could excuse the steel unions for taking this slide. In fact, as their relative wage standing fell in the 1960s, overall production quadrupled, output per worker more than tripled, and profits soared (see Figure 3).[64]

The union's 1966 fundamental stance toward rationalization at NKK, as at other major mills, sought to peg wage demands to corporate gains in productivity and profit. It pledged to maintain working conditions and "fight to get a share of the profits brought by rationalization."[65] Based on this platform, unions and managers in the steel industry worked out programs to "recycle" productivity gains to the workers in the 1960s and early 1970s. These programs further tested the claim that cooperative unionists could win a fair share of the expanding pie.

NKK's unions in 1966 proposed that "all money saved by rationalization that involves staffing cuts be returned to the workers." After several months of discussion in the management discussion council, they agreed to a multi-level structure of recycling. If staffing cuts took place with no change in work method or equipment—that is, a speed-up—all the cost savings would be added to the output premium of the remaining workers. For staffing cuts accompanied by "slight" changes in equipment or technology, 70 percent of the cost savings went to wages of those still on the crew, while for staff reductions enabled by "major" change in production facilities, just 30 percent of the gain was recycled.[66]

Here, as in the new shift system, the devil was in the details. Who would distinguish a "slight" change from a "major" one? Unfortunately, the details of the NKK plan are scarce, but Matsuzaki Hiroshi has thoroughly analyzed the plan worked out at New Japan Steel in the 1970s to recycle productivity gains.[67] This program set up two separate pools of money, a general fund of savings generated by rationalization, which was distributed to all workers at a mill, and funds given only to work sites affected in a particular case. The company paid this latter fund for only one year after any given staffing cut, although continual streamlining of the workforce meant that new payments usually replaced old ones. These funds were calculated not by simply totaling the wages of workers whose jobs were eliminated and giving this out in equal portions to each remaining crew member. Complicated formulae involving unit prices and performance evaluations were used to set the amount of this wage pool and distribute it to individuals. Matsuzaki concludes that the union fell far short of its goal of returning 33 percent of wage cost savings to the remaining workers because the company controlled the parameters of the recycling formula; the union accepted harsher conditions at work in exchange for only a small share of the financial gains.[68]

Annual wage bargaining, the effort to reduce hours, and the push to share the economic fruits of rationalization all betrayed the stated goal of the NKK union to maintain existing working conditions and eliminate sacrifice. Relative wage levels fell even as the industry prospered. Showpiece achievements of labor-management accord won slightly more leisure time and a slight share of productivity gains but sacrificed the quality of working life.

Many Japanese unions since the 1960s, like the steelworkers, have acquiesced to aggressive staffing cuts, sometimes for recycled pay to those who remained in the crew, sometimes just for the promise that a more productive company would protect the remaining jobs in the long run. One could put it harshly and say that a union that accepts staffing cuts betrays its fundamental obligation to protect the jobs of its members, but a conviction and a method supported this heresy of accepting cutbacks. In principle no layoffs or dismissals resulted. Excess workers were transferred to shorthanded sites. In theory, individual preferences were respected in selecting the transferees from a slimmed-down crew. This, at least, was the ideal system of "lifetime employment" as justified by cooperative unions to their members and praised by supporters of Japanese-style management to the world.

In the messy world of practice, despite the boom in domestic and global steel markets in the 1960s and early 1970s, jobs at the Kawasaki-area mills at the heart of NKK were anything but permanent. Managers were determined to realize the promise of new technology and return profits on expensive investments, and they ceaselessly pushed supervisors to produce more steel with fewer workers. Total employment at Kawasaki, Tsurumi, and Mizue reached an all-time high of 24,000 in 1963 and has been declining ever since. At the same time, steel markets in Japan and the world were growing so fast that NKK had to expand its total capacity. It wanted to build a new mill on a proposed landfill island adjacent to the existing plants. But millions of Japanese people by the 1960s decided they could afford to oppose the environmental pollution that had once seemed the inevitable price of progress. Citizens of old industrial centers such as Kawasaki and Yokohama were in the forefront of the environmental movement. The company faced stiff resistance to local expansion, and it deferred the Ōgishima plan.

NKK instead constructed a huge state-of-the-art integrated mill six hundred miles southwest, in Fukuyama. It began operations with 3,000 workers in 1967, when the three Kawasaki-area mills together employed almost 20,000. Within a decade, Fukuyama joined the Kawasaki mills, which were combined in 1970 into the Keihin complex, as twin pillars of the company. Fukuyama and Keihin each employed 12,000 workers in the mid-1970s, and each produced comparable quantities of steel. From the start, Fukuyama was a constant presence in Kawasaki, both threat and safety net for the workers. Its capacity ruled out plans to expand production in Kawasaki, so that excess hands "freed" by the continual drive to produce more steel with fewer people could not be absorbed locally. At the same time, the need to staff the growing Fukuyama complex with experienced men offered these people a destination.

NKK presented its union with one plan after another to reduce the Keihin workforce. The entire process was framed by a grand agreement to "save" the Keihin mill almost as soon as it was created by consolidating its operations, after all, on the Ōgishima landfill site. This would not be designed as a platform for expansion, but would be a lean new home. In a brilliant piece of brinksmanship, the company threatened both the union and the local government with shutting down all Keihin operations and building a new mill on the far northern coast. Worried union leaders quickly agreed to cooperate with an unprecedented reduction of the Keihin-Ōgishima workforce, from 18,000 to 12,000 over just five years. Worried local government officials put aside fears of the environmental impact when the company promised to spend over one billion dollars to make Ōgishima a world model of clean steel production.

This plan admittedly uprooted some workers, but it saved thousands of local jobs. That, at least, is how the union made the case to its members and to posterity. Gotō Tatsuo looked back on the creation of the Keihin-Ōgishima complex as one of the greatest achievements of his brand of cooperative labor relations. Faced with the threat of a move north because of the pollution problem, he said, the union lobbied the local government as well as the company and helped keep the home operation going.[69]

Lacking access to the strategic thinking of all the actors, this claim is difficult to evaluate. But Konda Masaharu just laughed when he heard it years later. Konda had been transferred from the labor to the planning division at corporate headquarters by 1970, and he took part in discussions with local authorities (including Nakao Yasuji, recently elected to the prefectural assembly from the Japan Socialist Party) and union leaders such as Gotō. "Can you imagine how much trouble this would have involved, for how many people? To provide an infrastructure for 10,000 employees at that site? The company never seriously considered the move. If the union says it helped prevent it, this is a lie. They exaggerate their role."[70]

Both the general plan to consolidate operations at Ōgishima and the specific proposals to carry this out sparked great anxiety among employees. The easiest transfer to contemplate was a move to a similar job in the same section or division, where a man might know his co-workers. Even a cross-division move at the same mill meant learning a new routine, with perhaps a chance to expand skills but also the threat of a lower wage premium and the fear, especially for an older worker, that he would not meet expectations at an unfamiliar job. An assignment to a new mill in a distant city carried all these risks and more, and it was obviously the most difficult change to accept, especially for married men. Many workers looked to the union to defend their right to refuse such an order.

Each proposed reduction led to a round of management discussion council meetings at the mill or corporate headquarters. The union also convened unusually well-attended local meetings to report on company plans and hear reactions. At council meetings in September 1971, NKK announced plans to shut down two Keihin blast furnaces when a new blast furnace at Fukuyama came on line. The union quickly promised to cooperate in the transfer of 1,000 excess personnel to Fukuyama. Just five months later, NKK presented a long-range plan for the Keihin-Ōgishima consolidation that would eliminate an additional 4,000 jobs, the largest cutback in company history.[71]

The process of working out the details involved three groups of actors in frequent private and public discussions: managers seeking maximum flexibility with minimum disruption and cost; union leaders standing on a public commitment to resist dismissals, but committed as well to accepting and enforcing the plan; and a fearful rank and file. Meetings of union locals sometimes erupted in angry criticism of the leaders. Workers called on the union to guarantee equal or better wages to all transferred men and defend the individual's right to refuse a transfer. Although even the more militant locals ultimately voted to accept the transfer plan, NKK did adjust its initial proposal over the course of several months. Most important, managers abandoned their initial proposal to lay off some workers temporarily. But the company went ahead with a hiring freeze and an early retirement program. It also transferred workers not only to Fukuyama but to the shipbuilding division at Tsurumi and to several NKK subsidiaries where conditions usually fell short of the employee's existing job.

The union entered these discussions as a worker advocate, gently monitoring the conditions of cutback. It ended as a company partner, vigorously imposing the decision. The prospect that individuals might refuse an order to move was a threat to the union: if a few men could claim special circumstances, the entire deal might unravel. Informal group members played a critical role in the coercive politics of cooperation. They urged their fellow workers to understand that their personal survival depended on company survival, which in turn depended on the Ōgishima plan. By readily accepting their own transfers, group leaders built peer pressure that made others unwilling or unable to resist.[72]

One controversial part of this rationalizing process was the decision to spin off subsidiary work processes such as transport, materials handling, catering, furnace cleaning, and machine maintenance to subcontracting companies, some newly created for the purpose. Many of the employees "transferred" from the Keihin mill were in fact simply shifted to these subcontractors and continued their existing jobs at lower rates of pay. One noteworthy case involved the custodial crews in the mill, which included many older workers who had suffered injuries and could not continue at their production jobs. In 1972 NKK proposed firing all these workers and rehiring them at a newly created, wholly owned subsidiary, NKK Green Service Company, headed by Orii Hyūga. The union demanded that NKK keep the workers on the NKK payroll and designate them as being "on loan" to the subcontractor. It won this protection for some severe hardship cases. The rest became Green Service employees or quit.[73]

Similar transfer and subcontracting dramas played out at all the major steel mills.[74] From 1960 into the mid-1970s, the proportion of subcontract workers in the industry more than doubled. By 1976 they accounted for 44 percent of the total labor force and 57 percent at the newest works in the major corporations, such as Fukuyama.[75] Well before the two oil crises made streamlining the order of the day for corporate Japan in the 1970s, the superintendents of the cooperative workplace in unions and company offices had struck the following deal. Barring gross negligence, male union members would not be laid off. If the company decided that circumstances required, some workers would accept local or long-distance transfers within the company, whatever their family circumstances, and others would accept reassignment to a subcontractor, or they would resign. When these shifts alone did not suffice, some workers would accept offers to retire voluntarily. The union would convince the men to agree to the inevitable for the greater good. On the grounds that flexible deployment was a reasonable condition for job security, the courts reinforced and extended this system by rejecting lawsuits by workers who claimed a right to refuse transfer orders.[76] Unions, managers, and the courts thus defined the practical meaning of lifetime employment.

Looking back in 1983, the Sōyūkai's official account of the turbulent history of labor at NKK claimed confidently that its cooperative policies had brought the greatest good to the greatest number. But as one member admitted, this was a hard sell to fellow workers. "It's easy to push a move-ment that transfers responsibility, that blames the company and agitates for strikes irresponsibly, but a responsible movement of correct unionism is really tough."[77] Making deals in private, arguing at every turn against strikes, criticizing workplace activism, rejecting a vigorous defense of work-ing conditions, leaning on reluctant men to accept transfers, pressuring oth-ers to retire early in the general interest: these activities of "correct union-ism" were not likely to win broad-based enthusiastic support.

Instead, they hollowed out the union. In 1963 Odaka Kunio undertook his final survey at NKK, interviewing a large sample from every mill. The results alarmed the managers. The ideal worker, the man imbued with strong dual allegiance to company and union, was a vanishing species, just 13 percent of the workforce compared to one-third in the 1950s (see Figure 5). And the doubly alienated "con-con" employees had soared in number, from a scant tenth or less to 29 percent. Orii Hyūga took the labor division staff on a tense retreat to the resort town of Hakone to pin down the source of the steelworkers' discontent and formulate a response.[78] But several years later the labor division repeated this survey and discovered an even greater proportion of anti-company, anti-union types, so many that it kept the results secret.[79]

Fewer and fewer steelworkers viewed the union as a resource that might address their problems. A 1965 poll at one Fuji Steel mill found that just 15 percent of respondents were inclined to take complaints about work condi-tions to the union. Over half blamed the union for failing to win satisfactory wage increases.[80] A 1969 survey at the five major steel companies found considerable latent support for more militant unionism: 63 percent of members were dissatisfied with the union's activities, and exactly the same percent were willing to go on strike to support union demands.[81] At New Japan Steel union surveys in 1974 and again in 1979 found that only 2 per-cent of members believed the union "reflects my opinions well."[82]

Yet if cooperative unions were losing the hearts and minds of their mem-bers, they remained strong enough to neutralize alienated workers through their tight alliance with the company. In addition, both line supervisors and labor managers increasingly took over unionlike functions. One fifth of the Fuji Steel workers in 1965 said they would take up work-related complaints directly with the foreman, more than the number who relied on the union. A 1969 NKK manual on labor relations advised foremen to convene work-place discussions to help understand and address the discontents and prob-lems of subordinates. Unlike the gatherings of the same name in the 1950s, these were not union activities. They were weekly or monthly meetings usually held during work hours, but with overtime paid if not. Even harsh critics of exploitative management practice noted that supervisors at these meetings did more than argue the company case during wage negotiations. They also won trust by giving careful attention to complaints about hours or vacation days.[83]

The steel industry's unions promised to secure for their members a fair share of the growing pie produced by cooperative wage bargaining and the politics of consultation and trust. They enforced allegiance on doubters through informal groups working closely with the labor division, which offered preferential raises and promotions to loyal members and promised protection in tough times. They fulfilled their promise in the sense that union members shared in the general affluence of the high-growth era and the subsequent years of slow but steady expansion. In the 1970s they also offered members a chance at increased leisure time and some degree of job security, although relentless pressure to streamline work crews and contain labor costs in good times and bad meant that no regular employee could be sure of a long-term job.

The labor-management relationship that delivered these results was not bilateral but triangular. Both union leaders and labor managers feared the ghost at the conference table: without results to show members, the old style of union activism might return to life. This fear in large measure explains how the cooperative unionists sometimes did gain favorable wage adjustments, guaranteed conditions of transfer, or shorter hours. Such results convinced some workers to toe the company line more or less happily, while others took a darker view of the sacrifices that came with cooperation. Steelworkers not only accepted a decline in wages relative to other industries, a more tightly administered workplace, and the increased prospect of a disruptive transfer. As the price of affluence, they had to rule out the workplace as a site of democratic activism.

Aside from sullen resignation, dissenters from the politics of cooperation could find few politically viable avenues of protest, but cooperative labor-management relations have never been placid. At large private firms in Japan from the 1960s through the 1990s, the stability of the system has been that of a person treading water, who keeps in place through ceaseless churning. Managers reached out to and into the union, cultivated informal groups, convened countless meetings to work out the details of slimmed-down crews and downsized mills. This was slogging, costly work. They considered the alternatives, remembered the bad old days, and in sharp contrast to their American counterparts, they decided it was worth the effort.[84] With their union partners, they worked out a system with enough appeal on one hand and enough levers of coercion on the other to lead most workers to see the status quo as either desirable or unavoidable, in any case as the only world practically imaginable. Workers neither freely embraced the new order, nor were they brutally battered into submission. Rather—and this is the essence of any system of hegemony—the cooperative order has rested on the "coercive consensus" of choices taken under the pressure of a subtle combination of persuasion and power.[85]

8 *Mobilizing Total Commitment*

Parallel to the political drive to isolate and contain the remnants of activist unionism, corporate managers and their union partners fashioned a lean, flexible, meritocratic social order in the workplace. This corporate order withstood not only the late 1960s political challenges of the New Left, but also the more profound economic shocks of the oil and yen crises in 1972–1974 that marked an end to twenty years of unprecedented economic growth. These shocks forced some adjustments, but the superintendants of the established order had already anchored their workplace hegemony in a social as well as a political foundation. They had fashioned unions into unusually cooperative institutions, and made workplaces into sites demanding an unusually total commitment to the company.

In these ambitious efforts, managers and cooperative unionists were responding to the equally ambitious efforts of activists who had aspired to control the workplace at the grass roots. In addition, they were moved by a sharp sense of the need to keep pace with competitors at home and abroad. Workers offered this degree of commitment in part because they had long viewed the factory as the source of their community and identity as workers. As the possibility of maintaining this world through activist unions disappeared, they were tempted to shift their commitment to the company. They were pushed to do so in order to survive on the job, to win promotions and raises. For many male workers, this industrial relations of total mobilization offered a relatively secure and respected working life, but it forced them to accept the corporation's standards for judging their "merit" and agree to its pervasive claim on their energies.

Changes in technology and education prompted companies to take diverse initiatives to convince workers to identify the corporate mission as their own. In the iron and steel industry around the world in the 1950s and 1960s, larger blast furnaces, new basic oxygen and electric arc furnaces, and continuous casting and automated rolling equipment transformed work routines. One NKK labor manager in 1962 remembered the bad old days of the 1940s. In rolling mills, skilled workers drew two red-hot steel sheets at a time out of ovens with metal tongs and inserted them into the rollers. Each weighed over fifty pounds. "The production process required skill from start to finish. Looking back from today, it was continous, unimaginably cruel physical labor. I worked as a labor draftee in rolling for two years during the war. This was such hard work that in the summer we would put a large block of ice on our forehead and could not maintain our stamina without a special ration of salt to lick as we worked."[1] Such jobs disappeared from the steel mills in the late 1950s and 1960s. In their place came work that was less wearing and required less physical skill but a different sort of intense concentration. The typical steelworker by the late 1960s watched dials or television screens, moved levers, and pushed buttons, overlooking the furnace or rollers from a safe distance behind a window.[2]

Changed technology demanded a different sort of worker. New tasks called for a higher level of logical thinking, but given that, they could be quickly mastered. Orii Hyūga explained that at NKK beginning in the late 1950s, "the operation and maintenance of more sophisticated, complex equipment called for workers with broader knowledge and powers of judgment." He and his colleagues found these young men in the swelling ranks of Japanese high schools.

Before World War II, the typical factory worker, male or female, had completed no more than the basic compulsory course of six years' elementary education. The occupation authorities expanded compulsory education through middle school, so that postwar recruits were hired at age fifteen. In the early 1950s, the majority of students ended their formal education with middle school, and these youths comprised the vast majority of recruits into the blue-collar workforce, but by 1960 well over half of Japanese middle school students were proceeding to high school. By 1970 the proportion had jumped to 82 percent.[3]

The sturdy farm boys from places dubbed "Kōkan village" who had once been hired directly out of middle school through personal connections were suddenly as scarce and as valuable, in the idiom of the day, as "golden eggs."[4] In 1959, as it prepared to open the Mizue mill, NKK started systematic springtime hiring of high school graduates for blue-collar positions and gradually phased out entirely its recruiting program for middle-school grads. As Orii recalls, both supply and demand factors led to this change: the supply of "good-quality" middle school grads became scarce by the late 1950s, and the operation of the new, automated equipment required more educated employees.[5] NKK was soon staffing its production sites exclusively with high school graduates.

Despite the neat fit between the demands of technology and the supply from the schools, managers—their traumatic memories of the recent strikes still vivid—feared the worst from this more educated worker. One of Orii's subordinates, Takanashi Yukio, wrote in 1962 that "given changes in the composition of the work force at new plants, whether the loyalty of young workers goes to the company or to the union will certainly and decisively influence labor-management relations." Takanashi noted that the desirable pattern of dual allegiance to company and union was least common among younger workers. In the 1950s American social psychologist Theodore Purcell had discovered that young workers were fickle, Takanashi wrote, and "all sorts of surveys point this out in our country as well, where the company loyalty of young workers in new plants has weakened to an extreme degree."[6] If the proportion of the young was to further increase, the danger was all the greater.

Takanashi argued that in an earlier era when it took years to master the skills of iron and steel work, the higher wages of senior workers had appeared legitimate. At new mills, an average recruit could operate a basic oxygen furnace after one year. Younger men now did the same jobs as fifteen-year veterans. They felt themselves as skilled and productive. They complained about their much lower pay.[7] They chafed at the continued division of employees into categories of "staff" and "operative" and resented their place in the latter group. And thanks to their "new postwar education," these young men reportedly thought in a more rational, cut-and-dried fashion, with a strong sense of their rights. "We cannot expect unconditional loyalty to the company from them, nor perhaps can we place too much hope in a philosophy of labor-management cooperation."[8]

Having thus sounded the alarm, Takanashi quickly reassured his readers. The new breed of young workers would not necessarily turn against the company overnight. The managerial response would be decisive. Having identified the discontents of the workers, "depending on our programs of labor management, we should be able to provide rational grounds for heightened loyalty."[9]

The effort to make loyalty the rational choice began with supervisors. Since the early 1950s, labor managers had sought to establish a modern American-style division between the work of line supervisors—foremen and section chiefs—and staff specialists, but the reform had yet to bear fruit. Working closely with Orii Hyūga, Konda Masaharu was NKK's point man in the ongoing endeavor to redefine the role of the foreman. He began his efforts in the labor section of the Mizue mill in the early 1960s by devising new programs to help foremen nurture loyalty among recruits.[10] Writing in 1967, he recalled that "the 1959 strike was a costly experience, but it led to serious reflection on our entire labor management program. Due to efforts at all levels, we have not had major strikes since then. . . . The biggest factor in stabilizing labor relations was new, thorough communication of management goals to all employees through a thick pipe connecting labor-management staff and line supervisors."[11]

Between 1959 and 1966, first at Mizue and several years later at the other mills, NKK and its competitors redefined the job of foreman.[12] Until this time, responsibilities for the job had been imprecise and shared. Technical personnel had been deployed on the shop floor where they set standards and helped supervise work operations, but the foremen had shared this responsibility. In addition, under a system dating back to the prewar era, labor staffers, such as Watanabe Tatsuo, had been assigned to each work site to assist the foremen in keeping attendance and wage records and maintaining work discipline. Under the new system, the company pulled the technicians into a central office to coordinate production processes and focus on research. It charged foremen and section chiefs with simply implementing the standards set at the center. As confidence in the new foreman increased, managers also withdrew the dispersed labor staffers from the front lines of labor control.

The foreman's authority was thus narrowed but strengthened. No longer responsible for setting production standards, and with the labor section staff now remote supporters, he was to supervise work operations and manage his subordinates. Konda expected the foremen to "produce high efficiency with few people," prevent restless young workers from quitting, and nurture workers' "enterprise consciousness." He concluded, "The most important objective of this system was to give the front line supervisors self-awareness as members of the management side."[13]

These men also took on a new role in the 1960s as alumni overseers of the informal groups. Anxious to ensure that foremen gave primary loyalty to the company, steel managers insisted that the new foremen should not be union members. After some resistance, most unions agreed. Many foremen had served as both local union officers and informal group leaders. In their new status as union alumni, they acted as senior advisors to the informal groups and through them continued to influence the union.

As managers promoted the loyalty of veteran supervisors by integrating them more firmly into the corporate hierarchy, they also took important steps that appealed to the egalitarianism of rank-and-file workers. One crucial innovation was the practice of frequently rotating job assignments. By the 1980s, Westerners as well as Japanese experts were describing flexible deployment of employees as a defining feature of the Japanese workplace, but extensive job rotation was not a traditional practice.[14] In Japanese steel mills until the 1950s, much as in the United States, a worker would slowly climb a ladder of positions within a work crew, reaching the most skilled jobs and winning promotion to crew boss or foreman after ten or fifteen years, if ever.[15] Although new production technologies did not reduce every task to a common skill level, and practices of job rotation spread unevenly across each mill, the practice of rotating workers through all of the tasks at a particular job site, whether on an hourly, a daily, or a monthly basis, began to spread throughout the industry in Japan in the late 1950s.[16]

For some workers, rotation meant learning multiple, related skills. For others, it simply varied the routine at basically similar tasks. But the trend toward broad rotation was unmistakable. The practice was part of a trial-and-error strategy of managers like Orii and Takanashi to retain the loyalty of blue-collar operatives. New technology made rotation possible because it sharply reduced the time needed to acquire skills. It also made rotation desirable, for as jobs became simpler and often less interesting, switching could relieve boredom and boost morale. Further, rotation appealed to the democratic consciousness of younger workers, who saw the older hierarchy of job assignments as both inegalitarian and technically unjustifiable.[17] Professor Odaka's 1963 survey at NKK explored the attitudes of workers toward "single skill" and "multi-skill" work, and Orii Hyūga learned from it that a majority of older workers preferred "staying at one workplace and developing skill at a single job" while most of those under twenty-five hoped to "change workplaces and learn various jobs."[18]

Flexible rotation held both promise and risk for workers. It could enhance the short-run interest of the work routine and the long-run security of one's place in the company. It could also disrupt familiar routines and force workers to adapt to quickly changing assignments. If all employees at a site could perform multiple jobs, supervisors were likely to ask three workers to stretch to cover tasks previously handled by four. When this happened, unions could potentially intervene to maximize the benefits of job enlargement and resist streamlined work crews that brought a more intense pace, but they did not do so aggressively. Although cooperative unions negotiated over the terms of job *transfers*, with mixed results, they completely ceded to management control of job *assignments* within the workplace.

A second measure that more explicitly appealed to the egalitarian ethos of many workers was the abolition of the separate categories of white-collar staff *(shokuin)* and blue-collar laborer *(kōin)*. According to a Nikkeiren survey, in 1967 fewer than one fourth of 174 major manufacturing firms still divided their employees into these groups. A few had never made such a distinction. Of the majority that had abolished it, 42 percent had done so by 1953, in the years when powerful early postwar unions demanded abolition of the hated status system.[19] But NKK and other companies took half steps, such as introducing a common salary structure for employees in both categories without eliminating the separate categories themselves. Through the 1950s managers, determined to protect their just-revived authority, resisted making what would have seemed a concession out of weakness in an era of resurgent union militance; only 9 percent of status-system abolitions took place from 1954 through 1959. But in the 1960s, many corporations decided that unions had been tamed sufficiently so that managers could profitably satisfy this long-standing desire of workers; from 1960 through 1967, another 41 percent abolished their old status differentials. The key innovation was to combine the nominal equality of a single status, sought by workers, with more rigorous programs, sought by managers, to differentiate employees by ability.

NKK was one of these second-round reformers. The company had compromised with the early postwar union offensive by implementing separate but more or less equal wage structures for blue- and white-collar workers. By the early 1960s, as Orii Hyūga tells the story, it was time to take the next step. The grounds for the older divisions no longer held. New technologies had made white- and blue-collar jobs more similar, while postwar education had rendered white- and blue-collar recruits more alike. NKK's opinion survey of 1963 revealed that 64 percent of all employees, and 73 percent of blue-collar workers, favored "abolition of the terms *shokuin* [white-collar staff] and *kōin* [operative]." In addition, many senior blue-collar men were eligible for promotion to supervisory positions, and the company wanted a legitimate standard, besides seniority, on which to make decisions. Orii's solution, implemented between 1964 and 1966, was to abolish the old categories and make everyone at NKK an "employee" *(sha-in)*. He called this "a new employee system based on meritocracy." More colloquially, NKK dubbed this "labor management where the blue sky's the limit."[20]

The new label of "employee" for all conveyed an obvious symbolic message of equality. In practice, however, functional differences and hierarchy remained. The union noted sourly that new subcategories sustained a division between "office" and "technical" employees. Also, men and women, and recruits with different levels of education, were slotted differentially into a hierarchy of "first-class employee" through "seventh-class employee," and they advanced at different rates. But at least one wall had crumbled. It was possible for a blue-collar man to rise beyond the previous ceiling of foreman to serve as an assistant section chief or even a section chief. Until this time, such jobs had been the jealously guarded domain of high school and college graduates recruited as white-collar employees. Despite some misgivings, the union accepted this "employee system" as fulfillment of a longstanding demand.[21]

The first blue-collar man in NKK history promoted to assistant section chief was none other than Kudō Shinpachi, founder and distinguished alumnus of the Labor Problems Research Group.[22] When additional promotions were slow to come, a number of loyal leaders of the cooperative factions of the union complained that the reform was more cosmetic than real. Orii admitted that workers griped of "clouds in the blue-sky system."[23] But such discontent was at bottom a call for the company to heed its own newly meritocratic rhetoric. It was handily contained within the logic of the new system.

Many younger steelworkers were still frustrated. Job rotation added interest and the prospect of growth to their work. The common status of "employee" delivered a long-sought symbolic affirmation of social equality. The possibility of a white-collar promotion beckoned as a distant promise. But the accumulated weight of annual pay increases, even with merit rating figured in, gave senior men much higher pay than new recruits. As differentials in skill decreased and workers young and old found themselves rotating through the same jobs, this wage disparity could be galling. By taking the further step of moving toward a merit-based wage system, managers addressed this discontent.

Seniority wages are often said to be one of the "three sacred jewels" of traditional Japanese employment practice. This is a misleading claim. The Japanese word often mistranslated as "seniority" is *nenkō*. It is a compound whose two syllables denote "seniority" *(nen)* and "merit" or "achievement" *(kō)*.[24] True to these semantic roots, wage practice in Japan since the beginning of the century had been marked by tension between inclinations to link pay to seniority and to reward merit as the employer defined it. The Japanese state in wartime and the powerful unions of the early postwar era had tipped the balance toward seniority as the decisive factor.[25] Managers had believed that seniority roughly coincided with skill, and they had earlier included it as one element in setting pay. But they detested the inflexibility of the wartime regulations and the early postwar wage agreements.

Beginning in the 1950s, managers worked desperately to reduce the force of seniority and increase the weight of elements that, they believed, better reflected a worker's contribution to the company. As changing production technology weakened the rough correspondence between seniority and skills, their discontent only grew.[26] Despite union calls for open and objective rating systems, managers expanded the role of merit ratings in annual "seniority" raises. They took another step to disconnect pay from seniority when they introduced "job wages." This American-style innovation had tied a portion of a worker's pay to the company's assessment of the difficulty of his job.[27] After years of resistance, the newly cooperative union at NKK in 1963 accepted a substantial reform in which 15 percent of an average worker's pay would derive from a job wage.

But then the drive for job wages stalled. Unions had resisted the change because veteran members defended their accrued stake in the existing system.[28] In addition, almost as soon as they put job wages in place, managers such as Orii realized that this system could be as inflexible as straight seniority pay. Swiftly changing technology required ever-changing job design. Keeping job wages up to date required a large, expert staff to reassess job definitions continually. In a second round of innovation encouraged by Nikkeiren, managers shifted the focus of wage reforms from job wages to merit-based pay and promotion.[29] A Nikkeiren progress report from 1967 aptly summed up the spirit of the reform: "without question, we [managers] can no longer survive with the peace-at-any-price wage system. . . . We must instead promote and compensate on the basis of merit."[30]

Three years after setting it up, NKK labor managers in 1966 modified job wages in this spirit. Uniform job wages for all employees in a given job did not properly motivate workers. The job wage would not increase without a promotion, and there were not enough opportunities for promotion to reward all deserving workers. Further, the problem would get worse because the relative weight of the "job" portion of the overall wage was set to increase over several years. Orii's labor division squared this circle by creating several classes within each job category. This allowed NKK to raise an individual's "job pay" in accord with merit ratings even if his job remained the same.[31] NKK's competitors took similar steps.[32] The steel industry, among others, thus significantly modified the American practice of job wages. By setting pay on the basis of an individual's characteristics, whether seniority or merit, labor managers as well as employees were freed from concern with the impact of job redesign on pay. Managers believed merit-based raises would help win commitment from young workers unhappy with low starting wages.

In Japanese workplaces over the next three decades, merit came to be enshrined alongside seniority as a basic principle for setting wages. The shift from job wages to merit wages continued, and the overall weight of merit judgments steadily increased. In 1967 Nikkeiren grandly announced that the decade 1965–1975 "is the era for the renovation of personnel management. . . . We label the thrust of this renovation 'meritocracy.' "[33] In the survey that accompanied this proclamation, Nikkeiren found that most companies (80 percent) already used merit as one of several factors to make a "comprehensive" determination of the base wage. Nearly one third (28 percent) of those surveyed had created a separate merit component of the overall wage. Half of those responding planned to expand merit-based pay in the future.[34] At NKK, the newly meritocratic job wage of 1966 accounted for 18 percent of an average worker's pay. This reached 22 percent by 1970.[35] In 1973, NKK abolished output and job wages entirely, replacing them with merit pay reflecting managerial assessment of a worker's demonstrated and potential ability. This merit-based component accounted for about half of a typical wage. In addition, almost all of the rest of a worker's income derived from a base wage that also reflected the accumulated weight of merit ratings.[36]

Unions objected to some of these changes. Subjective merit ratings could be manipulated to penalize activists in ways that seniority could not. They could undermine community by forcing workers to compete for favorable assessments. The Secretary General of the Sōhyō federation, Iwai Akira, was speaking precisely of this danger in 1967 when he sharply noted that "the attack of monopoly capitalism used to oppress workers from afar, but today capital is bringing the ideas of the Liberal Democrats directly to the most intimate battlefield of the workplace."[37]

But such fighting rhetoric aside, practical resistance was halfhearted. Even if union leaders had been inclined to fight merit wages, they could not have built a united front. As early as 1962 the inclination of senior leaders of the NKK union to resist the push for job wages was tempered by awareness that large numbers of recently hired young men with a postwar education and a new consciousness of their rights, who would soon constitute the core of the workforce, were unhappy with the weight of seniority in wage decisions.[38] Odaka's all-company survey in 1963 found that workers accepted merit as a legitimate standard in deciding pay and promotions. A slight majority at NKK supported a system that gave primary weight to a worker's job and merit rating, with some additional reference to seniority.[39] A strong minority (44 percent) of union members surveyed at the top five steel companies in 1973 objected that recent meritocratic wage systems gave insufficient credit to age. But 62 percent simultaneously felt that merit was given appropriate or even insufficient weight.[40] By the early 1970s, unions in the Sōhyō federation had accepted the general drift toward merit-based pay and promotions and defined their role as making sure the company's standards were "fair." One can imagine assertive unions defining and imposing their own standards for fair merit ratings, but in practice unions have sought little substantive input and achieved less.[41]

Given the divided views of workers and the hands-off stance of unions, managers faced little opposition as they expanded meritocracy at work. At the same time, for managers at NKK or any major firm to have jettisoned seniority entirely would have offended a vital constituency, the successive cohorts of veteran workplace leaders. To retain their loyal support, Japanese managers have kept seniority as one element in setting wages. Efforts to satisfy the heterogeneous elements in the labor force account for the amalgam of seniority- and merit-based pay that remains at the heart of the Japanese wage system in the 1990s.

In the words of Ishida Mitsuo, a scholar who sees meritocratic wages as both important and admirable, Japan's corporations in the 1960s developed a truly "autonomous" managerial concept.[42] Certainly the wage system that evolved from the 1960s to the 1980s was innovative. Companies rejected the concept of equal pay for equal work, if "work" is defined by a particular job description. They claimed to offer equal pay for those displaying equal devotion, potential, and exertion over time, as well as measurable skills or results. Their judgments of merit were at base judgments of a worker's character. The self-declared goal of labor managers was to nurture the merit of employees—in other words, to help workers "realize their human potential."[43] As Nikkeiren summed up the essence of the meritocratic workplace in 1969, "it is natural for people to entrust their lives to the enterprise, to seek meaning in life through working there. . . . Work is more than a relationship where an employer sells labor power to an enterprise. . . . People work to satisfy their highest desires, that is, to develop their abilities/merit to the greatest degree."[44] Ishida's uncritical acclaim for this system avoids the question of who defines merit and on what grounds, but he makes an important point in concluding that the ideology of meritocratic management denies that workers are purely economic beings. If the informal groups are a sort of Leninism-through-the-looking glass, this concept of wages is a mirror image of socialist idealism concerned to make labor a fulfilling process to realize human potential.[45]

The campaign for quality control provided another context for such idealistic visions of Japanese-style management. As the workplace activism of the 1950s withered, the quality control movement took root and flowered as a powerful alternative form of participation. Managers, not unions, led this drive to mobilize employees to serve corporate goals. Driven by a belief that Japan's production quality lagged and was a key to victory in global economic competition, the Japan Union of Scientists and Engineers (JUSE) and the Japan Efficiency Association launched similar initiatives for quality control (QC) and "zero defects" (ZD). These involved both supervisors and employees in decisions at work. In the 1950s quality control had spread among technicians and foremen, and over the next twenty years small-group activities expanded dramatically to involve the entire workforce. They won worldwide attention as a defining feature of Japanese-style management. As with merit wages, unions played almost no role in monitoring or defining standards for appropriate procedures and objectives of QC activity.

In 1963 JUSE began to register quality control circles in a stepped-up drive to promote them. These circles were groups of eight to ten workmates who would meet regularly to address varied problems of workplace quality. JUSE registered 2,000 to 5,000 new groups annually from 1965 to 1968 and nearly 10,000 per year from 1969 to 1972. Momentum then stalled for a time, but the QC movement entered a second growth spurt from 1977 through the peak year of 1984, when nearly 30,000 new groups registered. Many groups disbanded after a time, but by the late 1980s over 2 million working men and women in Japan had been registered at one time or another in over 260,000 quality circles.[46] These groups encouraged workers to apply their own rich knowledge of their jobs to raise productivity, improve quality, or upgrade their skills.

Steelmakers had been at the forefront of the 1950s drive to improve quality through relatively conventional programs of expert analysis and engineering on an American model; between 1951 and 1958, four major producers including NKK won the annual Deming Prize for corporate quality programs.[47] All the major steel companies continued as pioneers in the quality campaign by starting QC circles in the 1960s, as practice in Japan began to diverge sharply from the United States. By 1972 the industry reported 221,000 workers at 39 companies registered in 28,000 circles, for a participation rate of 77 percent of all employees.[48]

NKK was a leader among the steelmakers. In the 1950s, hoping to standardize and improve the quality of its products, NKK had both centralized the activities of quality control experts and dispersed their knowledge by training line supervisors in the techniques of problem solving and quality control. Indeed, supervisors often took the initiative and asked to be involved. This was the first step in transforming quality control into a broadly based employee activity. In the early 1960s, before the formation of circles themselves, technical staff were encouraging production supervisors to organize workplace "self-inspection" teams that monitored product quality. These teams provided a social base for the QC circles.[49]

The forces propelling and controlling the QC movement were complex. Engineers, quality experts, and corporate managers pushed the movement from above and from the center, while eager workplace supervisors pulled the movement outward and lower in the company hierarchy. The years after 1963 witnessed further steps that took quality control beyond the province of expert industrial engineers. QC circles were formed at numerous production sites in order to "improve service to the next stage in the process." For a few years most participants and all the leaders were foremen and crew bosses, closely assisted by technical staff. Then in the mid-1960s, the company began to encourage rank-and-file workers to join circles. This was the breakthough that completed the transformation of an American-style of expert QC into a new program of companywide participation. At NKK's Kawasaki mill by 1967, 80 percent of all employees were members of QC circles. With the slogan of "self-management" NKK managers stressed the autonomous operation of these voluntary but nearly universal QC circles. By the early 1970s the scope of circle concern had broadened to include activities to sustain employee morale. By 1977 nominal participation reached an amazing 98 percent of the workforce registered in 1,500 circles.[50]

NKK promoted circles for all through a carefully arranged complex of training programs and oversight committees. The nerve center was a Foreman's Club, formed in 1970 with units in each division of the newly consolidated Keihin mill. True to the pretense that QC was an autonomous movement, the club was nominally independent of the corporate hierarchy. A companywide policy group to promote QC, composed of QC experts from the technical staff and seven foremen, one appointed from each production division, worked closely with this club. Foremen and crew bosses played a central role both as coordinators of circles and frequently as group leaders. The company's decision to charge them with these responsibilities built on the earlier reform of the foreman system and reflected a new belief that QC circles were tools of labor management as well as production management.

Balancing these dual functions of circles required close attention. By the mid-1970s managers felt the need to impose greater external direction on "self-management" activity. As one technical manager wrote, "before talking of QC as self-development or nurturing of human qualities, we must define clear and specific goals for self-management activities and must concentrate the strength of all 1,500 circles to meet the goals of the entire mill." In 1975 NKK began setting annual targets for the QC circles to reduce accident rates and achieve annual savings of nearly $20 million through greater operating efficiency. Clearly the autonomy of the QC circles was circumscribed with care. Managers sought to orchestrate and "pool all the strength" of circle activity toward corporate goals without dictating so forcefully that employees lost any sense of control over their "self-managed" endeavors.[51]

This balancing act rested on a tension between "dovish" groups concerned to improve work conditions, increase skills, and promote better human relations and "hawkish" groups seeking to raise efficiency by standardizing work routines, eliminating "wasteful" activities, and often reducing staffing or raising output norms. Some groups pursued both hawk and dove agendas at once. In 1967 workers in the NKK pipe section set out to save money by lengthening the life of grindstones used to sharpen cutting tools. From April to October their QC group exhaustively analyzed the factors contributing to grindstone wear and tear, revising and standardizing the protocols for their use. The members reported saving 200,000 yen per month. One fruit of this effort was deeper awareness of the properties of the tools of their trade and enhanced mastery in their use. At the same time, the group leader noted that "some complained that as a result of cooperating [to standardize procedures], they were restricted by the standards, and the work routine became more difficult." Such voices, it seems, were either ignored or overcome.[52]

The next year a foreman led a group of ten co-workers in an effort to cut down on the frequent malfunction of rolling equipment. Through small-group brainstorming they identified the core problem as a decline in the aggregate skills and ability of the work group due to the recent transfer of several men. The solution, worked out over several months, was to clarify the tasks at each point along the production line and rotate all group members through each position, improving overall skill and understanding of the rolling equipment and making each man capable of troubleshooting. In addition, the task of spot-checking the rollers every ten minutes was added to the cooling platform operator's job, and the number of men performing checks increased from one to three. Some resistance to change in long-established work customs was noted but overcome. The result was said to be improved teamwork and a new sense of responsibility among the workers. Here, too, the circle apparently gave workers a sense of involvement, variation, and mastery on their jobs, but the newly added tasks meant greater pressure on some.[53]

Since 1963, thousands of such reports have been published in the official JUSE magazine, *Workplace and QC*. Each one appears under the group leader's name, with his picture, conveying to the many readers that this was valuable work. Circle leaders also presented their accomplishments at companywide, regional, and national QC conventions. At the end of a day packed with sober presentations would come hours of beer drinking and enthusiastic song, capped by the national QC circle song. Sociologist Robert Cole concluded that such camaraderie taught workers that "we are all, regardless of company affiliation, participating in a wider social world beyond the workshop." It broke down barriers among workers and firm and created "a sense of fellowship."[54] The quality control campaign became a social movement led by management, with a scarcely muted missionary zeal among promoters that swept up many participants.

The human impact of QC activity was mixed, and its attraction to workers rested on positive and negative pressures. On one hand, both a relatively upbeat analysis of QC activity at New Japan Steel in the 1970s as well as a sharply critical view of the NKK program in 1984 agree that group members defended an informal consensus to resist activities that would lead directly to staffing cuts or a more intense work pace.[55] Indeed, only 6 percent of circles at NKK in 1976 took up "labor cost reduction" as their primary theme. One third focused on reducing energy costs and 15 percent sought to conserve on operating material costs. A smaller proportion aimed to lower defect rates. A similar distribution continued into the 1980s.[56] One labor analyst generally hostile to management nonetheless found strong evidence that cost-cutting circles of steelworkers in 1971–72 built morale and solidarity among members and sometimes improved their skills.[57]

Some of the high school graduates who had high expectations for challenging work viewed circles as a way to give greater meaning to routine jobs that in themselves offered little sense of responsibility.[58] A survey by Tekkō Rōren in 1981 and another by the Japan Productivity Center in 1985 reported widespread agreement that circles both cut costs and raised morale.[59] Many employees welcomed the chance to participate in making decisions about their jobs.

On the other hand, an additional one third of the NKK circles in 1977 were classified vaguely as seeking "efficiency," a goal that could easily lead to a more demanding work routine. The two JUSE reports from NKK, written with a strong bias in favor of the project, offer strong between-the-lines evidence of pressure to dissolve customary practice and accept more demanding or restrictive work habits. These reports invariably discount such evidence and conclude that streamlined work routines resulted from working smarter, not harder. But Kumazawa Makoto, who has read hundreds of these reports, argues persuasively that the details often belie this claim.[60] When asked their opinion of QC activities, steelworkers in 1970 reported in large numbers that "I become busier and feel increased mental stress" (32 percent) or "I feel a slightly increased burden, but there is nothing to be done about it" (39 percent).[61] A survey the previous year reported that 67 percent of steelworkers believed self-management activites were a burden.[62]

Supporters of small-group activities inadvertently offer some good reasons why workers might well feel burdened. A report on the ZD movement fended off critics with a puzzling claim that their groups made the work pace "denser without imposing a speed-up."[63] Others frankly noted that constant pressure was needed to ensure participation. At NKK the actual rate of participation lagged about 10 percent behind the nominal one. Playing on the fact that "QC" and "idle" are both pronounced *kyūshi* in Japanese, one manager lamented that "we unfortunately still have 'QC' circles that are 'idle' circles." He concluded that although coercing others to join violated the voluntary spirit of QC, leaders must nonetheless "use all possible means to create a context where subordinates have no choice but to join."[64]

An implied threat that nonparticipation or even halfhearted contributions would damage a worker's merit ratings or promotion chances was certainly one such means; circle membership could only reach rates of 80 to 100 percent through a combination of attraction and coercion. In 1977 a worker at New Japan Steel died during a physical test administered as part of a small-group activity, and his workmates—not the union—sued to have this recognized as a work injury. The company denied the claim, saying the group was a voluntary activity. The court sided with the workers' contention that joining the circle was in effect compulsory. The union was reported to be even more upset than the company, for its basic stance had been that members participated on their own, so there was no call for the union to monitor the circles.[65] Unlike German unions, which have monitored and set limits on appropriate QC activity, Japanese unions defined small-group activities as voluntary and as part of production control, not labor management; for both these reasons, they contend, such activity is outside their jurisdiction.[66]

For employees concerned with the quality of their work life as well as the productivity of the workplace, small-group activities have been gifts wrapped in clashing colors: a controlled autonomous movement, a mandatory volunteer activity, and work that was somehow "denser" but not more intense. It would be a mistake simply to condemn these projects. They appealed to the pride of those who cared about their work and offered opportunities that many valued. Even harsh critics note that managers in Japan transcended the scornful philosophy that reserved the privilege of thinking for managers who ordered workers to do as they were told. Managers pulled off their balancing act and devised a new sort of worker participation that offered many benefits to the company. But it would be equally misleading to overlook the pressures that enabled QC activity to spread or the stresses that resulted. As practiced in Japanese workplaces, QC conferred both benefits and substantial burdens on the workers.

Most of these managerial reforms were inspired by American practice. A sharper division between line and staff functions, more explicit definition of the foreman's role, wages pegged to the substance of specific jobs, and the campaign for quality control were all introduced into Japanese workplaces in the 1950s as state-of-the-art techniques of the world's most productive manufacturers in the United States. All of these innovations had substantial impact, but they were all modified as they crossed the Pacific. Job wages were transformed to merit-based pay. This meant that income continued to derive from qualities of particular workers and not their particular jobs. But the objective characteristics of seniority and age, prominent in earlier wage-setting practice, did decrease in weight, while subjective judgments of the diffuse quality of "merit" grew in importance. Sharper divisions between line and staff were put in place, but supervisors and technical staff had been accustomed to working together, and the borders remained porous. The quality control campaign created networks that crossed this line-staff divide at many places. Foremen worked closely with production and quality engineers, and they drew the entire workforce into the QC circle movement. In dialectic fashion, managers used foreign models, but they built on existing institutions and expectations. The latter constrained and structured "foreign" innovations, even as managers modified existing practice substantially.

In addition, managers took steps to better mobilize workers that had no obvious foreign inspiration. They introduced extensive job rotation. For many production workers, quick mastery of multiple skills—or at least multiple tasks—at multiple sites gradually replaced mastery of a ladder of jobs at a single site as the typical career path. Managers also merged the dual-status ladders for blue-collar and white-collar employees into a single-status hierarchy that promised an open path to advancement to all regular male workers.

The Orii Hyūgas and Konda Masaharus of corporate Japan devised this distinctive social order in the workplace with the traumatic battles of the past fresh in their minds. They were determined to make investments pay and to compete domestically and abroad, and they were anxious to prevent a revival of activist unions that would set their own standards for wages or work conditions. They succeeded in both efforts. They convinced cooperative unions to cede nearly total control over job rotations, standards for merit pay and promotions, and quality control activities, and they internalized in workers a will to serve corporate goals. Employees had little choice but to accept the industrial relations of total mobilization. Unions told workers that corporate success was the surest guarantee to a secure, abundant future. Careful monitoring by supervisors and union leaders, extensive job rotation, the promise of promotion and preferential raises for all employees who developed their human potential and showed "merit," the opportunity and obligation to figure out how to work smarter (and harder) in QC circles—all this both directed and invited workers to offer a total commitment to their jobs, to perform to the utmost at all tasks and at all times.

9 *Managing Society for Business*

No corporation could sustain hegemony over its core employees in isolation, especially as the Japanese lived through a peaceful social revolution in the decades of high-speed growth. As in the rest of the advanced capitalist world, not only did new technologies change the experience of work. New affluence and the abundance of consumer goods changed behavior and expectations at home and in the community. More people sought higher education as a ticket to the middle class, and this schooling in turn spurred expectations of advancement. In Europe and North America by the 1960s, scholars of the left were predicting that these trends would work as an opiate upon the "embourgeoisified" masses.[1] But in the late 1960s and 1970s a surprising conjuncture of rising expectations, economic frustration, and social alienation confounded this view. People previously on the margins of many unions, especially women, ethnic or racial minorities, rural migrants, and foreign workers, began to join union activities with unprecedented vigor. One result was an explosion of workplace activism and union militance, especially in Western Europe; in the United States, the wildcat resistance of demoralized workers was a prominent response, as in the emblematic cases of General Motors' plants at Lordstown and Linden.[2]

In Japan, unionists of the old and new left hoped to profit from the similar discontent of a new generation of impatient youth. Student radicals took over university campuses and fought fierce battles with the national police. Some young people spoke of "escaping from salary" and rejecting the company-centered work ethic of their fathers. The environmental movement generated an impassioned critique of the "GNP banzai" mentality of postwar society. But in the end, neither a European-style outburst nor an

174

American sort of secession occurred in the workplace. To the contrary: while corporate managers and cooperative unionists successfully appealed to a new breed of workers, the state, the schools, and the mass media built institutions and sent messages that deepened the reach of the corporate-centered society. The powerful claim of Japan's manufacturing giants on the hearts and minds of its workers came to be snugly nested in a broad array of institutions, social policies, and laws, supported and bolstered by a set of "common-sense" ideas about the natural virtue of meritocratic competition and divided gender roles.

Large companies devoted huge amounts of time and money to educating workers. By the 1970s the education division at NKK offered so many courses and seminars for employees at every stage of their careers that one visiting European social psychologist chided Orii Hyūga that he was over-educating the workers.[3] But in one area the company reduced its role. As high school attendance became nearly universal, NKK and other major employers in the 1950s and 1960s abandoned in-house programs of formal schooling for middle school graduates that had been founded in the prewar years.[4] As they started to hire high schoolers "off the shelf," they expected these youths would bring with them basic skills and proper attitudes; but state bureaucrats as well as personnel managers worried whether schools would be able to socialize high school youths to be satisfied with blue-collar work.

To make sure they were not taking damaged goods, business leaders in the early 1960s pushed their concerns to the forefront of expert policy committees on education. A famous 1962 report of the government's Economic Advisory Council, comprised of top corporate figures, called for two-track schooling in which a small elite (the report specified precisely 3 percent of students) would be groomed in universities for top managerial positions. The mass of workers had no need for college, the report said, but they did need to master a consistently high level of basic skills to enable them to cope with rapid technological change in the workplace.[5]

The Ministry accepted this advice; and over the following years it proved quite successful, in the frank language of a retrospective government view of 1991, at "creating a large number of workers of standardized quality."[6] To be sure, the notion of a lopsided two-tier system and a 3 percent college elite flopped completely. The mothers and children of the new middle class feverishly sought the elite credential of college, and the proportion of youth going on to four-year or two-year colleges actually doubled from 1960 to 1975, reaching 35 percent by the latter year. But the schools nonetheless came to serve the corporate world nicely. They imparted basic skills widely and effectively. They made exam-based competition the universal standard for success while simultaneously teaching the value of teamwork and cooperation.[7] For at least thirty years, many in Japan have complained bitterly about the pressures of "examination hell," the colloquial term for the system of entrance exams reaching even to preschools, but the exams have conferred a powerful aura of fairness on the selection process.

Competition that began in the schools continued at work. The legitimacy of entrance exams reinforced that of meritocratic selection in the workplace, and vice versa. Successful students were socialized for careers in large organizations that expected employees to display day-to-day teamwork even while they competed vigorously for promotions and raises. Orii Hyūga tells of operatives eagerly buying technical books that explained new steelmaking processes, and he relates the story of a young worker's wife who complained to Orii "with a mixture of annoyance and pride that 'my husband doesn't look after the kids much on his day off because he's always studying.'"[8] The examination at the major steel mills for promotion to foreman was particularly demanding, prompting a comic-book circle at the Tsurumi mill to publish a cartoon in the mid-1960s titled "Building Character." An elementary schoolboy with textbooks packed into his backpack walks alongside his father, whose briefcase bulges with a protractor and textbooks written in English. The caption reads "Technical training for Dad; entrance exams for Son."[9]

Concern about "getting ahead" and "self-cultivation" resonated with traditions of competition and learning that reached back at least until the Meiji era. It permeated the school system, with its increasingly weighty appendage of private, after-school cram schools, and Nikkeiren's publications on meritocratic management. Values of self-cultivation and competition generally proved a dynamic combination. They focused the energies of successive generations of company men on developing their skills and forging ahead in pursuit of personal and corporate goals alike.

If education connects to workplace society above all at the point of entry, social welfare shapes the thinking and strategy of employees and managers over the long run of an employee's career. The array of retirement, severance, and injury benefits takes on particular importance at the point of exit. It also reinforces the interdependence of gender roles and the workplace. Beginning in the late 1940s, the architects of Japan's social welfare programs designed a comprehensive system of unemployment and disability insurance, health insurance, public and private pensions, and poor relief.[10]

The system as a whole has suppressed social spending in favor of capital accumulation, particularly in the 1950s when corporations acutely needed funds to purchase foreign technology. The system also has assumed that the family would play an active role by saving for illness and old age and by caring for ailing and elderly members. Behind the abstraction of "the family" stood particular wives and mothers; social policy reinforced and relied on a sharply gendered division of labor. The wife provided social service to others, and she gained her own social security, whether pension or health insurance, primarily through her husband. The family was a site of intersection between education, welfare, and labor policies. The Ministry of Education made this clear in a mid-1960s report that charged both schools and families with combating the alienation of the workplace, the former by socializing youth to the value of perseverance, the latter by providing a supportive refuge from the stress of the job.[11]

Social policymakers have been consistently unwilling to extend equal entitlements to all citizens. They have designed universal but hierachical systems of unemployment insurance, old-age pensions, and health insurance that forced workers to depend less on the state and more on employers, especially large companies, for social security. The health insurance system, put in place between 1957 and 1961, provided universal support, but it did so through a hierarchy of company- and state-run insurance unions, the former generously subsidized and inexpensive for members, the latter charging higher premiums and offering less comprehensive benefits. The pension system likewise took on its basic two-tiered shape in the 1950s and early 1960s. It offered a meager basic pension to all citizens, to wives only as dependents of husbands, and encouraged corporations to top this off with generous tax-advantaged pensions for long-term employees.[12] An employee who depended on such largesse was of course discouraged from supporting a union that sharply challenged his provider, and dependent wives were also hard pressed to challenge the gender hierarchy that still undergirds the corporate system.

Buttressed in these ways by social policy, the hegemony of the corporation rested on and reinforced the assumption that women would manage the homes while men operated steel mills and banks. Married women had rarely worked as employees outside of family businesses before World War II. Some were drafted into factories and offices during the war, but most left these jobs when the war ended. They accounted for only one fifth of all female employees in 1955.[13] Well below one in ten wives of male factory workers in Kawasaki held jobs outside the home in the 1950s. Although young, unmarried women by the thousands had worked for wages in factories since the late nineteenth century and millions of them worked in factories and offices in the postwar era, well into the 1960s almost all large employers required women to "retire" at marriage.[14]

If women at any point had rebelled against this system by demanding wage-earning careers on a par with men, the gendered foundation of the enterprise-centered society would have been shaken. In fact, some women in the 1960s successfully opposed forced retirement at marriage, and by the 1980s such policies had vanished from most workplaces. By 1975 over half of women employees in Japan were married, a huge increase from the 20 percent who were married in 1955. By 1982, over half of all married women worked outside the home in addition to shouldering the major burden of housework.[15]

But there is less to this change than meets the eye. One social survey found that the proportion of women who quit their jobs upon marriage in the 1980s was identical to that in the 1960s.[16] If one graphs the workforce participation of women by age, in most societies the line takes the shape of an M, starting with high employment rates for young women, dropping through the years of marriage and child-rearing, then rising once more. Through the 1990s women in Japan traced the deepest "M curve" of any major capitalist society.[17]

The overwhelmingly male leadership of unions agreed with the corporate and bureaucratic elites that women had a primary obligation to manage the family. The courts reflected this belief as well in taking a consistently narrow view of what constituted employment discrimination.[18] And large numbers of women continued to accept this "natural" duty. A 1987 survey found that over 75 percent of women nationwide believed it proper that they leave the work force either permanently or temporarily when their children were young.[19]

This remarkable continuity in gender consciousness is both cause and effect of the fact that in the 1970s and 1980s businesses continued to devise informal and formal means to pressure women to accept their subordinate status at work.[20] They satisfied the letter of the 1985 Equal Employment Opportunity Law (EEOL) by eliminating nominal gender tracking, and they offered career-oriented women access for the first time to the forbidding "comprehensive" track toward a managerial career. But in fact employers pressured the great majority to accept jobs on the implicitly female "general" track, and they also began hiring middle-aged married women as part-time workers in large numbers in the 1970s. From the 1950s through the 1980s, more women entered the workforce for a greater portion of their lives than ever before. But constrained by tax policies, social policies, and cultural expectations that made the general track and part-time work the "natural" choice, their labor was neatly integrated into a social system resting on a durable gendered division of labor: women as household managers were pillars of a corporate order that monopolized the waking energy of blue- and white-collar men.

As men and women made new uses of their time off the job and outside the home, corporations in the high-growth era continued to pay close attention to employees at play. Like the 1950s politics of workplace struggle, the politics of union-company cooperation spilled over into the community. The control of employee leisure had been part of the contest for the workplace since 1945, and through the 1950s corporations were hard pressed to channel employees in "safe" directions after hours.

When cooperative informal groups solidified control of union offices, many grassroots dissidents shifted their energy into cultural and recreational circles as sites to revive activist unionism. Communist Party youth groups, called Minsei, worked through semi-independent front organizations. In the 1960s their corporate foes dubbed this tactic a "recreational pink approach" (as opposed, it seems, to a political red one).[21] Minsei recruited through the established networks of music appreciation circles (Rō-on, or Sound of Labor) and Singing Voice choruses. Its members joined independent reading groups and founded circles to help troubled youths turn themselves around. Minsei also turned to sports, sponsoring annual field days beginning in 1962. It even sought to capture the mid-January national holiday for youth, the coming-of-age ceremony in which young women and men wore their finest (or only) kimono or suit to a moralizing lecture on civic responsibility. Not to be outdone, the Japan Socialist party and the Sōhyō federation stepped up competing efforts to sponsor community and workplace circles from sports and mahjong clubs to the traditional arts (flower arranging, tea ceremony) to photography or poetry writing.[22]

Minsei did not publicize its membership totals. According to a 1963 Nikkeiren manual on "how to combat Minsei," the group surged from a low of 1,500 members in 1958 to 80,000 by 1963. The authors might have exaggerated to stir their corporate audience to counterattack, but an analysis by partisans of the largest network of circles in Japan, the Sound of Labor, confirms that Rō-on gained support among young employees of large companies in the early 1960s, reaching an all-time peak of 638,000 members nationwide in 1965.[23]

At this point, Japan's captains of industry sounded the alarm. Nikkeiren

and the Japan Recreation Assocation began organizing workshops and publishing books of exemplary and cautionary case studies with no-nonsense
titles: *Workplace Recreation, with Special Reference to Managing Youth*
(1963) or *The Power of the Left in the Workplace: Cases Studies and Countermeasures* (1972 and 1975).[24] The first of these began by noting that new
technologies had made both family and workplace more productive, in turn
granting more leisure time to employees. Companies must therefore "promote the effective consumption of leisure" which has recently been con-
sumed in a passive, other-reliant way as trends, from the de-skilling of work
to the spread of mass media, have weakened "self-generated" recreation.
Companies should train "recreation leaders" and sponsor "free and democratic" groups for both "cultural" and "physical" leisure activities to make
sure that "ideological elements promoting class struggle" do not gain control of the workers through their myriad circles. In the majority of cases
where the enterprise union was in cooperative hands, the recommended
strategy was for company and union to jointly sponsor "independent"
leisure circles.[25]

These authors presented NKK's as a model of corporate recreation policy.
In 1963 the steelmaker sent ten employees to one of the first leadership
training seminars run by the Japan Recreation Association. At first, the
trainees' "consciousness was very low." They thought "recreation just meant
playing," and workmates scoffed that trainees were getting paid to play. But
the program reportedly convinced the trainees that leisure was serious business, a means to improve work morale, build a "healthy" workplace atmosphere, and promote positive human relations. Criteria for choosing leaders
were good health, a likable, cheerful personality, a sense of responsibility,
"healthy ideas," and a good work record. By 1967 NKK had built a cadre of
229 certified recreation leaders, all graduates of this three-day course, and
the company aimed to double their number for a ratio of one leader for
every thirty employees.[26]

Companies used their recreation groups to squeeze out "ideological" circles, an epithet that covered autonomous community groups and those
sponsored by socialists, communists, or nonpartisan dissenting unions.
"Rec" leaders were taken on retreats just like those for the informal group
vanguard. They were given the mission of identifying and isolating revolutionary elements in the workplace. They learned tricks such as how to flush
out subversives by launching a subscription drive for the conservative
Sankei newspaper. Those who refused would be marked as potentially dangerous elements. Labor managers also used the rec groups in tandem with

informal groups to mobilize workers to oppose strikes and support appropriate candidates in union elections.[27]

The drive to win hearts and minds through leisure focused primarily on the young. Opinion surveys by Tekkō Rōren echoed numerous others in discovering that the youth of the 1960s and '70s saw leisure, more than family or work, as the main source of pleasure and value. Such surveys identified better-educated, privately focused young men and women, who were likely to watch TV or play pachinko on their days off, as members of an alienated new generation in danger of turning its back on both union and company.[28] By 1969 NKK's Acorn Club saw apathy as a bigger threat than the left. In the old days, one man wrote, the enemy was clear and so was the goal, but today's workers see little glamour in the Acorn Club. To induce such youths to join their group, he identified sports as the most promising recruiting tool.[29]

Advocates of partisan leisure on the left viewed their dilemma in remarkably similar terms. The sober old-left founders of Sound of Labor circles were baffled by the younger generation, members of a global youth culture of the 1960s who wanted a "place we can relax, have fun, talk freely."[30] The young members called for free-spirited folk jamborees rather than somber classical concerts. Rō-on leaders were horrified at their casual attitude toward sex and their anarchic, privatized view of "liberation." Looking back from 1986, a collective of culture critics sensibly noted that Sound of Labor had thrived in an early postwar era of scarcity. Commercial music, whether in concerts or recorded form, had been too expensive for most people. Sound of Labor's subsidized concerts had invited top performers from the Soviet Union as well as sympathetic Japanese performing artists. The group had offered unparalleled access to both a supportive community of friends and the world's best musicians. Then in the 1960s, scarcity gave way to dreams of plenty. Stereos and LPs were affordable, if still a stretch for many workers. To counter Rō-on, the business world founded a competing organization called Onkyō, which subsidized concerts with big-name foreign orchestras. Japanese performers were less willing than before to play at cutrate fees for Sound of Labor audiences, and workers could afford an occasional splurge for a commercial concert as well. Later, the proliferation of *karaoke* machines in tiny bars further undercut the attraction of union-sponsored singing groups. The Sound of Labor developed an image as a stiff, sectarian society. Beginning in 1966 its membership plummeted.[31]

As organized circles of the business world and the left thus fought a culture and leisure war, Japanese society in the 1960s underwent a cultural revolution that rendered the mobilizing efforts of both sides less effective and less relevant. The products of a commercialized mass-culture industry became directly accessible to common people. The spread of television came quite suddenly toward the end of the 1950s. Private pleasures, such as driving "my car," owning "my home," or taking family vacations, became part of blue-collar life in the mid-1960s and beyond. As a more private and commercialized style of play took root, one might imagine executives would rejoice at the turn away from the politicized cultural circles. But the managers who had fought these circles began to lament that a self-centered privatism was drawing employees away from wholehearted devotion to the job.[32]

This fear proved excessive because these changes were neither politically neutral nor especially damaging to work motivation. Both right and left might lament the apathy of youthful seekers of private pleasures, but as long as the advocates of the politics of cooperation controlled the workplace, a quietly grumbling rank and file posed little threat. Union activists had trouble drawing new generations of workers into their fold, while managers proved well able to integrate the lifestyles of a mass consumer society into the hegemony of the corporation. In addition to sponsoring company recreation programs and commercial alternatives to circles of the left, employers could benefit from a logic of consumerism that diluted any latent threat from alienated, pleasure-seeking workers. Quite simply, a young man had to work hard and long to afford a car, not to mention a house, and increasingly his wife believed she had to work as well.[33] One field survey in 1971 reported that steelworkers as in the past were jealous of the abundant overtime of their co-workers in the busiest divisions of the mill. But the reasons for envy were new. A few men with large families still needed the overtime for basic necessities, but many others were intent on saving for major purchases, above all for cars.[34]

As the massive advertising industry and the examples of neighbors and friends conspired to redefine desires as needs, Japanese working people from the 1970s through the 1990s pushed themselves to "work like mad to stay in place."[35] The data are not entirely consistent, but reliable surveys suggest that actual hours at work increased in the 1960s, in particular for married men.[36] All sources agree that hours on the job, including reported overtime, increased from 1975 through 1987. Government statistics reported total annual working hours per person in the late 1980s to be more than 2,100, making Japanese by far the busiest workers in the advanced capitalist nations. The recession of the 1990s brought on a reduction that unions had been calling for, to no avail, for years. By 1993, average hours fell to 1,920 per person.[37] At the same time, managers under pressure to cut costs pushed employees to offer more unreported, unpaid "service overtime." Workers had little choice but to comply. They feared negative performance reviews or even pressure to "voluntarily" retire if they resisted, and unions were rarely willing to defend them. Careful estimates in the early 1990s placed annual unpaid overtime per employee in the vicinity of 100 to 200 hours.[38] In other words, a typical worker supplied two to five weeks of unpaid labor! To share the wages of affluence, working people in the 1970s, '80s and '90s could ill afford to question their commitment to fulfill their own needs by meeting the demands of the company.

The assumption that such a commitment was wise and proper rested on an implicit understanding that the company would make every effort to protect the jobs of loyal men. For the hegemony of the enterprise to endure, it was important that male employees trusted employers to honor this deal. Japanese managers in the 1970s and 1980s usually recognized the practical value of doing so. But when times were tough, executives were tempted to cut costs by cutting jobs, and the accumulated precedents of law played a key role in constraining this desire. Beginning with some forty cases between 1948 and 1950, judges defined the ground rules of personnel policy concerning dismissals and job security when unions or individual workers protested firings in court.[39] Unions won 90 percent of these cases.[40] In addition, labor lawyers hit on the ingenious tactic of seeking, and winning, "provisional dispositions" that prevented dismissals from being implemented for the duration of the usually prolonged case.[41]

The courts established as legal doctrine a practice that unions were trying to enforce at the same time through strikes: a company can dismiss workers only as a last resort. To do otherwise constituted "an abusive exercise of a right," in this case the employer's right to terminate a labor contract.[42] Although the courts recognized "business necessity" as a valid reason for dismissing workers, over several decades they established very high standards for an economic "need" to fire. Before taking this drastic last step, the employer had to exhaust a comprehensive set of remedies that have been specified with increased detail over the years: "transfers, farming out of workers to other companies, temporary layoffs, the solicitation of retirement requests, and the like."[43] Today in Japan, the business section of any major bookstore displays numerous "how to trim your business without really firing" manuals that describe these remedies in exacting detail.[44]

By imposing strict predismissal obligations, Japanese judges since the late 1940s supported workers in their claim of an implicit right to their jobs.

Especially in the egalitarian climate of the first two postwar decades, judges were part of society, not above it. They experienced the same hardships and emotions that led NKK workers to seek equality and attack status discrimination at work. The leading Japanese analyst of the matter has argued that judges in the early postwar era were underpaid and literally undernourished, so that "in regard to unjust dismissals they flamed with anger and a sense of justice."[45]

Whatever their motives, judges firmed up the job security so ferociously sought by unions, but this is not a one-way story of state intervention. If unions and their members had not viewed dismissals, even in arguably desperate economic situations, as an affront to be resisted, the courts would not have been faced with the need to develop such precedents. Yet the ironic long-run impact of these decisions was to weaken activist unions of the sort that resisted dismissals in the first place. By restraining "abusive exercise" of employer rights, the courts reinforced the social legitimacy and thus the hegemony of the corporation. As employers became aware of the legal impediments to dismissal and grew wary of challenging them, it was rarely necessary for unions to fight for their members' jobs, and workers had one less reason to view their unions as instruments of struggle against the corporation. Labor-related case law thus reinforced the peculiar institution of long-term employment security for regular male workers. It stabilized the corporate system against the cruder instincts of executives who would have preferred a freer hand.

In numerous related decisions in the 1970s and 1980s, however, the courts affirmed that such a high degree of job security came with a price: extensive managerial authority over the deployment of employees. These cases struck down challenges to managerial actions such as long-distance transfer orders or overtime assignments.[46] By giving legal force to what was concurrently taking root as an implicit customary bargain, judges helped retard the growth of the shop-floor union activism that had challenged NKK so vigorously in the 1950s, and the legal system thus promoted the industrial relations of total commitment.

In the high-growth decades corporate ideology took on the force of hegemony at work and in society. In Japan, as in Europe or the United States, those seeking to incite a new militance among workers faced a daunting task when they looked for a way to turn passive alienation to action. For a brief time in Japan they had some cause to hope. The global wave of political protest in the late 1960s and early 1970s broke across the nation with considerable force. The student movement peaked in 1968–69 with building takeovers, pitched battles with police, and canceled entrance exams at Tokyo University, the citadel of the elite. The New Left looked to the workplace as well, and a new generation of activists found some support even in the strongholds of informal groups and cooperative unions.

At NKK, younger workers with a high school education and an urge to advance provided a base for scattered sharp protests. Within the Acorn Club, younger members provoked a minor crisis in 1965 by arguing for a strike, a move eventually choked off by group chairman Kitazume Shun and his allies in Kudō Shinpachi's Research Group. In 1969, the Communist Party cell at NKK's Kawasaki mill caused a sensation with a pamphlet charging that NKK's average monthly wage lagged 6,000 yen (roughly 10 percent) behind Yahata's and Fuji's. With strong support in many workplaces, the Comrades Club (Socialist) minority on the union executive committee joined with frustrated junior members of the Acorn Club to force an extraordinary out-of-season drive for a special wage adjustment. The union executive committee authorized a detailed, on-site survey of wages at the three companies. After a dozen collective bargaining sessions—not meetings of the discussion council—from July through October, the company admitted that wages lagged an average of 2,000 yen. Facing the prospect of the first serious strike in a decade, NKK offered a one-time increase in base and incentive pay of this amount.[47] These energies carried forward for several years, during which a renewed atmosphere of confrontation and accusations of company bad faith marked wage and bonus negotiations at all three mills. In all cases, however, agreements were reached without strikes.[48]

A similar renewal of activism could be seen across the region and the nation. A powerful grassroots organizing drive erupted to protest Japan's role as staging area for American troops in Vietnam. Antipollution movements built unprecedented and effective networks to press claims on behalf of pollution victims.[49] According to a fearful report at Toshiba, the electronics giant located close to NKK, younger workers in particular were gripped by a new consciousness of political crisis. Their work motivation was failing. Communist Party and independent leftists managed to win a majority of positions on the Toshiba union's young men and women's division in 1968, and the CP continued to gain support at least through 1974, when several of its candidates for union office won 30 percent vote totals. This event provoked Toshiba's personnel office in 1974 to found a secret companywide association, the Ōgi (Fan) Club, out of a scattering of existing factory-based informal groups. Within several years, the Ōgi Club had devised a potent array of tactics to intimidate dissenters. Membership in the club had become a ticket to a fast-track career, and the forces of union-company collaboration were back in firm control of the Toshiba union.[50]

Related activism spread to subcontractors and smaller factories in the 1970s. Workers in at least five NKK subsidiaries founded locals of militant union federations such as the National Metalworkers Union (Zenkoku Kinzoku, or NMU), among the most assertive groups in the Sōhyō camp. Carrying forward the "workplace struggle" tradition of the 1950s, the NMU in the 1970s organized smaller workplaces with tens or hundreds of employees. Calling for "absolute opposition" to rationalization, it often won contracts that required prior union approval for any changes in work hours, staffing levels, or transfers. Managers believed themselves paralyzed. Union leaders viewed these activist locals as building blocks of a regional and national movement to transform Japan. To make sure such unions did not spread through its network of subcontractors, NKK took the drastic step of closing some of these companies rather than launching uncertain drives to retake control of their workforces.

But dissolving a company was no easy trick. It was extremely difficult to dismiss outright any workers willing to fight in court. NKK managers knew that judges would consider the resources of a parent company when deciding if "economic need" justified a decision to shut down a facility and fire workers. From 1977 to 1980, Watanabe Tatsuo took on the toughest assignment of his career as an NKK labor manager. He was dispatched as an executive to the Kōkan Trading Company (Kōkan Shōji, or KSK), a regional distributor of NKK products in western Japan consisting of warehouse and sales employees. In 1972, 40 of 330 workers at the Osaka warehouse had organized a union local and affiliated with the NMU. Angry at conditions that even Watanabe admitted were "poor," the union led several strikes in the following years. It won better pay and veto power over virtually all personnel decisions.

Watanabe's mission was to shut down KSK and negotiate severance agreements with union members while avoiding a long, expensive court battle. It took him three years. He sponsored the company baseball team and organized games of sales versus warehouse staff to open contact with the workers. He met secretly after hours with individuals or small groups to beg them to accept severance payouts. In the end, NKK was able to dissolve KSK without a court fight only by swallowing its pride and agreeing that the four most stubborn and radical holdouts could start their own small metalworking company, to be supported by orders from another NKK subsidiary.[51]

Activism on the margins of giant corporations, and occasional sparks of resistance at their center, caught the attention of left-leaning Japanese academics. Orthodox leftist writers produced a genre of labor analysis that is extremely useful in its detail but painfully predictable in its conclusions. After detailing new challenges from alienated young workers or underpaid subcontractors, these analysts concluded hopefully that the contradictions of the capitalist system were ripening, that a new era of class struggle and social transformation was not far off.[52] Their descriptions of scattered protests in the present were more accurate than their predictions for the future.

To be sure, the surge in world oil prices of 1973–74, coming on the heels of the "Nixon shock" of a suddenly devalued dollar, dramatically ended twenty years of double-digit economic growth and momentarily promised the objective conditions for such a transformation. Inflation briefly surged out of control. Although steelworkers remained on their jobs, the spring wage offensives of 1974 and 1975 in other industries and in the public sector were unusually spirited. Public sector employees in industries ranging from the national railways and tobacco monopoly to telecommunications and postal services spearheaded the contentious spring labor offensive of 1974, and unions won huge wage hikes that broke precedent by outpacing both inflation and productivity growth. The power of organized workers in the public sector reached a peak the following year, when more than one millon employees in public sector unions joined a week-long "Strike for the Right to Strike."[53]

But in the wake of these episodes, cooperative union leaders, top industrialists, and state officials moved with remarkable speed to restore business as usual, in part by fashioning new instruments of national economic and political coordination for private sector corporations. In addition, the general strike of public sector employees failed completely, largely because the labor movement could not win public support as it had in the 1950s. The government criticized the union assertion of power in the workplace as antidemocratic "minority egoism." The media and the public seemed to accept this claim, and the former articulated the hegemonic understanding of the day: in contrast to small business and nonunion workers, employees in public enterprises were privileged, with little ground for complaint; combative unions were a drag on the national economy, a symptom of the British or, in a new twist, the American disease of nonproductive economies. At the same time, most Japanese saw the managerial call for freedom to assess individual merit and diligence and to promote competition within the workplace as entirely reasonable.[54]

Some have identified the mid-1970s as a watershed marking the start of a new political economy and the heyday of Japanese-style "flexible production."[55] They call it "post-fordist," meaning a production system that transcended the deep divison of labor between technicians and managers who design things and make decisions, and workers who simply follow orders. But this moment of crisis and the ensuing adjustments should not be blown out of proportion. The politics and sociology of the cooperative mobilized workplace predated the 1970s and survived its shocks with minor scrapes but no grave wounds. It has been even less challenged since then.

The decades from the 1960s through at least the early 1990s were a relatively uninterrupted golden era of the corporate-centered society. The sharp challenges to managerial authority raised by unions in strategic industries from 1945 through the 1950s had been turned back. Aggressively cooperative unionists worked closely with managers to extend their sway. They kept dissenters weak and marginal. The practices of Japanese-style management, from job rotation and the single status hierarchy of "employee," to pay systems of merit plus seniority, to small group activities for quality control mobilized employees to furious efforts on behalf of the company. Systems of education and social welfare, gender-divided policies, beliefs, and behavior, the rules of the job game as adjudicated in courts, the demands and dreams of the good consuming life all combined to reinforce this commitment.

The 1970s witnessed some noteworthy macroeconomic and political adjustments, and further micro- and macroeconomic innovations continued thereafter, but dramatic changes had already transformed the Japanese workplace by the 1960s. When high growth ended abruptly with the oil crises of 1973–74 and 1978, "streamlining" (or, in the language of the 1990s, "downsizing") became the order of the day. Most unions sharply moderated their wage demands, and, with rare exceptions, they accepted cutbacks without major protest. In large private sector workplaces in particular, corporate managers and the state had secured a foundation well able to absorb these shocks and episodes of subsequent erosion or external pressure. At Toshiba the Ōgi Club won the day. At NKK, the Acorn Club trembled but held together, and in the 1970s and 1980s the consolidated Sōyūkai held off occasional challenges. It continues to dominate union offices today.

In recent years challenges from within the core of the enterprise system have been rare. Once in a great while, clumsy corporate actions have generated among loyal employees a sense of betrayal great enough to lead even the most cooperative union to cry foul, raise a banner of resistance, and force the offending company to retreat. In a well-known case at the Sasebo shipyard in Kyūshū, the union accepted a call in summer 1979 for voluntary retirements and wage cuts to allow this embattled shipbuilder to survive a sharp recession. By November, when the company's fortunes had improved, the union changed its position and launched several months of ultimately successful strikes to restore initial wages and work hours. The Sasebo strike defined for the early 1980s the outer limits of worker tolerance for sacrifice on behalf of the company at a major unionized firm.[56]

The main worry of managers and cooperative union leaders of the 1980s and early 1990s was not that such isolated energies might career out of control. They worried instead that apathetic members, the "anti-company, anti-union" worker, would hollow out the union and make it harder for managers to elicit loyal support. Union leaders at NKK and other major industrial firms in 1991 and 1992 lamented, as before, that young workers found the union "useless." They made plans to offer services with a contemporary appeal, such as less rigidly programmed leisure activities. If such tepid initiatives seemed unlikely to generate a powerful new union spirit, the danger that passive alienation might turn to insurgency seemed equally remote. Some employees in large companies in the 1980s and 1990s resisted mandatory overtime. In some highly publicized cases where devoted company men in their prime literally "worked to death" *(karōshi)*, their survivors sued for compensation. Other workers protested forced retirements that betrayed implicit promises of job security. But mainstream unions were slow to pick up these causes. Dissenters usually took their cases to court with support from ad hoc struggle groups, or they founded small new unions.[57]

In the iron and steel industry, the years after the dramatic appreciation of the yen in 1986 saw a tremendous corporate push to contain labor costs and reduce excess capacity so as to remain competitive with Korean mills and other new challengers. The top five steelmakers announced plans in 1986 to cut employment by roughly one third and shut down 15 percent of blast furnace capacity over five years to make it possible to operate profitably at lower volumes. A surge of demand in 1987 delayed some of these shutdowns—although not the cutbacks in employment. Until 1991, output and profit rose sharply, even as record numbers of workers were transferred to subcontractors or took voluntary retirement with union cooperation.[58] As earlier, critics of cooperation wrote of intense anger in the workplace over job cuts and wage restraint. They predicted that "the bird [of protest] is about to sing once more." But no mechanisms existed to transform into action the griping that showed up to an unprecedented degree in a new

1989 round of opinion surveys of steelworkers.[59] When the steel boom ended in 1990, unions proved as cooperative as ever in working out plans to cut costs and eliminate jobs.[60]

In the nation's smaller workplaces, at both independent producers and subcontractors to huge firms, militant and creative unions were quicker to act in defense of jobs, wages, work conditions, or the right to organize. Not only at Kōkan Shōji in the 1970s, but at several other NKK subcontractors, unions affiliated with the National Metalworkers Union won formidable control over work conditions well into the 1980s. Dozens of small unions launched determined, lengthy struggles against layoffs and shutdowns, in many cases taking over bankrupt firms. The *Asahi* newspaper reported 54 such struggles in progress in 1977, while one "self-managed" firm "counted 94 unions fighting bankruptcy" in 1982.[61] Measured against the thousands of small companies that went bankrupt each year, self-management was a minor trend. But it symbolized the possibility that working people might defend an independent common interest against that of the corporation. The options open to workers at such companies, and the responsibilities of parent companies to subsidiaries, remained controversial at the end of the 1990s.[62]

The environmental activism of the energetic citizens' movement that had emerged in the 1960s offered another potentially important ground upon which to restrain corporations in later decades. In the city of Kawasaki, by 1968 well-organized groups of citizens were holding frequent demonstrations and calling for justice for pollution victims. One of the first major tests of Kawasaki's environmental movement had been the struggle over pollution standards for NKK's new Ōgishima plant. In 1969 the company threatened to relocate if it could not release up to three times the legal limit for sulfur emissions. Local residents called the company's bluff, something the union had feared to do. Several groups formed an Association to Return the Blue Sky to Keihin, and by the summer of 1970, NKK had agreed to build Ōgishima to operate within the limits of the pollution laws.[63] The following year, Itō Saburō won election as Kawasaki's mayor with the support of the Japan Socialist and Japan Communist parties and a broad array of progessive citizen's groups. He held this position until 1989.[64]

In Kawasaki as in major cities throughout Japan, this surge of enthusiasm among citizens concerned with environmental protection and consumer rights helped "create small political and ideological spaces all over Japan separate from the logic of, and the order of, the corporation."[65] NKK ultimately appropriated the environmentalist mantle, boasting of its huge investment to make Ōgishima the very model of "a clean, green steelworks."[66] The business world as a whole came to speak an environmentally friendly language, and most large-company unions, which depend on potential polluters for jobs, have little interest in environmental activism. But concern for pollution victims and the environment remained at least potentially a latent source of alternative perspectives on the corporate-dominated society.

Women seeking to end discrimination at work were another ongoing source of potential challenge to corporate hegemony. They had joined the first wave of early postwar democratic activism, although they were segregated into the young men and women's division in most unions. In 1954, young textile workers at the Omi silk spinning factory staged a series of successful strikes demanding an end to what they condemned as "premodern" practices: required religious observances, rigid dormitory curfews, and even company censorship of their mail. In 1959–1961 nurses led strikes at hospitals nationwide to demand higher wages and protest similar dormitory restrictions as well as mandatory retirement at marriage.[67] Encouraged by one conscientious male union activist, female office workers at the Kyoto City Hall in 1963 led a "revolt of the tea pourers." Spurred by years of accumulated resentments, they one day simply stopped serving tea to their male colleagues as part of a protest against expectations that they offer such service to male colleagues as part of their jobs. For a time they changed customary practice, in their section only, but their long-run gains were limited.[68] Women at banks throughout Japan in the 1950s and 1960s seem to have fared better in challenging customary expectations that they run errands, clean handkerchiefs, shine shoes, or clean out the lunchboxes of male co-workers. Through the 1960s and beyond, women at many companies resisted compulsory retirement at marriage, through unions and in the courts. They won most of these battles.[69]

Some of these gains came with the support of the labor movement, but unions led by men usually have been passive allies at best in women's quest for equal opportunity at work. In an increasingly meritocratic workplace, a man anxious to advance would not be enthusiastic about opening the door to female competitors. After all, he would reason, they did not need the higher pay and security that a primary wage earner did. Of necessity as much as by choice, women have thus focused on the courts. If anything, the relative weight of civil as opposed to industrial actions has increased since passage of the EEOL in 1985.[70] Although the law only required employers to "make efforts" to end employment discrimination, it gave social legitimacy to legal demands for equal status.

Through such activities from the 1950s through the 1990s, women in Japan undeniably improved their conditions at work. The most blatant forms of discrimination disappeared, and increasingly responsible positions opened up for a determined minority. But on the whole, the work of women remains directed along familiar tracks. At the end of the 1990s, the vast majority of female employees occupied part-time or "general" positions that were no longer openly marked "for women only" but were widely understood as such. As the workplace order demanded from men a single-minded commitment to the company, it came to require from women a double commitment. They had to manage their homes with professional efficiency aided by a flood of new appliances. And they were needed for millions of lower-level positions in offices, stores, and assembly lines. Most women responded to these needs and pressures, and their own desire for disposable income, by taking jobs but also rejecting the dubious privilege of competing on the managerial track. In a 1992 survey by the Ministry of Labor, only 7 percent of women answered "definitely yes" when asked if they wanted the kinds of jobs men had. About 65 percent said they "wouldn't want them." They seemed to be saying, "If the only way to advance is by turning into a total company person, who needs a promotion?"[71]

Nevertheless, a minority of women determined to persist has been able to accumulate expertise, seniority, and some job security in both blue- and white-collar work. In the late 1990s women's groups pushed to revise the Equal Opportunity Employment Law by transforming the requirement that firms show "effort" to end discrimination into a requirement that they show results. Parallel legal actions attacked discriminatory promotions and sexual harassment at work. In one 1996 decision, the Tokyo district court awarded thirteen veteran female bank workers a total of nearly one million dollars to compensate for the "clear and extreme differences in promotions for men and women. The bank's personnel policies are definitely not permissible under current law."[72] This was a noteworthy precedent, but Japanese managers are likely to prove adaptable enough to accommodate some women demanding such access to the male domain at work, so long as they accept principles of meritocratic competition and so long as other women (or their mothers) tend to affairs at home. Nonetheless, more than their quiescent male co-workers, women remain a potential source of disturbance to the calm surface of the corporate order.

The late 1980s and early 1990s witnessed yet another round of speculation that in addition to assertive women a new breed of youth was about to break the rigid mold of the corporate-dominated society. The popular media called these youths "aliens" *(shinjinrui)*. Pundits in these booming years of the economic "bubble" noted that many young people were choosing freelance work for high hourly wages rather than entering the oppressive hierarchies of large companies. One social scientist on the left commented in 1992 that "although trends among young people won't bring the battle directly to the heart of large enterprises ... in the long run they will be an important force for change of the Japanese-style corporate society. At present, young people are more likely to escape than to fight, so long as they have someplace to escape to. ... The solidarity of the escapees should be able to obstruct the further spread of the domination of Japanese-style management throughout society."[73] Similar comments had marked the phenomenon of dropouts "escaping from salary" during the heady days of high-speed economic growth in the 1960s. But the recession of the 1970s had squelched such talk, and the even more prolonged stagnation of the 1990s powerfully concentrated the minds of many free-spirited youths on the tasks of settling down and finding a secure niche at work. The solidarity of those who opt out, then and now, seems a weak base for any movement to chip away at the hegemony of the corporate system.

The economic bubble of the 1980s intensified some old problems for working people, such as long hours and unpaid overtime. It also generated severe new ones. After decades in which Japan could boast of relatively high equality of income and assets, the gap between the haves and have-nots began to widen. The tightest labor market in postwar history offered a favorable context for organized workers to protest this turn, but the dominant tone at the highest levels of the labor movement, where steel unionists continued to speak with authority and occupy important offices, was one of complacent boasts about the unprecedented aggregate wealth of the nation. The Rengō federation's target for reducing average work hours was even less ambitious than that of the Labor Ministry. A government "Five Year Plan" of 1989 called for a reduction from an annual average of over 2,100 hours to 1,800 hours a year by 1992, but Rengō set its goal as 1,800 hours by 1993. Indeed, Nikkeiren came to identify a new "enemy" in its annual reports of the 1990s. The problem for big business was no longer the union movement, even the slightly militant public sector workers. The problem was rather the state. Faced with pressure from the Labor Ministry and other agencies for new policies to reduce hours, protect older workers and employees of small businesses, and extend equal opportunity to women, Nikkeiren identified the heavy hand of government regulation as the new threat to capitalism in Japan.[74]

None of these sources of pressure on the margins, neither occasional insurgencies of small company unions, nor environmental activism, nor protests by women or the young, nor a reform-minded state, constituted a major threat to the corporate-centered society, whether singly or in combination. Bolstered by institutions and laws that reinforced corporate hegemony, managers in Japan have used coercive powers when they deemed it necessary, especially by creating new informal groups to isolate minority unionists. They simultaneously were sufficiently flexible to make strategic concessions, such as the new system of nominally gender-blind career tracks, to prevent incipient challenges from gaining force. The hegemony of the enterprise was neither brittle nor steady and placid. It was gyroscopic, capable of withstanding, co-opting, or deflecting a range of challenges and righting itself.

But one additional source of pressure in the 1990s did render the continued resilience of the Japanese workplace order and the larger system of corporate hegemony more uncertain than in the past. This was a new degree of international pressure, both political and economic.[75] The Japanese system was choking on its surpluses. As the then chairman of Sony Corporation, Morita Akio, noted in 1992, the high value of the yen and the trade barriers of quotas and market agreements being erected around the world ruled out Japanese-style business as usual.[76] Such foreign pressures might come in the form of political demands by other nations; the notion of the United States as the most powerful "opposition party" in Japan was hardly a joke in the 1990s.[77] They might come in the economic form of capital flows and currency fluctuations. In any case, they constituted a set of wild cards that could erode the system, especially as they intensified the pressure of various domestic carriers of mild challenge.

10 *Japan's Third Way*

The story of the ascendance of the corporate-centered society in Japan shares much with the histories of working people across the advanced capitalist world. In the early years after World War II few Japanese people had strong faith in the prospects for capitalist survival, not to mention hegemony. In this respect, the Japanese and European experiences were the same. Visions of apocalypse or deliverance were common not only in the immediate post-surrender turbulence in Japan, but well into the 1950s. NKK's union newspaper of these years advertised for the collected works of Marx, Lenin, and on occasion even Stalin. It published surveys of industrial production showing the socialist world outpacing capitalist economies.[1]

Postwar experience in Japan is part of a global postwar history because for some years a self-conscious movement of the working class was very important. Unions and managers confronted each other in what they called "all-out wars of labor and capital." Eventually many in Japan's working class melted into a broader mainstream society, or came to believe they had done so. But for fifteen years or more, workplaces in Japan as in other nations were sites of a distinct social world where the customary practices, expectations, and interests of workers often opposed those of corporate managers. The emerging hegemony of the corporation pushing to control the workplace did not easily overcome the vigorous movements of organized employees who hoped to protect customary work routines and resented new forms of evaluation.

But no ads for Stalin appeared in the NKK paper after 1955, and in the 1960s new graphs of production began to appear, showing the Japanese line first catching, then surpassing, those of Britain, West Germany, and then the

United States. In Japan, and in industrial economies of the West, American technology and American-style business unionism appeared to have headed off explosive class conflict by delivering the goods. Thus, another feature common to Europe, Japan, and the United States is that uncertainty about the viability or desirability of a capitalist future gave way to a hegemony of the values of the corporation. A series of labor-capital accords was reached in many countries that promised to sustain this hegemony, and corporate values penetrated the body politic, the system of education, and the words and images of the mass media.

In these three respects—the early postwar sense of crisis, the salience of class conflict, the eventual achievement of capitalist hegemony—Japanese experience is part of a history that is international more than it is peculiar to Japan. To recognize this common ground is important in the face of seemingly endless portrayals of Japan as exceptional. But it is equally important not to end with a banal conclusion that life has been essentially the same in the past fifty years across the industrial or postindustrial world, that neither a nation's institutions, historical experience, nor culture amount to much.

Although part of a larger shared history, experience in Japan presents a number of particular features. These do not set Japan apart from the rest of the world in a consistent fashion. Early postwar uncertainty was everywhere, but it was surely greater in Japan and Europe than in the United States. Class conflicts crystallized in Japan, as elsewhere, but in Japan they developed in a way that made them particularly likely to dissolve. Labor-capital accords were reached in many societies, but the United States and Japan came to harbor extreme (although very different) versions of the corporate-centered society, in contrast to Europe, where social democracy sunk deeper roots, or the Third World, where the challenge to capitalism was far more profound.

One difference stands out. Corporate hegemony has been stronger and more enduring in Japan since the early 1960s than anywhere in the world. Despite tensions similar to those found elsewhere, large Japanese companies integrated the social worlds of employee and enterprise in a remarkably total fashion. Certainly managerial hegemony was challenged at times in Japan. But elsewhere these challenges erupted into great crises—in Italy in the Hot Autumn of the late 1960s through the 1970s, in Germany in the late 1960s and 1970s, in France in 1968, in Britain with its coal and steel strikes of the 1970s and '80s, in the United States with its Rust Belt industrial collapse of the same decades. Even in Germany, where a relatively enduring accord of business and unions was restored, organized workers have continued to defend comparatively independent positions in their ongoing negotiated settlements. At every turn in Japan, however, the corporate and bureaucratic superintendants of order managed to make adjustments and keep the lid on. The ultracooperative stance of mainstream unions has persisted and been extended.

In early postwar workplaces in Japan an informal sense of "us" versus "them" shaped an employee's view of the boss, but this attitude was not durably linked to a militant or a radical unionism. Rather, managers reconstructed the workplace and nurtured allies within unions and among the employees at large so as to tightly integrate the "us" of the workplace world with the "us" of the company (and the company's union), setting "us" against a "them" of other companies (or other unions). As they internalized a total commitment to corporate success, workers in Japan came to participate in corporate activities outside day-to-day work routines more extensively than in other nations. Rather than continuing to bargain in an adversarial relationship, unions began to participate in labor-management consultation over numerous managerial issues, and managers drew millions of workers into small-group activities to increase productivity.

Early in the twentieth century, the American union leader Big Bill Haywood made the pithy and accurate claim that "the manager's brains are under the workman's cap."[2] Japanese managers from the 1950s through the present have not merely removed workers' "brains" through industrial engineering that simplified work (although such endeavors were part of the story). Managers maintained hegemony in the workplace by mobilizing workers' intelligence toward corporate goals; they drew them into the analysis of work even as they imposed expert analysis upon them.

Japan's postwar contest for the workplace gave way to the unusually total hegemony of a corporate-centered society because of a particular confluence of global and local structures and pressures. The legacy of World War II provided one critical piece of the context. Bombs demolished factories and cities, extraordinary inflation leveled differentials of wealth, and the occupation authorities initially planned to demand stiff war reparations. These disasters fostered a widely held belief that "we are all in this together." This sense of common fate, prodded by the precedent of the all-inclusive wartime patriotic labor front, helps explain the distinctive decision of so many postwar unions to include as members white-collar workers, even to the level of section chief.

Wartime devastation and postwar uncertainty fostered an intense concern first with economic survival, then with recovery. Unions of all stripes worried about more than wages and work conditions. Their members felt it

natural to concern themselves with what managers were doing to revive
production, to find new materials to replace colonial resources and new
markets to replace military demand. Unions joined managers to create a
network of industrial, regional, and national recovery councils in 1947, and
at many companies early postwar collective bargaining led to the formation
of management councils, in which unions held decision-making power.
The union seat on such bodies was never secure. Some councils quickly collapsed, while the mandate of others shrunk drastically under management
pressure. But the practice of labor-management consultation on a broad
range of issues, and the idea that such matters were the business of unions,
an idea that was only weakly developed in prewar or wartime Japan,
remained widespread and persists to the present.

Beyond the immediate shock of war and defeat, Japan's place in the international political economy had a continuing impact. A global American
geopolitical hegemony shaped postwar Japan during and long after the
Allied occupation, and the Americans played both sides of the street. They
legalized labor unions in 1945, and then helped the managerial elite back
onto its feet three years later. They gave communist labor leaders a crucial
opening in 1945 and 1946, then authorized the Red Purge in 1950. They
nurtured the Sōhyō federation as an anticommunist bulwark in 1950 and
1951, but when Sōhyō embraced workplace activism, Americans in 1954
and 1955 helped Japanese government and business leaders launch a productivity movement that attacked Sōhyō and promoted cooperative labor
leaders. American policy in Japan did much to intensify the contest for the
workplace and to determine the outcome, and the shifting American pressures produced abundantly ironic consequences. Inside observers as early as
the 1960s recognized that cooperative unions in Japan were unexpectedly
threatening American economic interests.

The state was another element in the conjuncture that shaped the Japanese workplace. The law and its interpretation by the nation's ruling
bureaucrats inhibited the growth of the sort of union that challenged NKK
so vigorously in the 1950s and promoted the ultracooperative unions that
emerged in later years.[3] It also codified the implicit guarantees of long-term
job security that were at the heart of the accords worked out between cooperative unions and management.[4] Here the state both responded to labor
activism and constrained its future course. Equally important in transforming labor-management relations and sustaining the hegemony of the corporation were public policies indirectly connected to labor in areas of education and social welfare.

Technology shaped the contest for the workplace, even as its deployment was influenced by it. Steel managers saw the import of new technologies as vital to enable their companies to compete in domestic and international markets, and many key innovations in management strategy were driven by the need to exploit these technologies effectively. Managers' perception of this need was accelerated by the threat of the labor movement in the 1950s and 1960s, which led them to see new technologies and plants as tools to regain control of the workplace. NKK, for example, used its new Mizue plant as a wedge to divide and transform the union. More generally, the determination to make good use of new equipment, combined with fear that alienated young recruits would turn against the company, encouraged new practices such as multitask training and job rotation.

The perceived need to quickly master new technologies can be seen as part of a related cluster of "late development" effects. Early in the century, Thorstein Veblen articulated a notion of late development without using the term, and Alexander Gerschenkron laid out a theory of "economic backwardness" derived from Euro-American history.[5] Ronald Dore more recently applied similar ideas to Japan.[6] The key point is that the timing of a nation's industrialization influences a wide range of matters: the economic role of the state, the role and structure of corporations, characteristics of the labor market and the labor movement, social ideas and policies.

The impact of late development on Japan's modern experience reaches back over a century. The nation's modern industries first came of age in the late nineteenth century when few Japanese possessed the technical or managerial skills demanded by the high-tech industries of the day. In the 1870s the government had to import foreigners who had these skills. The scarcity of skilled workers then led the larger firms to train native operatives, technicians, and managers on the job or in company training programs. Related to such impact on recruiting and training, late development further influenced the attitude of employers and employees toward wages, job switching, skills, and labor organizing. It led prewar managers to introduce annual but variable wage increments to induce scarce skilled workers to stay with a firm. It encouraged workers to organize factory-based unions rather than community-based craft unions, since relevant crafts were not widely spread in the community. It meant that corporations had difficulty recruiting extensive staffs of industrial engineers, and the resulting blurriness of line-staff divisions influenced strategies for controlling labor, production, and quality. These practices remained important throughout the prewar and wartime periods. They provided a firmly embedded set of precedents as a point of departure for postwar Japanese employers and employees: wages reflecting a mix of merit judgments and seniority, close ties between engineering experts and veteran workplace bosses, and the assumption that workplace locals were the natural unit of labor organizing.

Another important factor in the dynamics of the postwar ascendance of the corporate-centered society, even—or especially—in the man's world of steelmaking, was the system of gender roles. The ability of management to mobilize the energies of male workers so totally on behalf of corporate goals, and to marginalize those who would question such commitments, depended on a profoundly gender-divided workplace and society and reinforced it in turn. The so-called corporate warrior, even of the blue-collar ranks, was able and willing to make his professional commitment at work because his wife was secure in a homemaker's role, now defined as a modern, scientific contribution to building a new Japan. NKK was a pioneer in the drive to rationalize the consuming and reproducing functions of employee wives, and especially in the 1950s and 1960s, women were socialized into this role by bureaucrats and educators, both male and female, with significant help from the major companies themselves.

In this and other ways, family life, gender, and consumption shaped the corporation-centered society. The spread of mass higher education changed the expectations of new recruits in ways that managers anticipated more effectively than activist unions. Increased competition for entrance to high schools and college reinforced and reflected more intense competition for advancement within the firm, as attested by those cartoons of the 1960s showing father and son both studying side by side. These social characteristics are defining features of postwar Japan itself, and one cannot easily separate cause and effect. Intensified competition in the schools, the re-creation of the family system, and the spread of consumerism were both result as well as cause of the hegemony of the corporation in society.

The war, the state, late development, and gender roles were bound up in a cultural matrix that heightened the intensity of the contest and reinforced the hegemony that resulted. The war and the United States profoundly influenced Japanese culture, for while militarism was a core cultural value in the 1930s, defeat, the atomic bomb, and American occupation combined to render it marginal and to make pacifism a deeply felt value. The concepts of "peace" and "democracy" (and of "culture" itself) came to be central components of Japanese culture in the 1950s. They provided rallying points for the union movement.[7] But other durable ways of thinking and finding meaning in everyday life had some different effects. Longstanding concern with status, "human treatment," and terms of membership in the enterprise remained central interests of workers in the postwar era and provided fertile ground for companies to safely absorb employee demands. Likewise, late development had a cultural dimension that cut against the militance of early postwar unions. A discourse of personal sacrifice on behalf of a national endeavor to "catch up" had a powerful tug on people, while calls for struggle within the factory could be scorned as selfish in the midst of what many saw as a transcendent national struggle.

In sum, wartime devastation and American power, late development, and accumulated prewar patterns of factory organization and labor-management relations constituted a social context that limited the range of choices available to postwar workers and managers. It created a social and cultural field that made some decisions likely, as when workers chose to organize factory-based unions. It made others improbable, such as management creation of a sharp divide between industrial engineering and quality control staff on one hand, and line managers, foremen, and workers on the other. The international context ruled out some things in short order, such as openly communist leadership of unions, while it gradually worked against others, such as Sōhyō's brand of unionism. Within all these contexts, to paraphrase Marx, Japanese workers and managers made their own history, but they did not make it just as they wished.

What they made, eventually, was the hegemonic corporate order. In the 1940s and 1950s in Japan, one finds not hegemony but two opposed ideologies fighting it out on cultural as well as material turf. Key tenets of the managerial understanding of reality, shared by an important minority of employees, included the following articles of faith. The good of the company was the good of all its members and of society at large. The interests of workers and managers, of labor and capital, were in basic accord. Unions had a legitimate role as watchdog, but resorting to open conflict was destructive. Efficiency, quality, and productivity were sacred values, and rewards to workers should reflect the value they gave to the company. Those men who made a full commitment to the company should be looked after to the best of a corporation's ability, and the proper role for women was to help them offer this commitment. The active participation of all members of the corporate community would help the company, the society, and the nation.

Against these notions, many unionists through the 1950s argued fervently for a different order at work and in society. The company existed to provide a livelihood to employees and their families, not the reverse. Jobs for men were to be protected at all costs. Pay ought to reflect need-related factors, such as age, and should rise predictably with seniority. To achieve these results, union members should organize from the base of the work-place. They should have a voice in decisions at work, and they should set independent standards for work conditions that would take precedence over pursuit of profit. This unionism assumed that the interests of workers and capitalists were opposed, conflict was natural, and the long-term objective of organized employees was to share or control managerial functions.

In the major steel mills, the last hurrah of this union agenda came in the strikes at the end of the 1950s. Throughout the nation's major workplaces, the managerial *ideology* of the 1950s became the *hegemony* of the 1960s and after. One source of its longevity was the very intensity and totality of the clash that produced it. Unions in early postwar Japan were not as secure in their power as those elsewhere, but their aspirations were grand and radical, their tactics bold and militant. To the extent that unionized workers saw the company as "their" community and sought to control it, they both provoked managers to resist fiercely and offered an opening and an inspiration for a corporate project to totally mobilize employees on behalf of "our" company.

A second, related source of the relative durability of Japan's corporate order and the totality of its embrace has been its ability to absorb elements of the union challenge. For all their talk of job- and then merit-based wages, managers have continued for forty years to give important—if steadily decreasing—weight to seniority in setting pay. While insisting on a free hand to transfer employees and ease out the excess, they have institutional-ized an important degree of job security for loyal men, both blue and white collar. They answered calls for participation with consultation and QC cir-cles. They met calls for equality with the single-status hierarchy of "em-ployee." More recently, they have offered some women access to career posi-tions. Sustaining hegemony has been a dynamic process of appropriating opposing positions and incorporating them safely.

Naysayers and Celebrants of the Japanese Workplace

Japanese scholars in the first postwar decade presented the history of capital-ism in their country as a tale of distorted development, picking up where the mainstream of prewar Marxism left off. Their students wrote a postwar labor history of social tragedy and the betrayed promise of liberation. They lamented the destruction of a unionism that sought secure jobs, pay reflecting worker needs, and authoritative participation in decision-making at work.

The point of departure for this critical narrative has been disappointment that the labor movement abandoned revolutionary goals and accepted the value system of capitalism and that unions have been integrated into the snug embrace of the corporation. Shimizu Shinzō, a union activist turned scholar with experience in the national headquarters of Tekkō Rōren in the 1950s, put it this way in 1982: "In the 20 years of high-speed growth . . . regular workers in large corporations followed a course from loyalty to the enterprise to subordination by it, snared by the framework of QC circles plus raises and promotions based on meritocratic individual competition. Ultimately they were absorbed completely into the corporate-centered society, and the corporation is today the most powerful social unit in Japan." The mainstream of the labor movement "makes the corporation the base of its existence," whereas a proper "society of workers and labor unions can only come to life founded on values that are completely different from those of the corporation."[8]

Kumazawa Makoto elaborated on this critique. He condemned as a pernicious extension of corporate domination new systems of merit rating in the 1970s in which employee self-evaluations were the basis for wage and promotion decisions. Proponents described the evaluations as a means of "expanding the potential of human beings." On the contrary, he argues, they gave even greater legitimacy to "merit" assessments and led employees to further internalize the norms of the corporation: "no space remains for a worker consciousness that even questions, much less attacks, meritocracy." For Kumazawa and colleagues such as Hyōdō Tsutomu or Watanabe Osamu, a proper labor movement would have resisted the meritocratic spirit of a competitive individualism that inevitably leaves some co-workers behind. Proper unionism would have put forward an agenda to improve conditions at work and "protect people's livelihoods by standing on a principle of equality that transcends the national common sense of bourgeois society."[9]

As Japan's factories flooded the world with goods of quality and sophistication, and Japan's economy outpaced that of its rivals, it was inevitable that a more positive assessment of what Koike Kazuo called "the progressive nature of Japanese industrial relations" would find powerful advocates. Koike is the godfather of this interpretative stream, an important scholar of the same generation as critics such as Kumazawa and Hyōdō. Beginning in the 1970s, he has been supported by a younger cadre of commentators. They have recast the history of labor and management relations as a social miracle unfolding in tandem with the more famous economic one, and indeed enabling it. In their rendition, practical workers cooperated with farsighted managers to overcome divisive polarization and radical unions. They replaced foolish confrontation with Japanese-style cooperation and won affluence for their nation and better lives for themselves. Koike judges this congruence a "fortunate" development and concludes that Japan's "skill formation and industrial relations have put it a step ahead of world trends"; he also apparently believes that the corporations and the individuals who work there have been equally "fortunate."[10]

Among a younger generation of scholars, Nitta Michio is a leader in extending Koike's argument. He argues that cooperative unions have a "fairly high level of voice" in matters ranging from staffing, transfers, safety, work conditions, and wages to corporate policies and investment decisions. One of his "fundamental messages" is that workers and labor unions in Japan at every level from small production teams to corporate headquarters "speak out and participate actively and substantially."[11] His like-minded colleague, Ishida Mitsuo, goes further in seeing the system as good for its participants as well as the bottom line. He writes to "defend the fervor of the Japanese worker." While critics of merit-based wage setting call for a movement to resist meritocracy, Ishida embraces it as "a good thing" and calls for a "movement to realize meritocracy in its true form."[12]

Writing at the end of the 1980s, Ishida presented himself as "pouring cold water on the critical consensus of the day," but his assessment was in fact close to the mainstream of public opinion at that time.[13] By the mid-1980s, declarations elevating a Japanese style of labor management to the status of a model to the world were common. One such euphoric statement came from a professor of management at Hitotsubashi University who wrote, "I believe that the time has come for those concerned with Japan's long-term prosperity to consider seriously the feasibility of exporting certain elements of Japanese civilization that have resulted in Japan's leadership in the production of goods—most notably, its corporate system."[14] The eminent sage of Japanese-style quality control, Karatsu Hajime, happily agreed: "I believe that the results of Japan's experimentation [in industrial management] should be disseminated throughout the world. . . . More fundamentally, Japan should offer a positive challenge to the Cartesian assumptions underlying Western business methods."[15]

Such affirmative perspectives seemed to have won the day in the 1980s; but a combination of economic stagnation, international criticism, and a renewed critique from the domestic left leaves us with both contending views of the virtues and defects of the Japanese workplace system of the present and contending prescriptions for the future. From 1992 to 1998, the worst recession since the 1940s sobered the celebrants of Japanese-style management. Most of the newly negative voices in popular management literature deplore the rigidity of long-term job security or seniority-based wages. They want corporate Japan to be even leaner and meaner. But the then-chairman of the Sony corporation, Morita Akio, in 1992 asked his compatriots to be kinder and gentler. He drew wide attention (and not a few charges of hypocrisy) for a refreshing blast at corporate Japan for "sacrific[ing] consideration for their employees, shareholders, and local communities" in an excessively "single-minded pursuit of economic efficiency." He called on companies to "thoroughly review their fundamental business practices" and grant employees more holidays, fewer working hours, and higher pay.[16]

On the other side, self-declared critical scholars have been moved to reformulate their arguments by the surprising resilience of the economy through the 1980s.[17] They seek to credit Nitta's evidence that some cooperative unions made a difference and Ishida's contention that many workers accepted meritocratic work regimes, and yet sustain a critical interpretation. One means to this end was a feminist critique, forcefully advanced by Ōsawa Mari. She mostly avoids the question of whether cooperative unionism benefits the men at the system's core, although she does note that these men sacrifice freedom and family life for the sake of their privileges. She rather emphasizes three simple points. First, a distinctive and fundamentally discriminatory gender relationship "lies at the foundation of Japan's corporate-centered society." Second, social policies premised upon and supporting a division of labor by age and sex have only reinforced this society since the 1970s. Third, so-called reforms such as the Equal Opportunity Employment Law in fact "perfectly fit the patriarchal character of the enterprise-centered society."[18]

More familiar anti-establishment voices refashioned their critiques in a somewhat penitent tone. Kumazawa Makoto even titled a recent work "Light and Shadow in Japanese-Style Management."[19] He admits that "the liberation of desire and the achievement of a certain degree of personal material security" are among "the most authentic components of postwar democracy." But in Kumazawa's grammar, a subordinate clause noting the "bright light of postwar democracy" is always linked to a stressed clause describing the shadow of an "incomplete formation, or indeed the destruction, of a communal society able to reconcile the clash of private rights."[20]

In an important comparison of labor unions at Toyota and Nissan in the 1980s, Hyōdō Tsutomu and Totsuka Hideo confess to having held an excessively monolithic view of the degree to which cooperative enterprise-based unions in large private companies allowed managers a free hand to deploy labor power. "In the course of our research," they wrote, "we discovered a clear difference" between Nissan and Toyota. Nissan's union turns out to be a classic case of reverse colonization, where the reputedly captive union for many years exacted a formidable price for its "cooperation." It consolidated substantial authority to "regulate the workplace."[21] But the authors are critical of this union's regulatory power. They emphasize its undemocratic roots. Foremen were the authorities who counted, able to force their will on subordinates as well as on managers. They conclude by noting that Nissan management was finally able to destroy much of this power at the end of the 1980s.

Totsuka Hideo joins with labor economist Tokunaga Shigeyoshi in perhaps the clearest statement of a renewed critical synthesis, close to my own view. They divide postwar labor studies into three eras: an early postwar criticism; a dissenting view of the social dynamics of the high-growth era, of which they were part; and a more recent affirmative view. They admit that their earlier critiques failed to anticipate the stability and endurance of the cooperative system of labor-management relations. They recognize the "clear fact that this [system] has been one factor supporting the productive power of Japanese capitalism and contributing to the competitive advantages of Japanese corporations in world markets." Nonetheless, they are not persuaded by their upbeat colleagues. Despite its productive power and competitive edge, "we cannot see in the system of Japan's corporate-centered society the requisite social principles to make it a model for contemporary human society." They stress that productive dynamism in itself is not a "social principle" and argue that intrinsic traits of the Japanese system, such as long hours, the intensity of labor, and the low status of women and foreign workers are violations of the norms of international organizations such as the United Nations, the International Labor Organization, and international union federations.[22]

People outside Japan face the daunting task of navigating this rich and impassioned debate to find meaning for themselves. For those comfortable with a trickle-down social miracle, the Japanese system has something to recommend it. In the early years of the economic miracle, unprecedented rates of investment and savings meant deferred gratification for working people, who endured long hours, dangerous conditions, cramped housing, and harmful pollution. But eventually gratification did arrive, in the form of a vigorous consumer culture offering substantial material benefits, if not to the veteran workers of the early postwar era, then to their children. Japanese people in the high-growth era enjoyed increasing social equality. Although pollution victims suffered horribly, the majority of people were healthier and better clothed and fed than ever. Stores large and small overflowed with an array of increasingly affordable, enticing consumer goodies. Within the workplace, QC circles and job rotation enhanced the interest of some jobs and the sense of engagement of some employees.

Further, it is undeniable that the Japanese industrial order has handled the pressures of recession more gently than has the United States, at least. Long-range transfers are surely a hardship for many, but the thousands of American steelworkers in the Monongahela Valley in the early 1980s who lost their jobs on short notice and collected meager unemployment checks or were forced to take low-wage service jobs might have been delighted had U.S. Steel acted like NKK and moved them at wages close to their old pay, even to unfamiliar jobs at a new plant in some remote place like Houston. The Japanese workplace of cooperative unions and productivity-minded managers did offer some valuable life supports to loyal workers and home-makers who bought into the system and accepted their place.

Yet a measure of security brought a high degree of dependence. With the single status of employee came strict discipline and hierarchy. With merito-cratic wages came constant evaluation and pressure to measure up to the company's standards or fall by the wayside. With cooperative unions came heavy-handed discrimination against dissenters. Workplace life in Japan has often been marked by a desperate quality of striving and by escalating demands placed on workers by managers as devoted to the bottom line as their counterparts elsewhere. By repudiating conflict as an unnatural state of being, mainstream unions willingly surrendered a vital weapon of the weak.

Perhaps such trade-offs were inevitable. Perhaps the only way to secure the wages of affluence was to accept dependence on the company and unre-strained corporate authority at work. If one compares the job security enjoyed by core workers in large Japanese firms to the traumatic insecurity of jobs in America during the manufacturing depression of the early 1980s or the chronic downsizings since then, living in a Japanese workplace looks inviting.[23] But one should insist on a more demanding comparison. One can look at what unions elsewhere have achieved, or imagine what might have been in Japan, and take a critical view of the costs of capitalist success.

One might, for example, compare the hands-off passivity of Japanese unions when managers introduced QC circles to the assertive participation of German employees through their works councils. In most German work-places, management and works councils negotiated the arrangements for implementing QC circles. They reached agreement concerning "selection of participants, the voice and training of discussion leaders as well as the eval-uation of work results." In addition, councils required measures to address "possible negative effects, the meeting of circles during working hours and the admission of the works council to QC circle meetings." Agreements at major German auto makers, for example, provided for the election of group leaders and specified procedures to remove leaders from their posts.[24] Had unions in Japan pursued such protections, they could have ameliorated the negative pressures of QC circles and revitalized their local organizations.

In similar fashion, one might compare the charade in which the NKK union bargained to head off a threatened move to northern Japan in 1970 to several cases where German works councils mounted extensive campaigns to force steel producers to retract plans for mill closings and invest to modern-ize plants instead. At NKK as well as at German steelmakers, the result was to keep an original facility in operation, and it is true that jobs were lost in the process in both countries. The difference is not so much in the results but in the transparency of the process of reaching a decision. In the NKK case, managers seem to have decided to consolidate operations at Ōgishima even before "negotiations" began, and so-called industrial democracy functioned behind closed doors, if at all. It is almost impossible to discern what marginal impact the union's cooperative stance had on softening the blow to employ-ment or work conditions. In the German cases, corporations announced shutdown decisions publicly and later retracted them. Jobs that would have been lost were evidently saved by the intervention of works councils.[25]

Japanese steel unions might have fared better in their negotiations, whether for wages in the 1960s, for the new shift system in 1970, or over the terms of transfers and downsizing in more recent years, had they been will-ing to threaten open resistance. Early postwar unions were committed to reviving the economy as well as controlling the workplace, and the activists of the 1950s spoke in favor of increasing productivity even as they opposed the productivity movement on political grounds. If such unionists had sus-tained their grassroots activism, they might have found a way to accept measures to increase productivity while protecting an independent labor voice on matters from wage setting to staffing to safety. Of course, we can-not turn back the clock to test this proposition, and even stating the hypoth-esis risks romantically exalting a lost cause. But in looking to the future, it is equally dangerous to acquiesce in the tyranny of a view that what actually happened was the best that can be imagined.

Even a booster of the status quo like Ishida Mitsuo ends his strong affirmation of meritocratic management with a call for unions to regulate more actively a truly "fair" meritocracy.[26] This seems a promising suggestion. It suggests that workers start with existing institutions that seem genuinely attractive to many, and improve them. But to answer Ishida's call to action, working people would have to define fairness on their own terms. For instance, they would have to establish a principle that effort matters more than results. Otherwise, they may as well let the personnel office continue to conduct merit ratings as it sees fit. And in a world that identifies the success of an employee with the success of the company, and that repudiates the very idea of conflicting interests, it is hard to imagine a body of organized employees defining and then imposing "fair" standards for merit ratings that do not defer to the demands of the corporation for efficient and profitable results.

For an observer who wishes to learn from the Japanese experience, one key is to recognize that working life in Japan has multiple aspects. Just as Japanese managers or engineers did with American practice in the 1950s, others should be able to disassemble the Japanese package and refashion attractive pieces to suit their own needs. As they do so, a second key is to be aware of position. The lessons taken away from the Japanese story by a CEO will be different from those absorbed by a minimum-wage worker, a skilled professional, or a union organizer. CEOs are concerned fundamentally with the bottom line. They will surely be—indeed they have for some time already been—excited by the potential for Japanese practices to raise productivity and cut costs. The others might share this concern, but they also have a powerful interest in democratic process as a good in its own right. They must search for ways to build upon the desirable elements of security, participation, and productivity found in the Japanese workplace without sacrificing an independent voice. German works councils took such an approach in their conditional cooperation with QC circles. It is a strategy available to anyone looking to learn from Japan.

Whither the Japanese Workplace: Becoming Like "Us"?

Possibly the long recession that began in 1992 will one day be seen as a more profound crisis than that of the 1970s, and the beginning of the end of the golden era of Japan's corporate-centered society. Certainly, this has been the common wisdom of trendy prognosticators advocating market orthodoxy in the 1990s. But the order of things in Japanese workplaces is adaptive and enduring.[27] The hindsight of the next generation of historians is likely to regard the foreign shocks and domestic recession of the 1990s as catalysts of a slight shift toward a less regulated but no less encompassing hegemony.

Observers have been predicting the disappearance of the institutions that mark life in Japanese workplaces for a long time. I remember vividly a visit to a Sony TV assembly plant during my first trip to Japan as a high school student in 1969. Our tour guide proudly told of the all-encompassing benefits bestowed on employees by the company, such as dormitories and after-work schooling for the young female operatives. He boasted of the company loyalty of all workers, men as well as women. He then concluded, "But this is all changing. The student movement is so strong. Younger workers are more individualistic. They want their own cars. The old loyalty is disappearing."

When high growth ended in 1974, the engine of transformation was no longer said to be changing values among employees. Pundits rather stressed the changing attitudes of managers, who were proclaiming "permanent employment" and "seniority wages" to be expensive luxuries doomed to extinction.[28] The booming 1980s then brought with it a return to the logic of the late 1960s. Labor shortages and abundance had produced an "alien" species of individualist, pleasure-seeking youth who were going to transform the system by rejecting secure careers with major companies. Then after the bubble burst and the 1990s "ice age" of hiring freezes and downsizing set in, the reasoning of the 1970s returned. Managers were once again the crusaders for change. The *Economist* in 1993 gleefully reported a decision by Pioneer, the large audio-equipment maker, to force thirty-five veteran employees to retire early. "Capitalism in Japan is becoming harder to confuse with socialism.... [The Pioneer decision] is seen as a signal that the post-1945 tradition of life-time employment in big companies is creaking under pressure from economic slowdown."[29] All these over-eager predictions are part of a cyclical logic of talking about Japan that parallels the business cycle precisely. In good times, labor shortages and affluence will lead employees to reject the status quo. In bad times, the pressures of the bottom line will lead bosses to "finally" move to a proper market-based system of employment.

In 1997, the Japanese economy seemed poised uneasily between recovery and renewed recession, which offered an opening to both sorts of logic at once. One day in February a local newspaper announced that "the Japanese economy has lost its luster" and described "one of the great role reversals of the modern era—the transformation of Japan from behemoth to bungler." In this telling, the corporations were abandoning their workers. "Japan's giant corporations . . . have been considered not only the engine of the Japanese economy but also the glue that held Japanese society together. But the ties between the corporations, their workers and suppliers are now weakening."[30] One month later a column in a daily digest of news from Japan predicted the same weakening ties, but for the opposite reason. With the economy reviving, "lifetime employment is out" and "an era of job-hopping for workers" was in.[31]

This ahistoric, shallow rhetoric of sudden change and collapsing institutions is deeply flawed. If the Japanese workplace is changing—which it assuredly is—that in itself is nothing new. The most profound transformations took place in the first twenty years after the war. In large private factories, workers in the late 1940s formed unions of unprecedented number and vigor, and they initiated the determined labor union offensive of the 1950s. This prolonged contest for the workplace ended with the most basic of changes, the triumph of "cooperative" industrial relations in the 1960s.

In the decades since, the state, corporate executives, and union leaders faced changes that led observers to predict at every turn the collapse and transformation of this new industrial order. But the superintendants of the state and business worlds, in partnership with understanding unionists, developed new reinforcing levers at the macroeconomic level, such as the "economically adjusted" wage policy of the 1970s. These same actors put in place new education and social welfare policies in the 1970s that bolstered the "natural" order of gender division and dependence on the corporation. In the 1980s the political and bureaucratic drive for administrative reform privatized the railroads and the telecommunications monopoly, thus extending the hegemony of corporate values deep into public sector workplaces.[32] In such ways, across the golden age of the corporate-centered society, the mobilized workplace order modified and renewed itself continually.

The rhetoric of change and collapse is also misleading because it misconstrues the institutions said to be on the brink of extinction. "Permanent employment" has been a misnomer since the term was invented in the 1950s. Mass dismissals in large companies and disputes over them were more common in that decade than at any point since. Since then, managers have been hemmed in by legal decisions and the accumulated weight of precedent, but they have also been aided by expanded state programs of "employment adjustment subsidies." They have carefully designed an impressive tool kit of techniques for the flexible deployment of workers and the trimming of workforces. Managers at the top five firms in the iron and steel industry reduced employment by one fourth from 1993 to 1996 without dismissing a single worker. Seen in this light, the early retirements at Pioneer hailed as signs of change by the *Economist* were simply business as usual.

The term "seniority wages" has been no less a misnomer. From the late 1940s to the present, the relative weight of age and seniority in pay setting has diminished, but it has remained significant. For this very reason, managers "streamline" workforces by pushing relatively overpaid senior employees to take early retirement. Conversely, although systems of merit rating have become more pervasive since the 1950s, from the early twentieth century to the present, with the brief and partial exception of the 1940s, merit judgments have always been part of the wage calculus. When the *Economist*, that intrepid drumbeater for Anglo-American market values, proclaimed in 1996 that "out of the late-feudal collectivism of the past 140 years will emerge a Japan based on the principles of individual enterprise and individual responsibility," it blithely misread the past as much as the future.[33] In the hegemony of corporate Japan, mechanisms such as job rotation and QC circles have indeed channeled individual energies toward collective goals, but exam-based education and merit-based raises and promotions have also for decades promoted fierce competition and "individual enterprise and responsibility." In that sense, the prototype for a managed but competitive future is firmly anchored in the past.

Finally, change should not be confused with the collapse of a hegemonic system distinguished by a gyroscopic or spongelike ability to absorb shocks and co-opt pressures. The efforts of the elites of corporate and bureaucratic Japan to command legitimacy and respect have rarely been complacent. Although custodians of order in the late 1990s found themselves forced at least to talk of reforming themselves, the core values of the corporate order—meritocracy and efficiency—were if anything more sacred than ever. The object of reform was to extend them. Japanese managers were improvising on familiar tactics to mobilize employees to the same determined efforts as in the past. Their desire to recruit a core group of the best and the brightest at the point of entry and keep them seems little diminished. Even the 1997 prediction of the end to lifetime employment admitted that "only one company in ten has actually instituted year-round hiring as needed."[34] As this report described a certain fraying at the margins of the workplace system, it offered a very familiar refrain.

The omnipresent talk of change at the end of the twentieth century was both predictive and prescriptive. Japan, people were told, both will and should radically transform itself to develop a "proper" multiparty political system and a properly individualistic economic order.[35] Such a statement is fundamentally misguided. It reflects a misreading of the past, putting forward a nonsensical view of a static, traditional Japan as the baseline against which change is measured. It shows a failure to understand the dynamism of corporate hegemony since the 1960s and its adaptive capacity. Blithe predictions of a brave new world overlook powerful commitments by authoritative institutions to restrict change. In the face of a world seen as threatening, the major national federations of management and labor are gingerly seeking a relatively modest adjustment of the status quo.

Nikkeiren, for its part, put forward the managerial vision of a deregulated, market-friendly future in its "Bluebird Plan" of 1996. To "restore international competitivity" the federation did call for "structural" reforms. It wanted to end many forms of public regulation, in particular those said to drive up the cost of the industrial infrastructure of utilities, distribution, and transportation. But Nikkeiren ended its clarion call with two strong notes of caution. First, consumers had to be re-educated. Their "obsessions with brand names and with fresh products" were partly to blame for the "high prices in our country." To bring Japanese prices in line with those elsewhere, consumers would have to change their attitudes to become more price conscious. Government and business would have to provide consumer information and education. So much for consumer sovereignty. Of equal importance, although "free market capitalism brings prosperity to industry and raises standards of living through the principle of free competition, it gives rise as well to evils such as low growth, high unemployment, imbalances of income, speculative bubbles, and excessive investment. That is, we need a system to manage risk and provide a check to the crises and problems inherent in capitalist market economies."[36] So much for unleashing market forces. Nikkeiren explicity presented the Bluebird Plan as its vision of a "third way" that would avoid the excesses of Anglo-American capitalism as well as the rigidities of social democratic systems.

Nikkeiren called on management more than the state to "check" the excesses of the market. It also called for a new "civilian power" of the citizenry at large to play this role. Unions are mentioned in passing in this familiar vision as cooperative partners who must help enterprises be all the more flexible in hiring, deploying and—it is implicitly assumed—easing out workers, and in setting wages in more "rational" fashion. The Rengō labor federation was unlikely to demur. The secretary general of the labor federation in 1997 was Washio Etsuji, formerly a union leader at New Japan Steel. Washio, a Tokyo University graduate, was a star of the cooperative union elite in the 1980s and 1990s. Interviewed for a front-page feature on "Private sector reform: the future of the corporation" in April 1997, he noted that "every company is shouting that this is an era of great competition and [is] trying to cut jobs. But careless cutbacks will actually hurt productivity."[37] His implication is clear. *Careful* pruning would grow the tree of productivity and ultimately yield jobs, and unions should cooperate.

These go-slow reformers of the managerial and union elite spoke for many. They found significant support in mass media suspicious of too single-minded a pursuit of an American model.[38] The very fact that Nikkeiren's manifesto for structural change came in the form of a coordinated plan is a fine indication that buzzwords such as "deregulation" and "globalization" would be given meaning within the boundaries of the managed meritocracy already so firmly entrenched.

If the predictions of change miss the mark, there is little to fear from the high-handed prescriptions that come with them, exhorting Japanese people to be properly free-market, risk-taking workers and capitalists. The prescriptions are as presumptuous and potentially damaging as the predictions are misleading. Is it really desirable to transform Japan into a proper mirror of "us"? The answer comes down to a question of who and where is "us." From the viewpoint of working people as consumers, cheaper rice and electricity is enticing. But a race toward the pot of gold at the end of the efficiency rainbow also promises even less security and more pressure to outperform neighbors and co-workers than the none-too-relaxed status quo.

The history of the Japanese workplace offers the possibility of an alternative scenario, one in which working people devise strategies and institutions to restrain corporate values rather than embrace them ever more fully. In postwar Japan unions ultimately did not do this. They pulled back from bottom-up activism, and they became tightly controlled institutions closely allied to managers. This brought economic gains but sacrificed the workers' own efforts to control their lives. One might imagine a different future, where unions would be more open and responsive to their members, willing to take a stance independent from the corporation and so extend the realm of democratic participation beyond the voting booth. Efficiency might be redefined in the process, but so would the meaning of worker autonomy and well-being.

Appendix: Figures

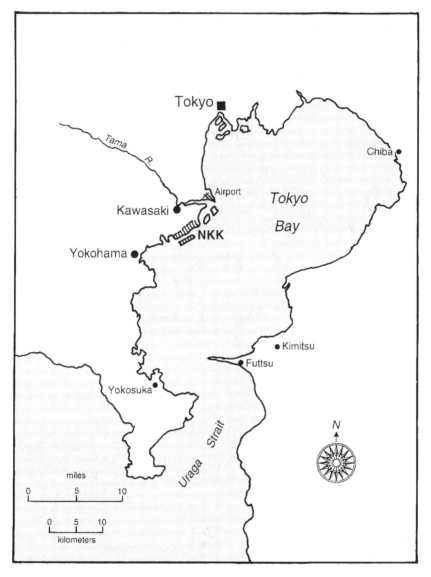

Figure 1. Map of the Tokyo region, 1970s–1990s.

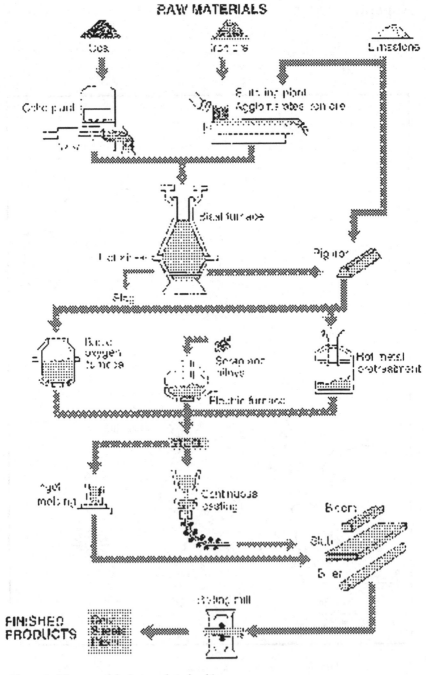

Figure 2. Diagram of the iron and steelmaking process.

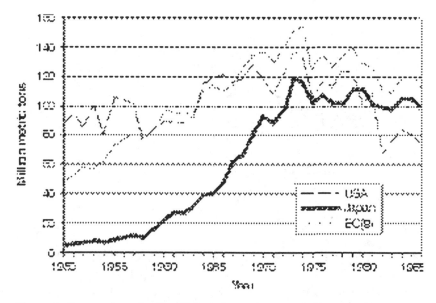

Figure 3. Raw steel production, United States, Japan, and European Community, 1950–1986. *Source:* American Iron and Steel Industry, *Annual Statistical Reports,* various issues. Cited in Thomas R. Howell, William A. Noellert, Jesse G. Kreier, and Allan William Wolff, eds., *Steel and the State* (Boulder: Westview Press, 1988).

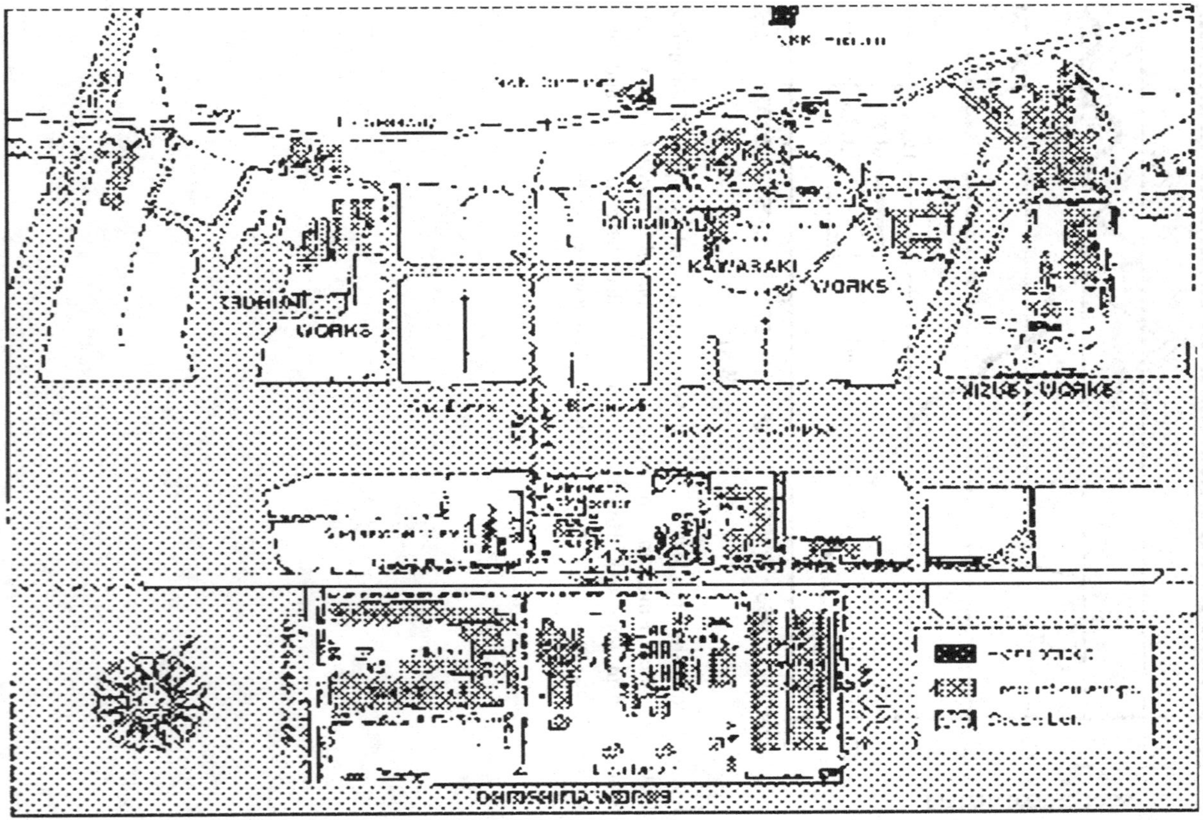

Figure 4. Layout of the NKK iron and steelmaking complex in Kawasaki.

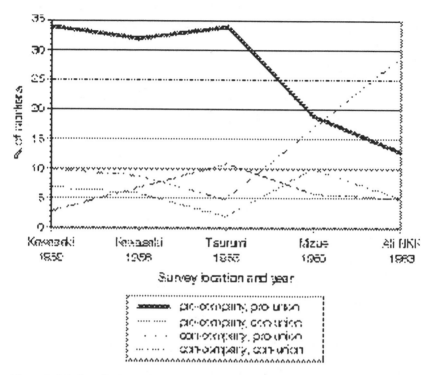

Figure 5. Worker allegiance at Nippon Kōkan, 1952–1963. *Source:* Adapted from Odaka Kunio, *Sangyō shakaigaku kōgi* (Tokyo: Iwanami shoten, 1981), pp. 512–513. (*Note:* The survey included another category, "neutral" attitudes toward either company or union. Responses in this category are not included here.)

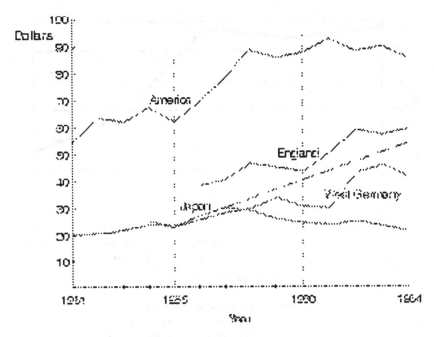

Figure 6. Relative labor costs per ton of steel production, Japan, United States, Britain, West Germany, 1951–1964. The dotted line extrapolates Japanese labor costs for 1958–1964, assuming the 1955–1957 trend had continued. *Source:* Adapted from Matsuzaki Tadashi, *Nihon tekkō sangyō bunseki* (Tokyo: Nihon hyōronsha, 1982), p. 17.

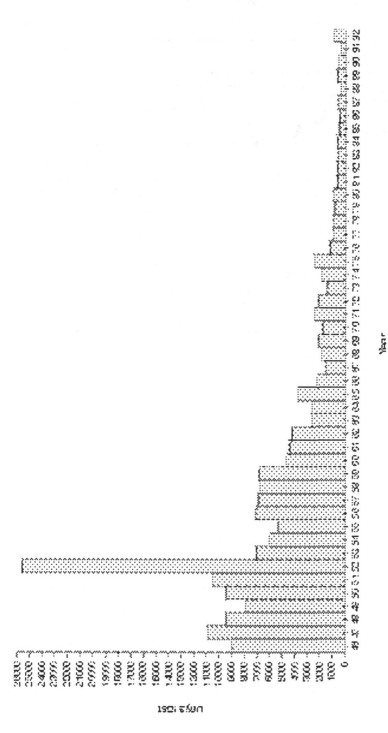

Figure 7. Strike trends in Japan: Days lost per dispute, 1946–1992. *Source:* Ōhara Institute for Social Research, *Nihon rōdō nenkan,* annual volumes, 1959–1993.

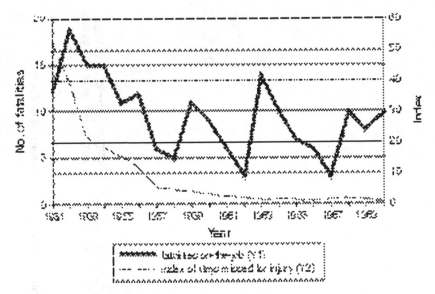

Figure 8. Accident rates at Nippon Kōkan, 1951–1970. *Source:* Orii Hyūga, *Rōmu kanri nijū nen* (Tokyo: Tōyō Keizai Shinpōsha, 1973), pp. 130–131.

Notes

1. Japan Reborn

1. Barshay, "Imagining Democracy in Postwar Japan."
2. Interview with Nakamura Kōgō, October 7, 1991.
3. "Drastic Steps Set to Fight Food Lack," *Japan Times,* June 6, 1946.
4. Cohen, *Remaking Japan,* pp. 171, 179.
5. Kawasaki rōdō shi, ed., *Kawasaki rōdō shi,* pp. 7–8, 410.
6. Comments of Japanese college students at a screening of one such program that I attended in 1989.
7. Dower, *Empire and Aftermath,* p. 294.
8. Johnson, *MITI and the Economic Miracle,* pp. 181–182. Gordon, *The Evolution of Labor Relations in Japan,* pp. 334–335.
9. Maier, "The Two Postwar Eras," p. 327; cites A. J. P. Taylor.
10. Moore, *Japanese Workers and the Struggle for Power* p. 104, Table 4.1.
11. Ibid., pp. 156–160.
12. Ibid., p. 104.
13. Cohen, *Remaking Japan,* Ch. 15.
14. Ohara Institute, *Nihon rōdō nenkan (1959)* p. 138.
15. See Cohen, *Remaking Japan,* pp. 271–272 for the example of Zen Keinosuke.
16. Takeda, *Ōji seishi sōgi,* pp. 36–38; and Ueda, "Kigyō kan kyōsō to 'shokuba shakai,'" pp. 1–16.
17. Gordon, "The Invention of Japanese Style Management."
18. Halberstam, *The Reckoning,* pp. 153–187.
19. Nippon Kōkan Tsurumi, *Tsurutetsu rōdō undō shi,* pp. 63–68. Cohen, *Remaking Japan,* pp. 221–222.
20. Kawasaki, *Kawasaki rōdō shi,* p. 85.
21. Nippon Kōkan, *Nippon Kōkan kabushiki kaisha 30 nen shi,* pp. 21–23.
22. Interview with Kamimura Hideji, October 14, 1992.

23. Interview with Nakamura Kōgō, October 7, 1991.
24. All quotes from interview with Kudō Shinpachi, April 12, 1992.
25. All quotes from interview with Isobe Toshie, September 11, 1992.
26. Orii, *Rōmu kanri nijū nen* pp. 4–5; see pp. i–ii for Orii's philosophy of labor management.
27. Interview with Konda Masaharu, February 28, 1992.
28. Matsuzaki Masanobu, cited in Aoki, *Nippon gisō rōren,* pp. 13–14.

2. Organizing the Steelworkers

1. Smith, "The Right to Benevolence," pp. 236–270.
2. Hyōdō, *Nihon ni okeru rōshi kankei no tenkai,* pp. 367–403; Nishinarita, *Kindai Nihon no rōshi kankei,* pp. 200–214; Gordon, *Labor and Imperial Democracy,* pp. 103–131; and Garon, *The State and Labor,* pp. 53–54, 92–93.
3. Nihon seisansei honbu, ed., *Nihon no rōshi kyōgi sei,* p. 5. Garon, *State and Labor,* p. 54.
4. Garon, *State and Labor,* pp. 211–214; and Gordon, *Labor and Imperial Democracy,* pp. 321–322.
5. Nihon seisansei honbu, *Nihon no rōshi kyōgi sei,* p. 7.
6. Nippon Kōkan Tsurumi, *Tsurutetsu rōdō undō shi,* pp. 47–50. Nippon Kōkan Kawasaki, ed., *Jū nen no ayumi,* pp. 2–5.
7. Kawasaki, *Kawasaki rōdō shi,* p. 56.
8. Nippon Kōkan, ed., *Nippon kōkan kabushiki kaisha 40 nen shi,* pp. 285–287.
9. Nippon Kōkan Tsurumi, *Tsurutetsu rōdō undo shi,* p. 51.
10. Ibid., pp. 52–54.
11. This workplace recharged batteries used to power forklifts.
12. Nippon Kōkan Kawasaki, *Jū nen no ayumi,* pp. 3–5, 33.
13. Ibid., pp. 6–7.
14. Interview with Matsuda Takezō, October 23, 1992. He compiled and wrote much of Nippon Kōkan Kawasaki, *Jū nen no ayumi.*
15. Nippon Kōkan Kawasaki, *Jū nen no ayumi,* p. 6.
16. Ibid.
17. Ibid.
18. Ibid., p. 8.
19. Ibid., p. 7.
20. Interviews with Kamimura Hideji, October 14, 1992, and Matsuda Takezō, October 23, 1992. Nippon Kōkan Kawasaki, *Jū nen no ayumi,* p. 8.
21. Nippon Kōkan Kawasaki, *Jū nen no ayumi,* p. 11.
22. Ibid., p. 10.
23. On the slightly different Yahata case, see Gibbs, "The Labor Movement at the Yahata Steel Works."
24. Nippon Kōkan Tsurumi, *Tsurutetsu rōdō undō shi,* pp. 57–74. Aihara, "Nippon kōkan no sōgi, 1946," pp. 97–106.

25. Aihara, "Nippon kōkan no sōgi, 1946," p. 100.
26. Ibid.. Nippon Kōkan Tsurumi, *Tsurutetsu rōdō undō shi*, p. 74.
27. Nippon Kōkan Tsurumi, *Tsurutetsu rōdō undō shi*, p. 60.
28. Ibid., pp. 72–73.
29. Ibid., p. 75.
30. Nippon Kōkan Kawasaki, *Jū nen no ayumi*, pp. 17–18.
31. Ibid., p. 18.
32. Ibid., pp. 18, 24.
33. Nippon Kōkan Tsurumi, *Tsurutetsu rōdō undō shi*, pp. 87–88.
34. Ibid., pp. 82–87.
35. Moore, *Japanese Workers and the Struggle for Power*, pp. 156–160.
36. Nippon Kōkan Kawasaki, *Jū nen no ayumi*, pp. 72–73, 219–234.
37. Ibid., p. 13.
38. Ibid.
39. Sōdōmei, *Go jū nen shi*, pp. 127–130. Aihara, "Nippon kōkan no sōgi, 1946," pp. 107–112.
40. Nippon Kōkan Kawasaki, *Jū nen no ayumi*, pp. 25–27. Sōdōmei, *Go jū nen shi*, pp. 130–134. Aihara, "Nippon kōkan no sōgi, 1946," pp. 107–112.
41. Nippon Kōkan Kawasaki, *Jū nen no ayumi*, p. 28.
42. Sōdōmei, *Go jū nen shi*, p. 134. Nippon Kōkan Kawasaki, *Jū nen no ayumi*, p. 29.
43. Nippon Kōkan Kawasaki, *Jū nen no ayumi*, p. 30.
44. Ibid., p. 71.
45. Ibid. Interview with Kamimura Hideji, October 14, 1992.
46. Nippon Kōkan Kawasaki, *Jū nen no ayumi*, p. 31.
47. Ibid., p. 239.
48. Ibid., pp. 49, 239.
49. Ibid., pp. 52–53.
50. Ibid., pp. 54–56, 241.
51. Interview with Matsuda Takezō, November 17, 1992.
52. Nippon Kōkan Kawasaki, *Jū nen no ayumi*, pp. 71–72.
53. Hayakawa and Yoshida, "Keizai Fukkō Kaigi," part 1, pp. 3, 6.
54. Ibid., p. 14
55. Ibid., part 2, pp. 3–12, 19–20; part 3, pp. 1–9.
56. Nishinarita, "Senryōki Nihon no rōshi kankei," pp. 206–209.
57. Nippon Kōkan Tsurumi, *Tsurutetsu rōdō undō shi*, pp. 150–151.
58. Ibid., pp. 151–153.
59. Ibid., p. 154.
60. Nippon Kōkan Kawasaki, *Jū nen no ayumi*, p. 43.
61. Ibid., pp. 40–43.
62. Ibid., p. 39. Emphasis added.
63. Nishinarita, "Senryō ki Nihon no rōshi kankei," p. 208. Tackney, "Institutionalization of the Lifetime Employment System," pp. 386–387.

64. Nakaoka, "Senchū, sengo no kagakuteki kanri undō (2)," pp. 55–57.
65. Dore, *British Factory–Japanese Factory,* Ch. 8.

3. Restoring Managerial and State Authority

1. Nippon Kōkan Tsurumi, *Tsurutetsu rōdō undo shi* (1956), pp. 142–145.
2. Nimura, "Nihon rōshi kankei no rekishiteki tokushitsu," p. 91.
3. Nippon kōkan, *Nippon kōkan 40 nen shi,* pp. 293–299, and *Nippon Kōkan 60 nen shi,* p. 160.
4. Nippon kōkan, *Nippon kōkan 40 nen shi,* pp. 300–320, and *Nippon kōkan 60 nen shi,* p. 160.
5. Interview with Takemura Tatsuo, June 10, 1992.
6. Nippon Kōkan Tsurumi, *Tsurutetsu rōdō undō shi* (1956), pp. 60–61.
7. Cohen, *Remaking Japan,* p. 262.
8. Orii, *Rōmu kanri nijū nen.* Basic biographical data is listed on the colophon. Interview with Okuda Kenji, November 27, 1992.
9. Orii, "Jūgyōin no kaisha ni tai suru ittaikan," pp. 100–101.
10. Orii, *Rōmu kanri nijū nen,* p. ii.
11. Interview with Konda Masaharu, February 18, 1992.
12. Ariiumi, "The Legal Framework," p. 93; and Woodiwiss, *Law, Labour, and Society,* pp. 113–116.
13. Miyake, *Reddo paaji to wa nani ka.*
14. Nakamura Seiji, *Nihon seisansei kōjō undō shi,* pp. 179–183, 192. Hyōdō, "Rōdō kumiai undō no hatten," pp. 113–114.
15. Maier, "The Politics of Productivity," p. 41.
16. Garon and Mochizuki, "Negotiating Social Contracts," p. 158.
17. Nakamura Seiji, *Nihon seisansei kōjō undō shi,* pp. 198–202, 207–208.
18. Sōhyō, *Sōhyō 30 nen: shiryō shu,* p. 345.
19. Nihon seisansei honbu, *Nihon no rōshi kyōgisei.*
20. Ibid., pp. 8–9.
21. Nihon keieisha dantai renmei, *Shokuba tōsō to sono taisaku,* pp. 50–98.
22. Williamson, *Coping with the Miracle,* p. 250.
23. Mita, "JC tanjō no hiwa," p. 102.
24. *Ekonomisuto,* vol. 41, no. 2 (January 15, 1963), p. 39.
25. Williamson, *Coping with the Miracle,* pp. 39–40.
26. Mita, "JC tanjō no hiwa," pp. 94–95.
27. Sōhyō, ed., *Sōhyō jū nen shi,* p. 474.
28. Nippon Kōkan Tsurumi, *Tsurutetsu rōdō undō shi,* pp. 363–365.
29. Interview with Nakao Yasuji, October 11, 1991.
30. Sōhyō, ed., *Sōhyō ni jū nen shi,* pp. 619–620.
31. Williamson, *Coping with the Miracle,* pp. 32–33.
32. Tilton, *Restrained Trade,* Ch. 6.

33. Kawasaki, *Kawasaki rōdō shi*, p. 309.
34. Ibid., p. 311.
35. Ibid., p. 375.
36. Ibid., pp. 398–400.
37. Interview with Kudō Shinpachi, April 12, 1992.
38. Sasaki, *Sengo shi daijiten*, pp. 462–463, entry "Population."
39. Kawasaki, *Kawasaki rōdō shi*, pp. 409–410.
40. Ibid., pp. 408–409 on savings, 414–415 on consumer trends. Horioka, "Consuming and Saving."
41. Kawasaki, *Kawasaki rōdō shi*, pp. 426, 433–435.
42. Garon, *State and Labor in Modern Japan*, pp. 236–237.
43. Woodiwiss, *Law, Labour, and Society in Japan*, pp. 101–117.
44. Cohen, *Remaking Japan*, p. 215. Woodiwiss, *Law, Labour, and Society*, pp. 103–104, 106–107. Gould, *Japan's Reshaping of American Labor Law*, p. 36.
45. Woodiwiss, *Law, Labour, and Society*, p. 110.
46. Gould, *Japan's Reshaping of American Labor Law*, pp. 31–33. Kettler and Tackney, "Light from a Dead Sun."
47. Woodiwiss, *Law, Labour, and Society*, pp. 157–159.
48. See Cole, *Strategies for Learning*, on quality control circles.

4. Reinventing the Steel Mill

1. Hein, "Growth versus Success," pp. 108–112.
2. Yonekura, *The Japanese Iron and Steel Industry*, p. 190.
3. Ibid.
4. Ibid., pp. 193–196.
5. Johnson, *MITI and the Japanese Miracle*, pp. 199–200.
6. Matsuzaki, *Nihon tekkō sangyō bunseki*, p. 50.
7. Dower, *Empire and Aftermath*, p. 316. Nippon Kōkan, *Nippon Kōkan 40 nen shi*, p. 382.
8. Havens, *Fire across the Sea*, p. 93. Nippon Kōkan, *Nippon Kōkan 40 nen shi*, p. 382.
9. Nippon Kōkan, *Nippon Kōkan 40 nen shi*, pp. 383–384. Yonekura, *The Japanese Iron and Steel Industry*, p. 197.
10. Yonekura, *The Japanese Iron and Steel Industry*, pp. 213–219.
11. Ibid., pp. 197–200.
12. Lynn, "Institutions, Organizations, and Technological Innovation," pp. 25–29.
13. Samuels, *Rich Nation, Strong Army*, pp. 52–56.
14. Lynn, "Institutions, Organizations, and Technological Innovation," pp. 124–133, 252. Yonekura, *The Japanese Iron and Steel Industry*, pp. 220–221.
15. Yonekura, *The Japanese Iron and Steel Industry*, p. 221.

16. Ibid., p. 216.

17. Orii, *Rōmu kanri nijū nen*, pp. 20–21.

18. Interview with Okuda Kenji, February 13, 1992. Orii, *Rōmu kanri nijū nen*, pp. 3–10. Nippon Kōkan Kawasaki, *Jū nen no ayumi*, p. 164.

19. Interview with Morito Akio, September 14, 1992.

20. Ibid. Orii, *Rōmu kanri nijū nen*, pp. 21–24. Nakamura Keisuke, *Nihon no shokuba to seisan shisutemu*, p. 199, n. 22.

21. Gordon, *Evolution of Labor Relations in Japan*, pp. 285–290.

22. Orii, *Rōmu kanri nijū nen*, p. 54.

23. Ibid., pp. 50–52.

24. Matsuzaki, *Nihon tekkō sangyō bunseki*, pp. 15–17.

25. Ibid., pp. 17, 67, 68–79.

26. Ibid., p. 17.

27. Ibid., pp. 93–94.

28. Interview with Imaizumi Masumasa, November 14, 1991.

29. Nakamura Keisuke, *Nihon no shokuba to seisan shisutemu*, pp. 143–44. Tsutsui, "W. Edwards Deming," pp. 295–325.

30. Interview with Imaizumi Masumasa, November 15, 1991.

31. Shimada, *Hyūman ueaa no keizaigaku*.

32. Nakamura Keisuke, *Nihon no shokuba to seisan shisutemu*, pp. 142, 144.

33. Ishikawa, *TQC to wa nani ka*, pp. 20–25.

34. "Kōjō kengaku to genba tōron kai: Nippon Kōkan Kawasaki seitetsujo, 5/10/56," *Hinshitsu kanri* 7, no. 7 (July 1956); emphasis added.

35. Interview with Imaizumi Masumasa, November 14, 1991.

36. "Dokutaa Juran, 4 kaisha, kōjō e iku," *Hinshitsu kanri* 5, no. 8 (September 1954): 17, cited in Nakamura Keisuke, *Nihon no shokuba to seisan shisutemu*, p. 198, note 10.

37. Nakamura Keisuke, *Nihon no shokuba to seisan shisutemu*, p. 147.

38. Interview with Imaizumi Masumasa, November 14, 1991.

39. Ishikawa, *TQC to wa nani ka*, p. 30. "QC katsudō no teichaku (3)," *Nihon keizai shimbun*, January 24, 1990.

40. Ōkōchi et al., *Rōdō kumiai no kōzō to kinō*, p. 123 and passim.

41. Konda, "Nippon Kōkan no rain ni yoru no rōmu kanri," pp. 6–8.

42. Orii, *Rōmu kanri nijū nen*, p. 31.

43. Konda, "Nippon Kōkan no rain ni yoru no rōmu kanri," p. 5.

44. Ibid.

45. *Shinseikatsu* 6, no. 6 (June 1959): 8–9 for list of these companies. Gordon, "Managing the Japanese Household," pp. 245–283.

46. Nippon kōkan, *Nippon Kōkan 40 nen shi*, p. 496.

47. Interview with Isobe Toshie, September 11, 1992.

48. Orii, *Rōmu kanri nijū nen*, p. 113.

49. "Kōjō, jigyōjo ni miru shinseikatsu undō no jirei: Kawasaki seitetsu jo to

hitachi zōsen no undō gaikyō," *Rōsei jihō*, no. 1358 (December 1955): 29–34. *Shinseikatsu* 1, no. 7: 2; no. 10: 2–3.

50. Kawasaki, *Kawasaki rōdō shi*, pp. 427–436, 511–513.
51. Hongo, "Toshiba 'jyōzu na kurashi no undō," pp. 30–31.
52. Kawasaki, *Kawasaki rōdō shi*, p. 513.
53. Nippon Kōkan Tsurumi, *Tsurutetsu rōdō undō shi*, pp. 271–272.
54. Ōkōchi et al., *Rōdō kumiai no kōzō to kinō*, p. 168.
55. Interview with Kamimura Hideji, October 14, 1992. Nippon Kōkan Kawasaki, *Tatakai no ayumi*, pp. 146–149.
56. Nippon Kōkan Kawasaki, *Tatakai no ayumi*, pp. 146–149. Nippon Kōkan Tsurumi, *Tsurutetsu rōdō undō shi* (1956), pp. 466–472 and (1970), p. 372.
57. Interview with Ōshima Ai, September 26, 1991.
58. Interview with Nakao Yasuji, October 15, 1991. Nipppon Kōkan Kawasaki, *Tatakai no ayumi*, pp. 105–106. Kawasaki, *Kawasaki rōdō shi*, p. 513.
59. Gordon, "Managing the Japanese Household."
60. Meyer, *The Five Dollar Day*, pp. 123–149.
61. Gordon, *Evolution of Labor Relations in Japan*, pp. 369–371.
62. Nihon seisansei honbu, ed., *Nihon no rōshi kyōgi sei*, pp. 6–10.
63. Ibid., p. 1.
64. Orii, *Rōmu kanri nijū nen*, p. 169.
65. Odaka, *Sangyō no shakai gaku kōgi*, p. 511. Orii, *Rōmu kanri nijū nen*, pp. 76–77.
66. Odaka, *Sangyō no shakai gaku kōgi*, pp. 544–547, and *Sangyō ni okeru ningen kankei*, pp. 348–362.
67. Orii, *Rōmu kanri nijū nen*, p. 169.
68. Orii, "Jūgyōin no kaisha ni tai suru ittaikan," pp. 112–118.
69. Orii, *Rōmu kanri nijū nen*, p. 170.
70. Interview with Watanabe Tatsuo, September 25, 1991.
71. Interview with Kondo Haruhiko, Okitsu Hideo, and Okuda Kenji, September 3, 1992.
72. Interview with Kudō Shinpachi, April 12, 1992.
73. Interview with Kondo Haruhiko, September 3, 1992.
74. Interview with Gotō Tatsuo, July 4, 1991.
75. Interview with Kitazume Shun, July 4, 1991; Shiinomi kai, ed., *Shiinomikai kessei 15 shūnen kinen*, pp. 6–7, 9–10.
76. Interview with Isobe Toshie, September 11, 1992.
77. Interview with Kihara Tsuneaki, November 23, 1992.
78. Hyōdō and Totsuka, eds., *Rōshi kankei no tenkan to sentaku*. In this book Company A is Nissan and Company B is Toyota. Halberstam, *The Reckoning*. Cusumano, *The Japanese Automobile Industry*, Ch. 3.
79. Interview with Kondo Masaharu, September 3, 1992. Interview with Ogura Shigemasa, May 13, 1992.

80. Interview with Kondo Haruhiko, September 3, 1992. Nippon Kōkan Kawasaki, *Jū nen no ayumi*, p. 250.

5. Forging an Activist Union

1. Hyōdō, "Shokuba no rōshi kankei to rōdō kumiai," pp. 211–225.
2. Cusumano, *The Japanese Automobile Industry,* Ch. 3. Takeda, "Minkan daiki-gyō ni okeru rōdō kumiai undō," pp. 1–25, and *Ōji seishi sōgi,* pp. 21–23. Ueda, "Kigyō-kan kyōsō to 'shokuba shakai,'" pp. 48–68. Ōkōchi et al., *Rōdō kumiai no kōzō to kinō.*
3. Ishida Hirohide, "Hoshu seitō no bijyon," pp. 88–97.
4. Nippon Kōkan Kawasaki, *Tatakai no ayumi,* p. 79. Nippon Kōkan Tsurumi, *Tsurutetsu rōdō undō shi* (1956), pp. 221, 267.
5. Nippon Kōkan Tsurumi, *Tsurutetsu rōdō undō shi* (1956), pp. 271–272.
6. Interview with Matsuda Takezō, October 23, 1992. Interview with Isobe Toshie, September 11, 1992.
7. Nippon Kōkan Tsurumi, *Tsurutetsu rōdō undō shi* (1956), pp. 273–275. See also Ōkōchi et al., *Rōdō kumiai no kōzō to kinō,* pp. 153–165.
8. Nippon Kōkan Tsurumi, *Tsurutetsu rōdō undō shi* (1956), pp. 275–276.
9. Interview with Isobe Toshie, September 11, 1992.
10. Takanashi, *Nihon tekkō gyō,* p. 338.
11. Nippon Kōkan Tsurumi, *Tsurutetsu rōdō undō shi* (1956) and Nippon Kōkan Kawasaki, *Jū nen no ayumi.*
12. Nippon Kōkan Kyōsantō, *Keihin no kōro kara.*
13. Ōkōchi et al., *Rōdō kumiai no kōzō to kinō;* Takanashi, *Chōsa kenkyū shiryō* and *Nihon tekkō gyō;* Meiji daigaku, *Tekkō sangyō no gōrika to rōdō.*
14. Nippon Kōkan Tsurumi, *Tsurutetsu rōdō undō shi* (1956), pp. 371–374.
15. Takanashi, *Nihon tekkō gyō,* pp. 322–323.
16. Ōkōchi et al., *Rōdō kumiai no kōzō to kinō,* p. 111.
17. Takanashi, *Nihon tekkō gyō,* p. 330.
18. Nippon Kōkan Tsurumi, *Tsurutetsu rōdō undō shi* (1956), pp. 367–368.
19. Takanashi, *Nihon tekkō gyō,* pp. 325–332.
20. Interview with Watanabe Tatsuo, October 25, 1991.
21. Nippon Kōkan Kyōsantō, *Keihin no korō kara,* p. 322.
22. Takanashi, *Chōsa kenkyū shiryō,* pp. 50–51.
23. Ibid., pp. 51–52.
24. Ibid., p. 52.
25. Ibid., pp. 53–54.
26. Ōkōchi et al., *Rōdō kumiai no kōzō to kinō,* pp. 106–107.
27. Interview with Nakamura Kōgō, October 7, 1991. Interview with Nakao Yasuji, October 15, 1991. Takanashi, *Chōsa kenkyū shiryō,* pp. 48–50.

28. Takanashi, *Chōsa kenkyū shiryō*, pp. 49–50.
29. Nippon Kōkan Kyōsantō, *Keihin no kōro kara*, pp. 323–324. Nippon Kōkan Kawasaki, *Jū nen no ayumi*, pp. 195–196.
30. Amadachi, *Nihon no rōdōsha*, pp. 9–10. Interview with Okuda Kenji, February 13, 1992.
31. Nippon Kōkan Kyōsantō, *Keihin no kōro kara*, pp. 324–330. Nippon Kōkan Kawasaki, *Jū nen no ayumi*, p. 197.
32. Nippon Kōkan Tsurumi, *Tsurutetsu rōdō undō shi* (1956), pp. 425–427.
33. Nippon Kōkan Kawasaki, *1957 nendo chintō jiko hihan*, p. 15.
34. Takanashi, *Chōsa kenkyū shiryō*, pp. 49–50.
35. Nippon Kōkan Kyōsantō, *Keihin no kōro kara*, pp. 318–319.
36. Interview with Nakao Yasuji, October 15, 1991.
37. Interview with Morito Akio, September 14, 1992.
38. Interview with Nakao Yasuji, March 5, 1992.
39. Nippon Kōkan Tsurumi, *Tsurutetsu rōdō undō shi* (1956), p. 375.
40. Ibid., pp. 376–377.
41. Nippon Kōkan Tsurumi, "Dai 24 ki undō hōshinsho," p. 31. Hirachi, "1959 sōgi to tekkōgyō 'rōshi kankei' no anteika," pp. 59–60.
42. Dower, "Peace and Democracy in Two Systems," pp. 3–6.
43. Nippon Kōkan Kawasaki, *Tatakai no ayumi*, pp. 189–197, 233–238, 249–251, 393–394.
44. Gotō Tatsuo, "Daily Calendar," 1957–1963.
45. Interview with Gotō Tatsuo, June 24, 1991.
46. Nihon tekkō sangyō rōdō kumiai, *Tekkō rōdō undō shi*, pp. 437–438 and passim. Report on the lower percent of NKK workers supporting a strike on the police law in Gotō, "Daily Calendar," October 1958.
47. Hazama, *Nihon rōmu kanri shi kenkyū*, pp. 295–298, 307–315, 373–379.
48. Nippon Kōkan, ed., *Nippon kōkan 30 nen shi*, pp. 393–394.
49. Nippon Kōkan, ed., *Nippon kōkan 40 nen shi*, pp. 570–571.
50. Shisō no kagaku kenkyū kai, *Kyōdō kenkyū: Shūdan*, pp. 3–4.
51. Kawasaki, ed., *Kawasaki rōdō shi*, pp. 225–228. Ōzawa, "Saakuru no sengo shi," pp. 73–74.
52. Kokumin bunka kaigi, *Nihon bunka no genjō to mondaiten*, pp. 178–183.
53. Ōzawa, "Saakuru no sengo shi," pp. 79–81.
54. Kokumin bunka chōsa kai ed., *Sayoku bunka nempō*, pp. 132–134.
55. Nippon Kōkan Kawasaki, *Jū nen no ayumi*, p. 192.
56. Ibid.
57. "Kumiai undō to utagoe," *Chisei* (October 1956), pp. 23–25.
58. Nippon Kōkan Kawasaki, *Jū nen no ayumi*, p. 192.
59. Tokyo yuibutsuron kenkyū kai, ed., *Sengo shisō no saikentō*, pp. 192–193. Nihon keieisha dantai, *Shokuba no rekurieishyon*, pp. 81, 140–142.

60. Matsuzaki, "Tekkō sōgi," p. 172.

61. Nakamura, "Tekkō rōren tōitsu chingin tōsō," pp. 288–289. Matsuzaki, "Tekkō sōgi," p. 173. Nihon tekkō sangyō rōdō kumiai, *Tekkō rōdō undō shi*, pp. 199–204.

62. Nakamura, "Tekkō rōren tōitsu chingin tōsō," p. 291.

63. Ibid., pp. 291–292.

64. Nippon Kōkan Kawasaki, *Jū nen no ayumi*, pp. 185–190. Nippon Kōkan Tsurumi, *Tsurutetsu rōdō undō shi* (1956), pp. 342–346.

65. Nippon Kōkan Tsurumi, *Tsurutetsu rōdō undō shi* (1956), p. 343.

66. Interview with Kondo Haruhiko, September 3, 1992. Nippon Kōkan Kawasaki, *Jū nen no ayumi*, p. 250. Nippon Kōkan Tsurumi, *Tsurutetsu rōdō undō shi* (1956), pp. 344–352.

67. Nakamura, "Tekkō rōren tōitsu chingin tōsō," pp. 294–297.

68. Nippon Kōkan Kawasaki, *Jū nen no ayumi*, p. 208.

69. Nippon Kōkan Tsurumi, *Tsurutetsu rōdō undō shi* (1956), p. 421.

70. Nippon Kōkan Kawasaki, *Jū nen no ayumi*, p. 210. Nippon Kōkan Tsurumi, *Tsurutetsu rōdō undō shi* (1956), p. 421.

71. Nippon Kōkan Kawasaki, *Jū nen no ayumi*, p. 210.

72. Nippon Kōkan Tsurumi, *Tsurutetsu rōdō undō shi* (1956), pp. 421–425.

73. Nippon Kōkan Kawasaki, *Jū nen no ayumi*, p. 210.

74. See, for example, Takeda, *Ōji seishi sōgi*, pp. 21–23.

6. Breaking the Impasse

1. Interviews with Konda Masaharu, February 18, 1992, Inoue Jutoku, August 28, 1992, and Isobe Toshie, September 11, 1992.

2. Nakamura, "Tekkō rōren tōitsu chingin tōsō," pp. 298–303. Nippon Kōkan Kawasaki, *Tatakai no ayumi*, pp. 158–165. Nippon Kōkan Tsurumi, *Tsurutetsu rōdō undō shi* (1970), pp. 128–131.

3. Nakamura, "Tekkō rōren tōitsu chingin tōsō," p. 302.

4. Nippon Kōkan Kawasaki, *Tatakai no ayumi*, p. 164. Nippon Kōkan Tsurumi, *Tsurutetsu rōdō undō shi* (1970), p. 128.

5. Nihon tekkō sangyō rōdō kumiai, *Tekkō rōdō undō shi*, pp. 376–378. Matsuzaki, "Tekkō sōgi," p. 173.

6. Matsuzaki, "Tekkō sōgi," pp. 167–171.

7. Nippon Kōkan Tsurumi, "1957 nendo chingin taishoku kin tōsō," p. 25.

8. Ibid., p. 28.

9. Matsuzaki, "Tekkō sōgi," pp. 191–192.

10. Interview with Konda Masaharu, February 18, 1992.

11. Matsuzaki, "Tekkō sōgi," p. 192.

12. Nippon Kōkan Kawasaki, "1958 nendo undō jiko hōshin," p. 7; and Nippon Kōkan Tsurumi, "Dai 23 ki undō hōshinsho," p. 32.

13. Hirachi, "1959 sōgi," p. 62. Nippon Kōkan Tsurumi, "Dai 23 ki undō hōshin-sho," p. 3.

14. Nippon Kōkan Tsurumi, "1957 nendo chingin taishoku kin tōsō," pp. 2–20.

15. Ibid., p. 10.

16. Ibid., p. 13. Nippon Kōkan Tsurumi, *Tsurutetsu rōdō undō shi* (1970), pp. 150–151.

17. Nippon Kōkan Tsurumi, "1957 nendo chingin taishoku kin tōsō," pp. 22–51. Nippon Kōkan Tsurumi, *Tsurutetsu rōdō undō shi* (1970), pp. 145–166. Nippon Kōkan Kawasaki, *Tatakai no ayumi*, pp. 166–188. Matsuzaki, "Tekkō sōgi," pp. 171–181.

18. Nippon Kōkan Tsurumi, "1957 nendo chingin taishoku kin tōsō," pp. 32–34.

19. Ibid., pp. 35–38.

20. Interview with Takanashi Akira, March 10, 1992. Nippon Kōkan Kawasaki, "1957 nendo chintō jiko hihan," p. 4.

21. Nippon Kōkan Kawasaki, "1957 nendo chintō jiko hihan," p. 4.

22. Nippon Kōkan Tsurumi, "1957 nendo chingin taishoku kin tōsō," p. 39.

23. Nippon Kōkan Kawasaki, "1957 nendo chintō jiko hihan," p. 8.

24. Ibid., p. 1.

25. Interview with Kamimura Hideji, October 14, 1992, and interview with Isobe Toshie, September 11, 1992. Nippon Kōkan Kawasaki, "1959 undō hōshin," pp. 3–5.

26. Interview with Gotō Tatsuo and Kitazume Shun, June 14, 1991.

27. Interview with Nakamura Kōgō, October 7, 1991.

28. Hirachi, "1959 sōgi," pp. 55–57. Matsuzaki, "Tekkō sōgi," p. 170. Nippon Kōkan Kawasaki, "1959 undō hōshin," pp. 2–14. Nippon Kōkan Kawasaki, *Tatakai no ayumi*, pp. 201–221. Nippon Kōkan Tsurumi, *Tsurutetsu rōdō undō shi* (1970), pp. 166–185.

29. Nippon Kōkan keihin rōdō sōyū kai, *Sōyū*, pp. 18, 20–21. Interview with Maehara Hideki, August 28, 1992.

30. Nippon Kōkan keihin rōdō sōyū kai, *Sōyū*, p. 20. Interviews with Isobe Toshie, September 11, 1992, Gotō Tatsuo, June 14, 1991, Miyata Yoshiji, June 1, 1992, Maehara Hideki and Inoue Jutoku, August 28, 1992.

31. Hoerr, *And the Wolf Finally Came*, pp. 101–104.

32. Interview with Nakao Yasuji, October 15, 1991.

33. Interviews with Gotō Tatsuo, June 24, 1991, and Oogi Shinichi, October 27, 1991.

34. Nihon tekkō sangyō rōdō kumiai, *Tekkō rōdō undō shi*, p. 422. Matsuzaki, "Tekkō sōgi," pp. 202–203. Interview with Nakao Yasuji, October 15, 1991.

35. Interview with Konda Masaharu, February 18, 1992.

36. Interviews with Isobe Toshie, September 11, 1992, and Kamimura Hideji, October 14, 1992.

37. Interview with Nakao Yasuji, October 15, 1991.

38. Interview with Isobe Toshie, September 11, 1992. Nippon Kōkan Tsurumi, *Tsurutetsu rōdō undō shi* (1970), pp. 175, 180–183. Nippon Kōkan Kawasaki, *Tatakai no ayumi*, pp. 210–216.
39. Interview with Kitazume Shun and Gōtō Tatsuo, June 14, 1991. Nippon Kōkan Kawasaki, "1959 undō hōshin," pp. 11–12.
40. Interview with Kudō Shinpachi, April 12, 1992.
41. Fujita, *Dai ni kumiai.*
42. Interviews with Kudō Shinpachi, April 12, 1992, Kitazume Shun and Gōtō Tatsuo, June 14, 1991, Inoue Jutoku, August 28, 1992, Kamimura Hideji, October 14, 1992, Kondo Haruhiko, September 3, 1992, and Watanabe Tatsuo, October 25, 1991.
43. Hirachi, "1959 sōgi," p. 62.
44. Ibid., p. 62.
45. Interview with Kondo Haruhiko, September 3, 1992.
46. Interview with Isobe Toshie, September 11, 1992.
47. Interviews with Watanabe Tatsuo, October 25, 1991, Konda Masaharu, February 18, 1992, and Kondo Haruhiko, September 3, 1992.
48. Nippon Kōkan Tsurumi, "Dai 24 ki undō hōshinsho," p. 31.
49. Hirachi, "1959 sōgi," pp. 62–64.
50. Interview with Kitazume Shun, June 14, 1991.
51. Nippon Kōkan Kawasaki, "1959 undō hōshin," pp. 21, 23.
52. Interviews with Kitazume Shun and Gotō Tatsuo, June 14, 1991, and Nakao Yasuji, March 5, 1992. Kitazume of the Acorn Club (5,499 votes) was one of the victorious vice-chairmen. Nippon Kōkan Kawasaki, *Tatakai no ayumi*, Appendix, pp. 106–107.
53. Nippon Kōkan Tsurumi, "Dai 23 ki undō hōshinsho," p. 34.
54. "Tekkō Suto: kōzai shikyō ni hibikazu: nagabikeba shikinkuri konnan ni," *Asahi shimbun*, November 1, 1957, p. 4.
55. Nippon Kōkan Kawasaki, "1957 nendo chintō jiko hihan," pp. 2–3, 12.
56. Interview with Inoue Jutoku, August 28, 1992.
57. Interviews with Takanashi Akira, March 10, 1992, Oogi Shinichi, October 27, 1991, and Kondo Haruhiko, September 3, 1992.
58. Interview with Okuda Kenji, January 11, 1991.
59. Interview with Takemura Tatsuo, June 10, 1992.
60. Interviews with Inoue Jutoku, August 28, 1992, Oogi Shinichi, October 27, 1991, and Okuda Kenji, November 22, 1992.
61. Interviews with Takemura Tatsuo, June 10, 1992, Inoue Jutoku, August 28, 1992, and Okuda Kenji, November 22, 1992.
62. Interviews with Konda Masaharu, February 18, 1992, and Takanashi Akira, March 10, 1992.
63. Interview with Inoue Jutoku, August 28, 1992.
64. Ibid.
65. Ibid.

66. Interview with Takemura Tatsuo, June 10, 1992.
67. Interview with Inoue Jutoku, August 28, 1992. The group was called the *Ittessukai*.
68. Interviews with Oogi Shinichi, October 27, 1991, and Konda Masaharu, February 18, 1992.
69. Occasional reports on these activities in Nihon tekkō renmei kai, *Tekkō kai*.
70. Interviews with Takemura Tatsuo, June 10, 1992, and Okuda Kenji, November 27, 1992.
71. Matsuzaki, "Tekkō sōgi," p. 191.
72. "Tsūsanshō ni seisaku kondankai," *Asahi shimbun*, October 15, 1957. "Yon bu mon ni jūten o: rainendo no zaisei tōyūshi," *Asahi shimbun*, November 9, 1957, p. 4. Nippon Kōkan Kawasaki, "1957 nendo chintō jiko hihan," p. 8.
73. Konda, "Tekkō no chin'age kaitō," p. 39.
74. Interview with Konda Masaharu, February 18, 1992.
75. Nippon Kōkan Tsurumi, "Dai 23 ki undō hōshinsho," p. 9. Emphasis added.
76. Interview with Miyata Yoshiji, June 1, 1992. Onomichi, *Kore ga rengō da*, p. 39.
77. Hirachi, "1959 sōgi," p. 58.
78. Ōkōchi et al., *Rōdō kumiai no kōzō to kinō*, pp. 166–172.
79. Ibid., pp. 232–233.
80. Hirachi, "1959 sōgi," p. 60.
81. Ōkōchi et al., *Rōdō kumiai no kōzō to kinō*, pp. 145–147. Hirachi, "1959 sōgi," p. 54.
82. Interview with Kudō Shinpachi, April 12, 1992.
83. Ōkōchi et al., *Rōdō kumiai no kōzō to kinō*, pp. 114–122.
84. Ibid., pp. 122–126, 165–180, 231–238. Hirachi, "1959 sōgi," p. 59.
85. Odaka, *Sangyō no shakai gaku*, pp. 534–535.
86. Interview with Nakao Yasuji, October 15, 1991.
87. Ibid.
88. Ōkōchi et al., *Rōdō kumiai no kōzō to kinō*, p. 146.
89. Interview with Gotō Tatsuo, July 4, 1991.
90. Interview with Watanabe Tatsuo, October 25, 1991.
91. Ōkōchi et al., *Rōdō kumiai no kōzō to kinō*, pp. 146–147.
92. Nippon Kōkan keihin rōdō sōyū kai, *Sōyū*, p. 8. Interviews with Kudō Shinpachi, April 12, 1992, and Watanabe Tatsuo, May 10, 1992.
93. Ōkōchi et al., *Rōdō kumiai no kōzō to kinō*, p. 145.
94. Michimata, "Tekkō rōdō undō." Takahashi Yūkichi, "Rōdō kumiai undō no gan," p. 165. Kinoshita Takeo, "Sangyō betsu zenkoku soshiki," pp. 11–25.
95. Aoki, *Nihon teki keiei no genba*, p. 226.
96. Ibid., pp. 233–236.
97. Interview with Kihara Toshiaki, November 23, 1992. Nihon Kōkan Kawasaki, *Tatakai no ayumi*, chronology (nempyō), p. 18.
98. Results can be found in relevant issues of *Kawatetsu Shimbun*.

99. Interviews with Kudō Shinpachi, April 12, 1992, and Nakao Yasuji, October 15, 1991.

100. Interview with Watanabe Tatsuo, October 25, 1991.

101. Hirachi, "1959 sōgi," p. 68, n. 52. Ōkōchi et al., *Rōdō kumiai no kōzō to kinō*, pp. 145–146.

102. Interviews with Isobe Toshie, September 11, 1992, Gotō Tatsuo, June 24, 1991, and Matsuda Takezō, October 23, 1992.

103. Nimura, "Nikkan rōshi kankei," pp. 2–9.

104. Hiwatari, "Japanese Corporate Governance Reexamined."

105. Interview with Inoue Jutoku, August 28, 1992.

106. Nippon Kōkan Kawasaki, "1959 undō hōshin," pp. 10–14. Nipon Kōkan Tsurumi, "Dai 24 ki undō hōshinsho," pp. 35–44.

107. Nippon Kōkan Kawasaki, "1959 undō hōshin," p. 12.

108. Ibid.

109. Ibid., p. 13.

7. Fabricating the Politics of Cooperation

1. Gramsci, *Prison Notebooks*, vols. 1 and 2. Williams, *Marxism and Literature*, pp. 108–114. Comaroff and Comaroff, *Of Revelation and Revolution*, pp. 13–32.

2. Comaroff and Comaroff, *Of Revelation and Revolution*, p. 25.

3. Kawabe, "Tekkō sangyō to tekkō rōren no ichi," pp. 20–27.

4. Yamamoto, "'Infuomaru soshiki' ni kansuru hito kōsatsu (1, 2)," p. 252. Miyata, *Kumiai zakku baran*, pp. 154–157.

5. Nippon Kōkan, "Kantoku nyūmon kōza: rōshi kankei," pp. 1–2.

6. Onomichi, *Kore ga rengō da*, pp. 37–39. Emphasis added.

7. Nippon kōkan keihin rōdō sōyūkai, *Sōyū*, inside front cover.

8. Interviews with Isobe Toshie, September 11, 1992, and Kondo Haruhiko, September 3, 1992. Nippon kōkan keihin rōdō sōyūkai, *Sōyū*, pp. 28–29.

9. *New York Times*, December 2, 1962. Mita, "JC tanjō hiwa," pp. 104–105. Reischauer, *My Life between Japan and America*, pp. 174, 234.

10. Mita, "JC tanjō no hiwa." Williamson, *Coping with the Miracle*, pp. 47–53.

11. Miwa, "JC tanjō no hiwa," pp. 100, 104–105.

12. Hyōdō, "Rōdō kumiai undō no hatten," pp. 131–132.

13. Onomichi, *Kore ga rengō da*, pp. 46–53. Miyata, *Kumiai zakku baran*, Ch. 7. Rekishigaku kenkyūkai, ed., *Nihon dōjidai shi*, pp. 22–24.

14. Ononmichi, *Kore ga rengō da*, pp. 54–67. Kinoshita Takeo, "Sangyō betsu zenkoku soshiki no bunretsu," pp. 24–40.

15. Koshirō, *Sengo 50 nen*, pp. 99.

16. Ibid., p. 100.

17. Yamamoto, "Daikigyō no rōshi kankei," and "'Infuomaru soshiki' ni kansuru hito kōsatsu (1, 2)." Yoshimura, *Jiritsu suru rōdō undō*, p. 128.

18. Gibbs, "The Labor Movement at the Yahata Steel Works," Ch. 9.

19. Nippon Kōkan keihin rōdō sōyūkai, *Sōyū,* p. 27.

20. Nippon Kōkan Mizue, *Jū nen no ayumi,* p. 312. Nippon Kōkan keihin rōdō sōyūkai, *Sōyū,* p. 25.

21. Interview with Kondo Haruhiko, September 3, 1992.

22. Interview with Watanabe Tatsuo, May 10, 1992.

23. Interviews with Ogura Shigemasa, May 13, 1992, and Konda Masaharu, February 18, 1992.

24. Interview with Konda Masaharu, February 18, 1992.

25. Hirano, "Rōdō kumiai no yakuin senkyo seido," pp. 41–45. Yoshizaki, "Ishi ga nagarete ki no ha," p. 23.

26. Takahashi, "Rōdō kumiai undō no gan," pp. 164–165. Rōdō mondai kenkyūkai, "Tekkō rōdōsha," Part 3, p. 113, and Part 6, pp. 83–84, 113. Interview with Nakao Yasuji, October 15, 1991.

27. Ishinomori, *Japan Inc.,* pp. 37–48. Watanabe, *Labor Relations.*

28. Michimata, "Tekkō rōdō undō," pp. 92–95, and *Gendai Nihon no tekkō rōdō mondai,* p. 46. Kawabe, "Tekkō sangyō," p. 31. Hirano, "Kyōchōteki rōshi kankei," pp. 84–89. Nippon Kōkan keihin rōdō sōyūkai, *Sōyū,* p. 82. Yamamoto, "'Infuomaru soshiki' ni kansuru hito kōsatsu (1)," p. 128.

29. Nippon Kōkan Mizue, *Jū nen no ayumi,* pp. 137–146. Nihon tekkō sangyō rōdō kumiai, *Tekkō rōdō undō shi,* pp. 541–549, 577–586.

30. Ishida, "Tekkō ōte go sha," pp. 66–67.

31. Konda, "Tekkō no chin'age kaitō," p. 46.

32. Ishida, "Tekkō ōte go sha," pp. 70–71.

33. Matsuzaki, *Nihon tekkō sangyō bunseki,* pp. 254–257, 262.

34. Ishida, "Tekkō ōte go sha," pp. 70–71.

35. Matsuzaki, *Nihon tekkō sangyō bunseki,* pp. 264–265.

36. Ishida, "Tekkō ōte go sha," pp. 71–73.

37. Rōdō mondai kenkyūkai, "Tekkō rōdōsha," Part 6. Tsubouchi X in *Donguri* (June 1965).

38. Higuchi, "Nippon kōkan keihin seitetsujo rōdō kumiai," p. 213.

39. Konda, "Tekkō no chin'age kaitō," p. 75. Ishida, "Tekkō ōte go sha," p. 45.

40. Nippon Kōkan Kawasaki, *Tatakai no ayumi,* p. 355.

41. Kawasaki, *Kawasaki rōdō shi,* pp. 776–778.

42. Nitta, *Nihon no rōdōsha sanka,* Chs. 2–4.

43. Nihon tekkō sangyō rōdō kumiai, *Tekkō sangyō no rōshi kankei,* pp. 34–37.

44. Interviews with Isobe Toshie, September 11, 1992, and Gōtō Tasuo and Kitazume Shun, June 24, 1991.

45. Interview with Nakao Yasuji, October 15, 1991.

46. Interview with Imaizumi Masumasa, November 15, 1991.

47. Matsuzaki, *Nihon tekkō sangyō bunseki,* pp. 184–185. Orii, *Rōmu kanri nijū nen,* p. 149.

48. Matsuzaki, *Nihon tekkō sangyō bunseki,* pp. 190–200.

49. Orii, *Rōmu kanri nijū nen*, p. 144.
50. Nippon Kōkan keihin, "Rōmu shiryō, No. 17."
51. In the three-shift, three-crew system, if each crew had seven workers, the total staff for that site was twenty-one. Simply adding a fourth crew raises the total 33 percent, to twenty-eight. But in the three-crew system, the seventh man allowed what was actually a six-person work team to rest a member each day. The seventh worker was not needed in a four-crew system, so total staffing would be twenty-four, an increase of 14 percent.
52. Matsuzaki, *Nihon tekkō sangyō bunseki*, 200–201.
53. Ibid., pp. 200–232.
54. Ibid., p. 217–221. Rōdōsha repootaaju, *Repootaaju: shokuba*, p. 20.
55. Orii, *Rōmu kanri nijū nen*, p. 150.
56. Matsuzaki, *Nihon tekkō sangyō bunseki*, p. 229. Rōdōsha, *Repootaaju: shokuba*, p. 24. Putnam, "Bowling Alone," pp. 65–78.
57. Nippon Kōkan Kawasaki, *Tatakai no ayumi*, p. 353.
58. Matsuzaki, *Nihon tekkō sangyō bunseki*, pp. 230–233.
59. Kawasaki, *Kawasaki rōdō shi*, p. 832.
60. Orii, *Rōmu kanri nijū nen*, pp. 130–131. Nippon Kōkan Mizue, *Jū nen no ayumi*, p. 255.
61. "Shokuba katsudō," p. 39. "Shihonka no shisō kōgeki," p. 50. Rōdō mondai kenkyūkai, "Tekkō rōdōsha," Part 2, pp. 62–64. Saitō, *Wa ga naki ato ni*, pp. 214–219.
62. Kawasaki, *Kawasaki rōdō shi*, p. 663.
63. Ishida, "Tekkō ōte go sha," pp. 63–65.
64. Matsuzaki, *Nihon tekkō sangyō bunseki*, pp. 114, 133, 147.
65. Nippon Kōkan Kawasaki, *Tatakai no ayumi*, p. 353.
66. Ibid.
67. Matsuzaki, *Nihon tekkō sangyō bunseki*, pp. 163–176.
68. Ibid., pp. 171, 174–175.
69. Interview with Gotō Tatsuo, July 4, 1991. Nippon Kōkan keihin rōdō sōyūkai, *Sōyū*, pp. 40–41.
70. Interviews with Konda Masaharu, February 18, 1992, and Nakao Yasuji, March 5, 1992.
71. Higuchi, "Nippon kōkan keihin seitetsujo," pp. 218–227.
72. Nippon Kōkan keihin rōdō sōyūkai, *Sōyū*, pp. 40–41.
73. Saitō, *Wa ga naki ato ni*, pp. 193–195.
74. Nitta, "Tekkō gyō," pp. 212–225.
75. Hasegawa, *The Steel Industry in Japan*, p. 90.
76. Foote, "Judicial Creation of Norms," pp. 667–670.
77. Nippon Kōkan keihin rōdō sōyūkai, *Sōyū*, p. 41.
78. Interview with Konda Masaharu, February 18, 1992.
79. Interview with Okuda Kenji, November 27, 1992.

80. Rōdō mondai kenkyūkai, "Tekkō rōdōsha," Part 6, p. 81.
81. Nihon tekkō sangyō rōdō kumiai, *Tekkō sangyō no rōshi kankei*, pp. 510, 530.
82. Ibid., p. 517.
83. Higuchi, "Nippon kōkan keihin seitetsujo," pp. 228–230.
84. Hoerr, *And the Wolf Finally Came*, pp. 326–327 and passim.
85. I borrow this phrase from Field, *In the Realm of a Dying Emperor*, p. 29.

8. Mobilizing Total Commitment

1. Takanashi, "Gijutsu kakushin to atarashii rōdō mondai," pp. 6–8.
2. Michimata, *Gendai Nihon no tekkō rōdō mondai*, pp. 95–137, esp. pp. 109–111. Yoneyama, *Gijutsu kakushin to shokuba kanri*, pp. 158–161. For a description of an identical change in Germany at the same time, see Lauschke, "Mobilität und Aufstieg in der Eisen- und Stahlindustrie," pp. 186–212.
3. Sasaki, *Sengo shi daijiten*, entry on *shingakuritsu*, p. 460. High school attendance rates in Kawasaki reached 95 percent in 1970. Kawasaki, *Kawasaki rōdō shi*, p. 619.
4. Rōdō mondai kenkyūkai, "Tekkō rōdōsha," Part 3, p. 112.
5. Orii, *Rōmu kanri nijū nen*, p. 98.
6. Takanashi, "Gijutsu kakushin to atarashii rōdō mondai," p. 13.
7. Meiji daigaku, *Tekkō sangyō no gōrika to rōdō*, pp. 58–60. Michimata, *Gendai Nihon no tekkō rōdō mondai*, p. 114. Yoneyama, *Gijutsu kakushin to shokuba kanri*, pp. 323–324.
8. Takanashi, "Gijutsu kakushin to atarashii rōdō mondai," p. 14.
9. Ibid., p. 15.
10. Interview with Konda Masaharu, February 18, 1992.
11. Konda, "Sagyōchō o chūshin to shita genba kanri," p. 5.
12. Orii, *Rōmu kanri nijū nen*, pp. 35–39.
13. Konda, "Sagyōchō o chūshin to shita genba kanri," pp. 7–8. Saitō, *Wa ga naki ato ni*, pp. 162–165. Orii, *Rōmu kanri nijū nen*, pp. 36–39.
14. Koike, *Shokuba no rōdō kumiai to sanka*, pp. 237–240, and *The Economics of Work in Japan*, pp. 54–61, 126–128.
15. Ōkōchi et al., *Rōdō kumiai no kōzō to kinō*, pp. 114–122.
16. Michimata, *Gendai Nihon no tekkō rōdō mondai*, p. 126. For Yahata, see Meiji daigaku, *Tekkō sangyō no gōrika to rōdō*, p. 60.
17. For NKK, see Takanashi, *Nihon tekkō gyō no rōshi kankei*, pp. 222–224. For Muroran, see Michimata, *Gendai Nihon no tekkō rōdō mondai*, pp. 96–137. For Yahata, see Meiji daigaku, *Tekkō sangyō no gōrika to rōdō*, pp. 58–61. Nihon tekkō sangyō rōdō kumiai, *Ōte seitetsujo no rōdōsha to rōdō kumiai*, pp. 1–18.
18. Orii, *Rōmu kanri nijū nen*, p. 87.

19. Nihon keiseisha dantai renmei, *Nōryoku shugi ni kansuru kigyō no jittai chōsa*, p. 5.
20. Orii, *Rōmu kanri nijū nen*, p. 40. In Japanese, *aozora no mieru rōmu kanri*.
21. Nippon Kōkan Kawasaki, *Tatakai no ayumi*, pp. 336–337. Nippon Kōkan Mizue, *Jū nen no ayumi*, pp. 248–250.
22. Interview with Kudō Shinpachi, April 12, 1992.
23. Nippon Kōkan Mizue, *Jū nen no ayumi*, p. 313. Orii, *Rōmu kanri nijū nen*, p. 47.
24. Kumazawa, *Portraits of the Japanese Workplace*, p. 35.
25. Gordon, *The Evolution of Labor Relations in Japan*, pp. 257–298, 374–386.
26. Kurahashi, "Sengo tekkō rōmu kanri shoshi," pp. 114–115.
27. Orii, *Rōmu kanri nijū nen*, p. 49–56.
28. Ibid., pp. 53–56.
29. The Japanese words here are *nōryoku* and *nōryokushugi*, which can be translated as "merit" and "meritocracy" or "ability" and "ability-ism." Because *nōryoku* refers to a diffuse set of abilities, including attributes such as attitude and effort as well as particular skills and achievements, I prefer to translate it as "merit."
30. Nihon keieisha dantai renmei, *Nōryoku shugi ni kansuru kigyō no jittai chōsa*," p. i.
31. Orii, *Rōmu kanri nijū nen*, pp. 66–67.
32. On Muroran, see Michimata, *Gendai Nihon no tekkō rōdō mondai*, pp. 151–158. On Fuji, Yahata, and NKK, see Kurahashi, "Sengo tekkō rōmu kanri shoshi," pp. 114–115.
33. Nihon keieisha dantai renmei, *Nōryoku shugi ni kansuru kigyō no jittai chōsa*," prologue (unpaginated).
34. Ibid., pp. 2, 14–15.
35. Orii, *Rōmu kanri nijū nen*, pp. 53–54.
36. Ibid., p. 62. Nippon kōkan, *Nippon kōkan 70 nen shi*, pp. 223–224.
37. Kurahashi, "Sengo tekkō rōmu kanri shoshi," pp. 114–115. Ishida Mitsuo, "Chingin taikei to rōshi kankei," pp. 40–41.
38. Nippon Kōkan rōdō kumiai kyōgikai, "Gyōmukyū ni tai suru dai ichi dankai no taisho."
39. Orii, *Rōmu kanri nijū nen*, p. 91.
40. Nihon tekkō sangyō rōdō kumiai, *Tekkō sangyō no rōshi kankei to rōdō kumiai*, pp. 507–508.
41. Ishida Mitsuo, *Chingin no shakaigaku*, pp. 62–63.
42. Ibid., p. 46.
43. Ibid., pp. 46–47.
44. Ibid., p. 49.
45. Ibid., p. 50.

46. Lillrank and Kano, *Continuous Improvement,* p. 1. On the zero-defect (ZD) movement, see Nihon nōritsu kyōkai, *1968 ZD hakusho,* p. 9.

47. Lillrank and Kano, *Continuous Improvement,* p. 211.

48. Saitō, *Wa ga naki ato ni,* p. 171. Kurahashi, "Sengo tekkō rōmu kanri shoshi," p. 118.

49. Nakamura Keisuke, *Nihon no shokuba to seisan shisutemu,* pp. 165–173.

50. Horiyone, "Keihin seitetsujo ni okeru shoshūdan katsudō," pp. 1–3. "Dōgyō-sha kan no QC saakuru kōryū: Nippon Kōkan to Kawasaki seitetsu," *Genba to QC,* no. 51 (January 1968), p. 62.

51. Horiyone, "Keihin seitetsujo ni okeru shoshūdan katsudō," p. 3.

52. Mori, "Kensaku toishi shiyō no teigen ni tsuite," p. 38.

53. Furukawa, "Shin'nin kantokusha ga QC saakuru de eta kyūkun," pp. 44–49.

54. Cole, *Strategies for Learning,* p. 290.

55. On New Japan Steel, see Nitta, "Tekkō gyō no 'jishu kanri katsudō,'" pp. 19, 31–32. On NKK, see Ōba, *TQC to no tatakai,* p. 19.

56. On 1976, see Horiyone, "Keihin seitetsujo ni okeru shoshūdan katsudō," p. 10; for 1982, Ōba, *TQC to no tatakai,* p. 11.

57. Michimata, *Gendai Nihon no tekkō rōdō mondai,* pp. 177–178.

58. Nitta, "Tekkō gyō no 'jishu kanri katsudō,'" pp. 26–28.

59. Kurahashi, "Sengo tekkō rōmu kanri shoshi," p. 119. Nihon seisansei honbu, *Senshinkoku byō to rōdō rinri no henyō,* p. 123.

60. Kumazawa, *Portraits of the Japanese Workplace,* Ch. 5.

61. Nitta, "Tekkō gyō no 'jishu kanri katsudō,'" p. 24.

62. Michimata, *Gendai Nihon no tekkō rōdō mondai,* p. 178.

63. Nihon nōritsu kyōkai, *1968 ZD hakusho,* pp. 31–33.

64. Horiyone, "Keihin seitetsujo ni okeru shoshūdan katsudō," pp. 7, 21.

65. Kurahashi, "Sengo tekkō rōmu kanri shoshi," pp. 118–119. Saitō, *Wa ga naki ato ni,* pp. 174–180.

66. On German unions and QC, Mueller-Jentsch and Sperling, "Towards a Flexible Triple System?" pp. 19–23.

9. Managing Society for Business

1. Mueller-Jentsch, "Labor Conflicts and Class Struggles," pp. 240–243.

2. Milkman, *Farewell to the Factory,* pp. 63–79.

3. Orii, *Rōmu kanri nijū nen,* pp. 103–104.

4. Ibid., pp. 97–99.

5. Watanabe Osamu, *Gendai Nihon no shihai kōzō,* p. 319.

6. Ōsawa, "Bye-bye Corporate Warriors," p. 9, cites the 1991 report of the Keizai kikaku chō, *Kojin seikatsu yūsen shakai o mezashite,* p. 45.

7. Watanabe Osamu, *Gendai Nihon no shihai kōzō,* pp. 321–322.

8. Orii, *Rōmu kanri nijū nen,* pp. 106–107.
9. Rōdō mondai kenkyū kai, "Tekkō rōdōsha," Part 3, p. 114.
10. Ōsawa, *Kigyō chūshin shakai o koete.*
11. Watanabe Osamu, *Gendai Nihon no shihai kōzō,* p. 320.
12. Ōsawa, *Kigyō chōshin shakai o koete,* pp. 185–200.
13. Kumazawa, *Portraits of the Japanese Workplace,* p. 160.
14. Upham, *Law and Social Change in Postwar Japan,* p. 132.
15. Kumazawa, *Portraits of the Japanese Workplace,* p. 160. "'Hataraku shufu' hansū o kosu," *Asahi shinbun,* July 11, 1983, p. 1.
16. Brinton, *Women and the Economic Miracle,* pp. 169–170.
17. Ibid., p. 29 for 1990 data.
18. Upham, *Law and Social Change in Postwar Japan,* pp. 135–136.
19. Brinton, *Women and the Economic Miracle,* p. 170.
20. Kumazawa, *Portraits of the Japanese Workplace,* pp. 169–196. Upham, "Unplaced Persons and Movements for Place," pp. 332–337. Ōsawa, *Kigyō chūshin shakai o koete,* pp. 151–157.
21. Matsumura, *Senjutsu tenkan suru minsei to kigyō no taisaku,* pp. 20–26.
22. Kokumin bunka kyōkai, *Nihon bunka no genjō to mondaiten,* pp. 190–192.
23. Tokyo yuibutsuron kenkyū kai, *Sengo shisō no saikentō,* pp. 180, 192, 195–196.
24. Nihon keieisha dantai renmei, *Shokuba no rekurieshion* and *Shokuba ni okeru sayoku seiryoku no jittai to sono taisaku.*
25. Nihon keieisha dantai renmei, *Shokuba no rekurieshion,* pp. 7, 12–13, 34–36, 193–194, and passim.
26. Ibid., p. 81. Kawasaki, *Kawakaki rōdo shi,* pp. 885–886.
27. Saitō, *Wa ga naki ato ni,* pp. 223–224. Rōdōsha chōsa kenkyū kai, "Infuomaru soshiki no jittai to mujun no kakudai," pp. 204–206.
28. Rōdōsha repootaaju guruupu, *Repootaaju: shokuba (1971),* p. 32. Nihon tekkō sangyō rōdō kumiai, *Tekkō sangyō no rōshi kankei to rōdō kumiai,* p. 480. Hyōdō, "Sengo Nihon no rōshi kankei," pp. 102–103.
29. Takahashi X, untitled column, *Donguri.*
30. Tokyo yuibutsuron kenkyū kai, *Sengo shisō no saikentō,* p. 199.
31. Ibid., p. 202.
32. "Seinen jūgyōin no seikatsu shidō ni tsuite," *Shin seikatsu.*
33. Kawasaki, *Kawasaki rōdō shi,* pp. 794–797.
34. Rōdōsha repōtaaju shūdan, *Repōtaju: shokuba,* pp. 33–36.
35. Kumazawa, *Portraits of the Japanese Workplace,* p. 249.
36. Kawasaki, *Kawasaki rōdō shi,* p. 833.
37. Kumazawa, *Portraits of the Japanese Workplace,* p. 251.
38. Morioka, "Zangyō oyobi saabisu zangyō no jittai," pp. 14–15. Fukushima, "Nihon no rōdō jikan no suikei," pp. 1–9.

39. Tackney, "Institutionalization of the Lifetime Employment System." Foote, "Judicial Creation of Norms in Japanese Labor Law," pp. 635–709. Tanabe, *Rōdō funsō to saiban.*

40. Tackney, "Institutionalization of the Lifetime Employment System," p. 425.

41. Ibid., pp. 418–420.

42. Foote, "Judicial Creation of Norms in Japanese Labor Law," p. 644.

43. See Sugeno, *Japanese Labor Law,* p. 408 for this quote and pp. 395–410 for a full account.

44. Foote, "Judicial Creation of Norms in Japanese Labor Law," p. 683 n. 192. Nevins, *Labor Pains and the Gaijin Boss.*

45. Tackney, "The Institutionalization of the Lifetime Employment System," p. 424 cites Tanabe, *Rōdō funsō to saiban,* p. 311.

46. Foote, "Judicial Creation of Norms in Japanese Labor Law," pp. 665–670.

47. Michimata, "Tekkō rōdō undō ni okeru uhateki chōryū," pp. 112–113. Nippon Kōkan Kawasaki, *Tatakai no ayumi,* pp. 367–373.

48. Michimata, "Tekkō rōdō undō ni okeru uhateki chōryū," pp. 112–113.

49. George, "Minamata: Power, Policy and Citizenship in Postwar Japan."

50. Yamamoto, "'Infuomaru soshiki' ni kansuru hito kōsatsu," Part 1, pp. 210–211 and Part 2, p. 128.

51. This extraordinary story is told in great detail by Watanabe Tatsuo in a 150-page handwritten "secret history" of KSK and his mission there, "Kōkan shōji no kaisha kaisan ni itaru made no keii."

52. Higuchi, "Nihon Kōkan keihin seitetsujo rōdō kumiai," p. 243. Hirano, "Kyōchōteki rōshi kankei no keisei," p. 108.

53. Gordon, "Contests for the Workplace," pp. 388–389.

54. Kumazawa, "Suto-ken suto," pp. 491–503.

55. Boyer and Durand, *L'apres fordism.* Maruyama, "Nihongata kigyō shakai to Nihon teki seisan shisutemu," pp. 122–129.

56. Yamamoto, "Sasebo jūkō rōdō sōgi (1979–80)."

57. National Defense Counsel for Victims of Karoshi 1990, *Karoshi.*

58. Kawabe, "Tekkō sangyō," pp. 36–40.

59. Ibid., pp. 40–42.

60. Kobayashi, "Tekkō gyō no risutorakucharingu to koyō chōsei," pp. 13–31.

61. Turner, *Japanese Workers in Protest,* p. 13. Inoue, *Nihon no rōdōsha jishu kanri.* On a case at a Tōshiba subsidiary, see Yamane, *Jishu seisan rōsō.*

62. Nakagawa, "Rōshi funsō shori, shin rūru tsukure," p. 2.

63. Kawasaki, *Kawasaki rōdō shi,* p. 977.

64. Ibid., p. 937.

65. Ozawa, "Saakuru no sengo shi," p. 89.

66. Nippon Kōkan, undated English-language publicity brochure, circa early 1990s, presents this as the "motto" of the facility.

67. Kumazawa, *Portraits of the Japanese Workplace*, pp. 164, 168. Sekitani, "Byōin sōgi," pp. 585–634.
68. Pharr, *Losing Face*, pp. 59–73, 189–194.
69. Kumazawa, *Portraits of the Japanese Workplace*, pp. 164, 168. Upham, *Law and Social Change in Postwar Japan*, pp. 129–144.
70. Kumazawa, *Portraits of the Japanese Workplace*, pp. 190–191.
71. Ibid., pp. 197–198.
72. "Shōkaku danjo sabetsu 'yurusarenu,'" *Asahi shinbun* (International Satellite ed.), November 28, 1996, p. 22.
73. Gotō Michio, "Zadankai: Nihon no kigyō to rōdō o tou," p. 19.
74. Watanabe, "*Yutaka na shakai*", pp. 16, 286.
75. Berger and Dore, *National Diversity and Global Capitalism*, pp. 12–25. Kahler, "Trade and Domestic Differences," p. 313. Watanabe, "Gendai Nihon shakai no ken'iteki kōzō to kokka," p. 222.
76. Morita, "Nihon gata keiei ga abunai," pp. 94–103.
77. See Kahler, "Trade and Domestic Differences," p. 313.

10. Japan's Third Way

1. *Kawatetsu shinbun*, January 1, 1955, p. 1, July 18, 1955, pp. 3–4 for graphs. Nippon Kōkan Tsurumi, *Dai 23 ki undō hōshinsho*, p. 28.
2. Cited in Montgomery, *Workers' Control in America*, p. 9.
3. Woodiwiss, *Law, Labour, and Society in Japan*.
4. Kettler and Tackney, "Light from a Dead Sun."
5. Veblen, "The Opportunity of Japan," p. 252. Gerschenkron, *Economic Backwardness in Historical Perspective*.
6. Dore, *British Factory–Japanese Factory*.
7. Dower, "Peace and Democracy."
8. Shimizu, "Sengo rōdō kumiai undō shi yosetsu," p. 10.
9. Kumazawa, *Portraits of the Japanese Workplace*, pp. 78–79, 81. Hyōdō, *Gendai no rōdō undō*, p. v. Watanabe, "*Yutaka na shakai*."
10. Koike, *The Economics of Work in Japan*, pp. 257–258, and *Rōdō kumiai to sanka*.
11. Nitta, *Nihon no rōdōsha sanka*, pp. 281–282.
12. Ishida Mitsuo, *Chingin no shakaigaku*, pp. 1, 65.
13. Ibid., p. 1.
14. Itami, "The Humanistic Corporation—An Exportable Concept?" p. 57.
15. Karatsu, "Japanese Know-how for American Industry," p. 64.
16. Morita, "A Critical Moment for Japanese Management," pp. 12–13.
17. Totsuka and Tokunaga, *Gendai Nihon no rōdō mondai*, pp. 2–3.
18. Ōsawa, *Kigyō chūshin shakai o koete*, pp. 19, 33, 232.
19. Kumazawa, *Nihon-teki keiei no meian*.

20. Kumazawa, *Portraits of the Japanese Workplace*, pp. 58, 81.
21. Totsuka and Hyōdō, *Rōshi kankei no tenkan to sentaku*, pp. 8–9.
22. Totsuka and Tokunaga, *Gendai Nihon no rōdō mondai*, pp. 4–5.
23. New York Times, *The Downsizing of America*.
24. Mueller-Jentsch and Sperling, "Towards a Flexible Triple System?" pp. 19, 23.
25. Vitols, "Restructuring in the German Steel Industry," p. 20.
26. Ishida Mitsuo, *Chingin no shakaigaku*, pp. 229–231.
27. Lincoln, "Japan Hasn't Really Failed."
28. Tsuda, "Nihon teki rōdō kankō to 76 nen shuntō," pp. 16–21.
29. "To Encourage the Others," *Economist*, January 16, 1993, p. 66.
30. Peter G. Gosselin, "Japanese Economy Has Lost Its Luster," *Boston Globe*, February 4, 1997, pp. A1, A7.
31. Doi, "Labor: Lifetime Employment is Out," p. 5.
32. Hyōdō, *Rōdō no sengo shi*, pp. 452–473.
33. "Tomorrow's Japan," *Economist*, July 13, 1996, p. 4.
34. Doi, "Labor: Lifetime Employment is Out," p. 5.
35. "Tomorrow's Japan," *Economist*, July 13, 1996, pp. 3–5.
36. Nihon keieisha dantai renmei kai, "Buruubaado puran kentō purojiekuto (BBPP)," cover sheet and pp. 9–10.
37. "Minkaku: kigyō no mirai o tou." *Asahi Shinbun* (International Satellite ed.), April 8, 1997, p. 1.
38. Lincoln, "Japan Hasn't Really Failed."

Works Cited

Aihara Shigeru. "Nippon kōkan no sōgi, 1946." In *Sengo rōdō sōgi jittai chōsa: tekkō sōgi*, ed. Rōdō sōgi chōsa kai. Vol. 7. Tokyo: Chūō kōronsha, 1958.

Amadachi Tadao. *Nihon no rōdōsha*. Tokyo: Tokyo University Press, 1953.

Aoki Satoshi. *Nihon teki keiei no genba*. Tokyo: Kōdansha, 1987.

———. *Nippon gisō rōren*. Tokyo: Aoki shoten, 1989.

Ariiumi Tooru. "The Legal Framework." In *Workers and Employers in Japan*, ed. Kazuo Ōkōchi, Bernard Karsh, and Solomon B. Levine. Princeton: Princeton University Press, 1974.

Barshay, Andrew. "Imagining Democracy in Postwar Japan: Reflections on Maruyama Masao and Modernism." *Journal of Japanese Studies* (Summer 1992): 365–406.

Berger, Suzanne, and Ronald Dore, eds. *National Diversity and Global Capitalism*. Ithaca: Cornell University Press, 1996.

Bernstein, Aaron. "The Difference Japanese Management Makes." *Business Week*, July 14, 1986, pp. 47–50.

Boyer, Robert, and Jean-Pierre Durand. *L'apres fordism*. Paris: Syros, 1993. Translated as *Afutaa fuodizumu*. Tokyo: Mineruba shobō, 1996.

Brinton, Mary. *Women and the Economic Miracle: Gender and Work in Postwar Japan*. Berkeley: University of California Press, 1993.

Cohen, Theodore. *Remaking Japan: The American Occupation as New Deal*. New York: Macmillan, 1987.

Cole, Robert. *Strategies for Learning: Small-Group Activities in American, Japanese, and Swedish Industry*. Berkeley: University of California Press, 1989.

Comaroff, Jean, and John Comaroff. *Of Revelation and Revolution: Christianity, Colonialism, and Consciousness in Southern Africa*. Vol. 1. Chicago: University of Chicago Press, 1991.

Cusumano, Michael. *The Japanese Automobile Industry: Technology and Management at Nissan and Toyota*. Cambridge, Mass.: Harvard University Council on East Asian Studies, 1985.

Doi, Ayako. "Labor: Lifetime Employment is Out, Job- and Employee-Hopping Are In." *The Japan Digest Forum* (March 20, 1997): 5.

Dore, Ronald. *British Factory–Japanese Factory.* Berkeley: University of California Press, 1973.

Dower, John W. *Empire and Aftermath: Yoshida Shigeru and the Japanese Experience.* Cambridge, Mass.: Harvard University Council on East Asian Studies, 1979.

———. "Peace and Democracy in Two Systems: External Policy and Internal Conflict." In *Postwar Japan as History,* ed. Andrew Gordon. Berkeley: University of California Press, 1993.

Ekonomisuto. 1950–1995.

Field, Norma. *In the Realm of a Dying Emperor.* New York: Random House, 1991.

Foote, Daniel. "Judicial Creation of Norms in Japanese Labor Law: Activism in the Service of—Stability?" *UCLA Law Review* 43, no. 3 (February 1996): 635–709.

Fujita Wakao. *Dai ni kumiai.* Tokyo: Nihon hyōronsha, 1955.

Fukushima Toshio. "Nihon no rōdō jikan no suikei." *Tōkei gaku,* no. 66 (March 1994): 1–9.

Furukawa Hosaburō. "Shin'nin kantokusha ga QC saakuru de eta kyōkun." *Genba to QC,* no. 68 (June 1969): 44–49.

Garon, Sheldon. *The State and Labor in Modern Japan.* Berkeley: University of California Press, 1987.

Garon, Sheldon, and Mike Mochizuki. "Negotiating Social Contracts." In *Postwar Japan as History,* ed. Andrew Gordon. Berkeley: University of California Press, 1993.

Genba to QC. 1965–1970.

George, Timothy. "Minamata: Power, Policy, and Citizenship in Postwar Japan." Ph.D. diss., Harvard University, 1996.

Gerschenkron, Alexander. *Economic Backwardness in Historical Perspective.* Cambridge, Mass.: Harvard University Press, 1962.

Gibbs, Michael H. "The Labor Movement at the Yahata Steel Works, 1945–1957." Ph.D. diss., University of California at Berkeley, 1990.

Gordon, Andrew. "Contests for the Workplace." In *Postwar Japan as History,* ed. Andrew Gordon. Berkeley: University of California Press, 1993.

———. *The Evolution of Labor Relations in Japan.* Cambridge, Mass.: Harvard University Council on East Asian Studies, 1985.

———. "The Invention of Japanese Style Management." In *Mirror of Modernity: Invented Traditions in Modern Japan,* ed. Stephen Vlastos. Berkeley: University of California Press, 1998.

———. *Labor and Imperial Democracy in Prewar Japan.* Berkeley: University of California Press, 1991.

———. "Managing the Japanese Household: The New Life Movement in Postwar Japan." *Social Politics* (Spring 1997): 245–283.

Gosselin, Peter G. "Japanese Economy Has Lost Its Luster." *Boston Globe,* February 4, 1997, pp. A1, A7.

Gotō Michio. "Zadankai: Nihon no kigyō to rōdō o tou." *Rōdō hōritsu junpō,* no. 1285 (April 10, 1992): 6–21.

Gotō Tatsuo. "Daily Calendar," 1957–1963.

Gould, William. *Japan's Reshaping of American Labor Law.* Cambridge: MIT Press, 1984.

Gramsci, Antonio. *Prison Notebooks.* Vols. 1 and 2. New York: Columbia University Press, 1991 and 1996.

Halberstam, David. *The Reckoning.* New York: Morrow, 1986.

Hasegawa, Harukiyo. *The Steel Industry in Japan: A comparison with Britain.* London: Routledge, 1996.

Havens, Thomas R. H. *Fire across the Sea: The Vietnam War and Japan, 1965–1975.* Princeton: Princeton University Press, 1987.

Hayakawa Seiichirō and Yoshida Kenji. "Keizai fukkō kaigi no soshiki to undō," Parts 1, 2, 3. *Hōsei daigaku Ōhara shakai mondai kenkyū jo kenkyū shiryō geppō,* nos. 283 (pp. 1–34), 284 (pp. 1–57), 292 (pp. 1–22) (February, March, and December 1982).

Hazama Hiroshi. *Nihon rōmu kanri shi kenkyū.* Tokyo: Ochanomizu shobō, 1978.

Hein, Laura. "Growth versus Success: Japan's Economic Policy in Historical Perspective." In *Postwar Japan as History,* ed. Andrew Gordon. Berkeley: University of California Press, 1993.

Higuchi Jirō. "Nippon kōkan keihin seitetsujo rōdō kumiai no soshiki to kinō." In *Gendai no rōdō kumiai undō,* ed. Kobayashi Yū. Tokyo: Otsuki shoten, 1972.

Hinshitsu kanri. 1955–1961.

Hirachi Ichirō. "1959 sōgi to tekkōgyō 'rōshi kankei' no anteika: Nippon kōkan, Tsurumi no jirei." *Kenkyū nempō: keizaigaku* 47, no. 1 (June 1985): 53–72.

Hirano Shōichi. "Kyōchōteki rōshi kankei no keisei to tekkō rōdō kumiai undō." *Rōdō undō kenkyū,* no. 58 (1976): 43–114.

———. "Rōdō kumiai no yakuin senkyō seido: 'sono jittai to mondai ten.'" *Rōdō nōmin undō* (August 1967): 40–50.

Hiwatari Nobuhiro. "Japanese Corporate Governance Reexamined: The Origins and Institutional Foundations of Enterprise Unionism." Paper presented at the Conference on Employees and Corporate Governance at Columbia University, Law School, November 1996.

Hoerr, John. *And the Wolf Finally Came: The Decline of the American Steel Industry.* Pittsburgh: Pittsburgh University Press, 1988.

Hongo Takenobu. "Tōshiba 'jyōzu na kurashi no undō' no ikikata," *Rōmu kenkyū,* 10, no. 12 (December 1957): 30–37.

Horioka, Charles. "Consuming and Spending." In *Postwar Japan as History,* ed. Andrew Gordon. Berkeley: University of California Press, 1993.

Horiyone Akira. "Keihin seitetsujo ni okeru shoshūdan katsudō: saakuru katsudō no mondai ten to taisho ni tsuite." Mimeograph copy of a lecture presented at Japan Productivity Center, September 27, 1977.

Hyōdō Tsutomu. *Gendai no rōdō undō.* Tokyo: Tokyo University Press, 1981.

———. *Nihon ni okeru rōshi kankei no tenkai.* Tokyo: Tokyo University Press, 1971.

———. "Rōdō kumiai undō no hatten." In *Iwanami kōza: Nihon rekishi 23, gendai 2.* 1977.

———. *Rōdō no sengo shi.* Tokyo: Tokyo University Press, 1997.

———. "Sengo Nihon no rōshi kankei." *Rōdō mondai kenkyū,* no. 3 (1981): 5–35.

———. "Shokuba no rōshi kankei to rōdō kumiai." In *Sengo rōdō kumiai undō shi ron,* ed. Shimizu Shinzō. Tokyo: Nihon hyōron sha, 1982.

Hyōdō Tsutomu and Totsuka Hideo, eds. *Rōshi kankei no tenkan to sentaku: Nihon no jidōsha sangyō.* Tokyo: Nihon hyōronsha, 1991.

Inoue Masao. *Nihon no rōdōsha jishu kanri.* Tokyo: Tokyo University Press, 1991.

Ishida Hideo. "Tekkō ōte go sha no dantai kōshō:kōshō senjutsu no kōsatsu." *Mitai gakkai zasshi* 61, no. 2 (February 1968): 55–81.

Ishida Hirohide. "Hoshu seitō no bijyon." *Chūō kōron* 78, no. 1 (January 1963): 88–97.

Ishida Mitsuo. *Chingin no shakaigaku.* Tokyo: Chūō keizai sha, 1990.

———. "Chingin taikei to rōshi kankei: Nihon no jōken." *Nihon rōdō kyōkai zasshi* (September 1985): 39–49.

Ishikawa Kaoru. *TQC to wa nani ka: Nihon teki hinshitsu kanri.* Tokyo: Nikka giren shuppankai, 1984.

Ishinomori Shōtarō. *Japan Inc.: An Introduction to Japanese Economics.* Berkeley: University of California Press, 1988.

Itami Hiroyuki. "The Humanistic Corporation—An Exportable Concept?" *Japan Echo* 12, no. 4 (1986): 57. Translated and abridged from "Bunmei o yushutsu suru toki." *Asuteion* (Autumn 1986): 40–50.

Johnson, Chalmers. *MITI and the Japanese Miracle.* Stanford: Stanford University Press, 1982.

Kahler, Miles. "Trade and Domestic Differences." In *National Diversity and Global Capitalism,* ed. Suzanne Berger and Ronald Dore. Ithaca: Cornell University Press, 1996.

Karatsu Hajime. "Japanese Know-how for American Industry." *Japan Echo* 13, no. 4 (1986): 64. Translated from "Beikoku keizai no hatan" (The collapse of the American economy). *Voice* (October 1986): 115–125.

Kawabe Heihachirō. "Tekkō sangyō to tekkō rōren no ichi." In *Nihon teki rōshi kankei no henbō,* ed. Makino Tomio. Tokyo: Ōtsuki shoten, 1991.

Kawasaki rōdō shi nensan iinkai, ed. *Kawasaki rōdō shi: sengo hen.* Kawasaki, 1987.

Kawatetsu shinbun. 1946–1955.

Keizai kikaku chō. *Kojin seikatsu yūsen shakai o mezashite.* Tokyo, 1991.

Kettler, David, and Charles Tackney. "Light from a Dead Sun: the Japanese Lifetime Employment System and Weimar Labor Law." *Comparative Labor Law and Policy Journal* 19 (January 1998): 101–141.

Kinoshita Takeo. "Sangyō betsu zenkoku soshiki no bunretsu, saihen to minkan "rengō" e no michinori." In *"Rengō jidai" no rōdō undō*, ed. Ōhara shakai mondai kenkyūjo. Tokyo: Sōgō rōdō kenkyū jo, 1992.

Kobayashi Ken'ichi. "Tekkō gyō no risutorakucharingu to koyō chōsei." *Keizai shirin* 62, no. 2 (September 1995): 13–31.

Koike Kazuo. *Shigoto no keizaigaku*. Tokyo: Tōyō keizai shinpō, 1991. Translated as *The Economics of Work in Japan*. Tokyo: Long Term Credit Bank International Library Foundation, 1995.

———. *Shokuba no rōdō kumiai to sanka: rōshi kankei no nichibei hikaku*. Tokyo: Tōyō keizai shinpō, 1977.

Kokumin bunka chōsa kai, ed. *Sayoku bunka nempō*. Tokyo, 1958.

Kokumin bunka kaigi, ed. *Nihon bunka no genjō to mondai ten*. Tokyo: Kokumin bunka kaigi, 1964.

Konda Masaharu. "Nippon kōkan no rain ni yoru rōmu kanri no jissai," *Rōmu kanri tsūshin*. 7, no. 23 (September 1967): 6–8.

———. "Sagyōchō o chūshin to shita genba kanri soshiki no gōriteki na unei." *Rōmu kanri tsūshin* 7, no. 23 (September 1967): 3–8.

———. "Tekkō no chin'age kaitō no konkyō to haikei." *Chingin repōto* 1, no. 1 (August 1967): 31–63.

Koshirō Kazuyoshi, ed. *Sengo 50 nen: Sangyō, koyō, rōdō shi*. Tokyo: Nihon rōdō kenkyū kikō, 1995.

Kumazawa Makoto. *Nihon-teki keiei no meian*. Tokyo: Chikuma shobō, 1989.

———. *Portraits of the Japanese Workplace*. Boulder: Westview Press, 1996.

———. "Suto-ken suto." In *Sengo rōdō kumiai undō shi*, ed. Shimizu Shinzō. Tokyo: Nihon hyōronsha, 1982.

Kurahashi Yoshinobu. "Sengo tekkō rōmu kanri shoshi." In *Nihon teki rōshi kankei no hikari to kage: Keizai hyōron bessatsu*. Tokyo: Nihon hyōronsha, 1982.

Lauschke, Karl. "Mobilität und Aufstieg in der Eisen- und Stahlindustrie nach dem Zweiten Weltkrieg." In *Mikropolitik im Unternehmen: Arbeitsbeziehungen und Machtstrukturen in industriellen Gro betriebe des 20. Jahrhunderts*, ed. Karl Laushcke and Thomas Welskopp. Essen: Klartext Verlag, 1994.

Lillrank, Paul, and Noriaki Kano. *Continuous Improvement: Quality Control Circles in Japanese Industry*. Ann Arbor: University of Michigan Center for Japanese Studies, 1989.

Lincoln, Edward J. "Japan Hasn't Really Failed: There's No Crisis So Don't Expect Radical Changes." *New York Times*, February 22, 1997, Op-ed page.

Lynn, Leonard H. "Institutions, Organizations and Technological Innovation: Oxygen Steelmaking in the U.S. and Japan." Ph.D. diss., University of Michigan, 1980.

Maier, Charles. "The Politics of Productivity: Foundations of American International Economic Policy after World War II." In *Between Power and Plenty: Foreign Economic Policies of the Advanced Industrial States,* ed. Peter Katzenstein. Madison: University of Wisconsin, 1978.

———. "The Two Postwar Eras and the Conditions for Stability in Twentieth Century Western Europe." *American Historical Review* 86, no. 2 (April 1981): 327–352.

Maruyama Yoshinari. "Nihongata kigyō shakai to Nihon teki seisan shisutemu." *Keizai hyōron* 42, no. 3 (March 1993): 122–139.

Matsumura Gen. *Senjutsu tenkan suru minsei to kigyō no taisaku.* Tokyo: Nihon keizai seinen kyōgikai, 1965.

Matsuzaki Tadashi. *Nihon tekkō sangyō bunseki.* Nihon hyōronsha, 1982.

———. "Tekkō sōgi." In *Nihon no rōdō sōgi: 1945–1985,* ed. Yamamoto Kiyoshi. Tokyo: Tokyo University Press, 1991.

Meiji daigaku shakai kagaku kenkyūjo. *Tekkō sangyō no gōrika to rōdō: Yahata seitetsu no jittai bunseki.* Tokyo: Hakutō shobo, 1961.

Meyer, Stephen, III. *The Five Dollar Day: Labor Management and Social Control in the Ford Motor Company, 1908–1921.* Albany: State University of New York Press, 1981.

Michimata Kenjirō. *Gendai Nihon no tekkō rōdō mondai.* Tokyo: Hokkaidō University Press, 1978.

———. "Tekkō rōdō undō ni okeru uyokuteki chōryū no taitō to yakuwari." *Rōdō undō shi kenkyū,* no. 57 (1974): 40–117.

Milkman, Ruth. *Farewell to the Factory: Automation in the Late Twentieth Century.* Berkeley: University of California Press, 1997.

Mita Katsuya. "JC tanjō no hiwa: denki rōren no maku." *Rōdō undō,* no. 212 (August 1983): 92–115.

Miyake Akimasa. *Reddo paaji to wa nani ka: Nihon senryō no kage.* Tokyo: Ōtsuki shoten, 1994.

Miyata Yoshiji. *Kumiai zakku baran.* Tokyo: Tōyō keizai shinpōsha, 1982.

Montgomery, David. *Workers' Control in America.* Cambridge: Cambridge University Press, 1979.

Moore, Joe. *Japanese Workers and the Struggle for Power, 1945–1947.* Madison: University of Wisconsin Press, 1983.

Mori Hideo. "Kensaku toishi shiyō no teigen ni tsuite." *Genba to QC,* no. 61 (November 1968): 32–38.

Morioka Kōji. "Zangyō oyobi saabisu zangyō no jittai to rōkihō kaisei no hitsuyōsei." *Keizai kagaku tsūshin,* no. 71 (November 1992): 14–25.

Morita Akio. "Nihon gata keiei ga abunai." *Bungei shunju* (February 1992): 94–103. Translated as "A Critical Moment for Japanese Management." *Japan Echo* 19, no. 2 (Summer 1992): 8–14.

Mueller-Jentsch, Walter. "Labor Conflicts and Class Struggles." In *Technological Change, Rationalisation and Industrial Relations*, ed. Bob Jessop, Hans Kastendieck, and Marino Regini. London: St. Martin's Press, 1985.

Mueller-Jentsch, Walter, and Hans Joachim Sperling. "Towards a Flexible Triple System? Continuity and Structural Changes in German Industrial Relations." In *German Industrial Relations Under the Impact of Structural Change, Unification, and European Integration*, ed. Reiner Hoffmann, Otto Jacobi, Berndt Keller, and Manfred Weiss. Dusseldorf: Hans Bockler-Stiftung, 1995.

Nakagawa Takao. "Rōshi funsō shori, shin rūru tsukure." *Asahi shinbun*, International Satellite ed., March 4, 1997.

Nakamura Keisuke. *Nihon no shokuba to seisan shisutemu*. Tokyo: Tokyo University Press, 1996.

Nakamura Seiji. *Nihon seisansei kōjō undō shi*. Tokyo: Keisō shobō, 1958.

Nakamura Takafusa. "Tekkō rōren tōitsu chingin tōsō." In *Sengo rōdō sōgi jittai chōsa: tekkō sōgi*, ed. Rōdō sōgi chōsa kai. Vol. 7. Tokyo: Chūō kōronsha, 1958.

Nakaoka Tetsurō. "Senchū, sengo no kagakuteki kanri undō (2)." *Keizai gaku zasshi* 82, no. 3 (1981): 43–61.

National Defense Counsel for Victims of Karoshi 1990. *Karoshi*. Tokyo: Madosha, 1990.

Nevins, Thomas J. *Labor Pains and the Gaijin Boss: Hiring, Managing, and Firing the Japanese*. Tokyo: Japan Times, 1984.

New Life Movement Association. *Shin seikatsu*. 1954–1985.

New York Times. *The Downsizing of America*. New York: Random House, 1996.

Nihon keieisha dantai renmei kai. "Buruubaado puran kentō purojiekuto (BBPP)." Tokyo, August 1996.

———. *Shokuba rekurieshion: toku ni wakanensō kanri no tachiba kara*. Tokyo, 1963.

———. *Shokuba tōsō to sono taisaku*. Tokyo: Nikkeiren, 1955.

Nihon keieisha dantai renmei kai, 1970 nendai rōmu kenkyū jo. *Shokuba ni okeru sayoku seiryoku no jittai to sono taisaku*. Tokyo: Nikkeiren, 1972 and 1975.

———. Kantō keieisha kyōkai. *Nōryoku shugi ni kansuru kigyō no jittai chōsa*. Tokyo: Nikkeiren, 1967.

Nihon nōritsu kyōkai, *1968 ZD hakusho*. Tokyo, 1969.

Nihon seisansei honbu. *Senshinkoku byō to rōdō rinri no henyō ni kansuru chōsa kenkyū*. Tokyo: Nihon seisansei honbu, 1985.

Nihon seisansei honbu, rōshi kyōgisei jōnin iinkai, ed. *Nihon no rōshi kyōgisei: sono rekishi, genjō oyobi mondaiten*. Tokyo: Nihon seisansei honbu, 1959.

Nihon tekkō renmei kai, *Tekkō kai*. 1955–1960.

Nihon tekkō sangyō rōdō kumiai rengō kai. *Ōte seitetsujo no rōdōsha to rōdō kumiai: tekkō rōren soshiki chōsa hōkokusho*. Tokyo, 1977.

———. *Tekkō rōdō undō shi*. Tokyo, 1971.

Nihon tekkō sangyō rōdō kumiai rengō kai and Rōdō chōsa kyōgikai, ed. *Tekkō sangyō no rōshi kankei to rōdō kumiai.* Tokyo: Nihon rōdō kyōkai, 1980.

Nimura Kazuo. "Nihon rōshi kankei no rekishiteki tokushitsu." In *Nihon no rōshi kankei no tokushitsu,* ed. Shakai seisaku gakkai. Tokyo: Ochanomizu shobō, 1987.

―――. "Nikkan rōshi kankei no shiteki kentō." *Ōhara shakai mondai kenkyūjo zasshi,* no. 460 (March 1997): 3–19.

Nippon Kōkan kabushiki kaisha, Keihin rōmuka. "Kantoku nyūmon kōza: rōshi kankei." (Pamphlet.) January 1970.

―――. *Nippon Kōkan kabushiki kaisha 30 nen shi.* Tokyo, 1942.

―――. *Nippon Kōkan kabushiki kaisha 40 nen shi.* Tokyo, 1952.

―――. *Nippon Kōkan kabushiki kaisha 60 nen shi.* Tokyo, 1972.

―――. *Nippon Kōkan kabushiki kaisha 70 nen shi.* Tokyo: 1982.

Nippon Kōkan Kawasaki seitetsujo rōdo kumiai. "1959 undō hōshin sho: chintō jiko hihan." Kawasaki, 1959.

―――. "1957 nendo chintō jiko hihan, 1958 nendo undō hōshin, hyōsan." Kawasaki, April 14, 1958.

―――. *Jū nen no ayumi.* Kawasaki, 1956.

―――. *Tatakai no ayumi: Nippon kōkan Kawasaki rōdō kumiai undō shi.* Kawasaki, 1970.

Nippon Kōkan keihin rōdō sōyūkai. *Sōyū.* July 1, 1983.

Nippon Kōkan keihin seitetsujo rōmu ka. "Rōmu shiryō, No. 17: 4 kumi 3 kōtai tokushū gō." October 1, 1970.

Nippon Kōkan Kyōsantō saibō, ed. *Keihin no kōro kara.* Tokyo, 1955.

Nippon Kōkan Mizue rōdō kumiai, ed. *Jū nen no ayumi.* Kawasaki, 1970.

Nippon Kōkan seitetsujo rōdō kumiai kyōgikai. "Gyōmukyū ni tai suru dai ichi dankai no taisho." July 12, 1962. (Held in the archives of the NKK Keihin labor union.)

Nippon Kōkan Tsurumi seitetsujo rōdō kumiai. "Dai 24 ki undō hōshinsho." Tsurumi, October 31, 1959. (Held in the archives of the NKK Keihin labor union.)

―――. "Dai 23 ki undō hōshinsho." Tsurumi: November 17, 1958. (Held in the archives of the NKK Keihin labor union.)

―――. "1957 nendo chingin taishoku kin tōsō keika hōkoku sho." Tsurumi: 1957. (Held in the archives of the Social Science Research Institute at Tokyo University as Rōdō chōsa shiryō, chōsa bangō 29–6.)

―――. *Tsurutetsu rōdō undō shi.* Tokyo: Shundaisha, 1956.

―――. *Tsurutetsu rōdō undō shi.* Tokyo: Tsurumi seitetsujo rōdō kumiai, 1970.

Nishinarita Yutaka. *Kindai Nihon no rōshi kankei no kenkyū.* Tokyo: Tokyo University Press, 1988.

―――. "Senryōki Nihon no rōshi kankei." In *Nihon no kindai to shihonshugi,* ed. Nakamura Masanori. Tokyo: Tokyo University Press, 1992.

Nitta Michio. *Nihon no rōdōsha sanka.* Tokyo: Tokyo University Press, 1988.

———. "Tekkō gyō ni okeru rōshi kyōgi no seido to jittai (1, 2)." *Shakai kagaku kenkyū* 32, no. 5 (March 1981): 151–225.

———. "Tekkō gyō no 'jishu kanri katsudō': dōin gata seisan, rōmu kanri no bunseki." *Nihon rōdō kyōkai zasshi,* no. 234 (September 1978): 13–32.

Ōba Hideo. *TQC to no tatakai.* Tokyo: Gakushu no tomosha, 1984.

Odaka Kunio. *Sangyō ni okeru ningen kankei no kagaku.* Tokyo: Yōhikaku, 1953.

———. *Sangyō no shakai gaku kōgi.* Tokyo: Iwanami shoten, 1981.

Ohara Institute for Social Research. *Nihon rōdō nenkan.* Tokyo: Tōyō keizai shinpō sha. Annual volumes, 1955–1997.

Oka Minoru. "Shihonka no shisō kōgeki to dō tatakau ka." *Gekkan: Tekkō rōren* 3, no. 7 (July 1958): 47–59.

Ōkōchi Kazuo, Ujihara Shōjirō, and Fujita Wakao. *Rōdō kumiai no kōzō to kinō.* Tokyo: Tokyo University Press, 1959.

Onomichi Hiroshi. *Kore ga rengō da: Sōhyō ga naku naru.* Tokyo: Takeuchi shoten, 1987.

Orii Hyūga. "Jyūgyōin no kaisha ni tai suru ittai kan wa ika ni shite takameru ka." In *Rōshi kyōryoku o meguru shomondai,* ed. Nihon keizai dantai renmei kai. Tokyo, 1954.

———. *Rōmu kanri nijū nen.* Tokyo: Tōyō keizai shimpōsha, 1973.

Ōsawa, Mari. "Bye-bye Corporate Warriors: The Formation of a Corporate-Centered Society and Gender-Biased Social Policies in Japan." Tokyo: University of Tokyo, Institute of Social Science Occasional Papers in Labor Problems and Social Policy, no. 18 (March 1994).

———. *Kigyō chūshin shakai o koete: gendai Nihon o "jiendaa" de yomu.* Tokyo: Jiji tsūshinsha, 1993.

Ōta Takeshi. "Shokuba katsudō o dō kaizen suru ka." *Gekkan: Tekkō rōren* 3, no. 7 (July 1958): 25–44.

Ozawa Shinichirō. "Saakuru no sengo shi." In *Kyōdō kenkyū: Shūdan: saakuru no sengo shisō shi,* ed. Shisō no kagaku kenkyū kai. Tokyo: Heibonsha, 1976.

Pharr, Susan. *Losing Face: Status Politics in Japan.* Berkeley: University of California Press, 1990.

Pinkwater, Daniel, "Japan Nosh." *All Things Considered,* National Public Radio. File no. 880505. 1988.

Putnam, Robert D. "Bowling Alone: America's Declining Social Capital." *Journal of Democracy* 6, no. 1 (1995): 65–78.

Reischauer, Edwin O. *My Life between Japan and America.* New York: Harper and Row, 1986.

Rekishigaku kenkyūkai, ed. *Nihon dōjidai shi.* Tokyo: Aoki shoten, 1990.

Rōdō mondai kenkyūkai, ed. "Tekkō rōdōsha," Parts 1–6. *Gekkan: Rōdō mondai* (December 1965–May 1966).

Rōdōsha chōsa kenkyū kai. "Infuomaru soshiki no jittai to mujun no kakudai." *Rōdō undō* (August 1978): 201–212.

Rōdōsha repootaaju guruupu. *Repootaaju: shokuba*. Tokyo: Shin Nippon shuppansha, 1971.

Saitō, Shigeru. *Wa ga naki ato ni, kōzui ga kitare: repootaju, kyodai kigyō to rōdō sha*. Tokyo: Tokuma shoten, 1974.

Samuels, Richard. *Rich Nation, Strong Army*. Ithaca: Cornell University Press, 1994.

Sasaki Takeshi et al., eds. *Sengo shi daijiten*. Tokyo: Sanseidō, 1991.

"Seinen jūgyōin no seikatsu shidō ni tsuite: sono jittai to mondaiten o saguru." *Shin seikatsu* (November 1965): 6–13; (December 1965): 6–15.

Sekitani Ranko. "Byōin sōgi." In *Sengo Nihon no rōdō sōgi*, ed. Fujita Wakao and Shiota Shōhei. Vol 2, 585–634. Tokyo: Ochanomizu shobō, 1963.

Shiinomi kai, ed. *Shiinomikai kessei 15 shūnen kinen: Donguri*. Kawasaki, 1969.

Shimada Haruo. *Hyūman ueaa no keizaigaku*. Tokyo: Iwanami shoten, 1988.

Shimizu Shinzō. "Sengo rōdō kumiai undō shi yosetsu." In *Sengo rōdō kumiai undō shi*, ed. Shimizu Shinzō. Tokyo: Nihon hyōronsha, 1982.

Shisō no kagaku kenkyū kai, ed. *Kyōdō kenkyū: Shūdan: saakuru no sengo shisō shi*. Tokyo: Heibonsha, 1976.

Smith, Thomas C. "The Right to Benevolence: Dignity and Japanese Workers, 1890–1920." In *Native Sources of Japanese Industrialization*. Berkeley: University of California Press, 1988.

Sōdōmei gojūnenshi iinkai. *Go jū nen shi*. Tokyo: Taiyō, 1964.

Sōhyō. *Sōhyō jū nen shi*. Tokyo: Sōhyō, 1961.

———. *Sōhyō ni jū nen shi*. Tokyo: Sōhyō, 1971.

———. *Sōhyō san jū nen shi: shiryō shū*. Vol. 1. Tokyo: Rōdōkyōiku sentaa, 1986.

Sugeno Kazuo. *Japanese Labor Law*. Translated by Leo Kanowitz. Seattle: University of Washington Press, 1992.

Tackney, Charles T. "Institutionalization of the Lifetime Employment System: A Case Study of Changing Employment Practices in a Japanese Factory." Ph.D. diss., University of Wisconsin, Madison, 1995.

Takahashi X. Untitled column. In *Shiinomikai kessei 15 shūnen kinen: Donguri*, ed. Shiinomi kai. Kawasaki, 1969.

Takahashi Yūkichi. "Rōdō kumiai undō no gan: infuomaru soshiki to dō tatakau ka." In *Nihon no rōdō kumiai undō (5): rōdō kumiai shoshiki ron*. Tokyo: Otsuki shoten, 1985.

Takanashi Akira. *Chōsa kenkyū shiryō, No. 45: tekkō ikkan meekaa ni okeru jigyōsho nai dantai kōshō*. Tokyo: Nihon rōdō kyōkai, 1961.

———. *Nihon tekkō gyō no rōshi kankei: dantai kōshōka no chingin kettei*. Tokyo: Tokyo University Press, 1967.

Takanashi Yukio. "Gijutsu kakushin to atarashii rōdō mondai" In *Gijutsu kakushinka no rōdō to rōdō hō*, ed. Nihon tekkō renmei. Tokyo: Nihon hyōronsha, 1962.

Takeda Makoto. "Minkan daikigyō ni okeru rōdō kumiai undō no tenkan." *Ōhara shakai mondai kenkyūjo zasshi,* no. 359 (October 1988): 1–25.

———. *Ōji seishi sōgi, 1957–1960.* Tokyo: Taga Publishing, 1993.

Tanabe Kōji. *Rōdō funsō to saiban.* Tokyo: Kōbundō, 1965.

Tilton, Mark. *Restrained Trade: Cartels in Japan's Basic Materials Industries.* Ithaca: Cornell University Press, 1996.

Tokyo yuibutsuron kenkyū kai, ed. *Sengo shisō no saikentō: Ningen to bunka.* Tokyo: Shiraishi shoten, 1986.

Totsuka Hideo and Hyōdō Tsutomu, eds. *Rōshi kankei no tenkan to sentaku: Nihon no jidōsha sangyō.* Tokyo: Nihon hyōron sha, 1991.

Totsuka Hideo and Tokunaga Shigeyoshi. *Gendai Nihon no rōdō mondai: atarashii paradaimu o motomete.* Tokyo: Minerva shobo, 1993.

Tsubouchi. Untitled column, Shiinomi kai, ed. *Shiinomikai kessei 15 shūnen kinen: Donguri.* Kawasaki, 1969.

Tsuda Masumi. "Nihon teki rōdō kankō to 76 nen shuntō: hyōmenka shita shūshin koyō sei hihan." *Gekkan: Rōdō mondai tokushū gō 1976 shuntō dokuhon* (February 1976): 16–21.

Tsurumi Shunsuke. "Hidaka Rokurō to no taidan: Ima minshushugi no ne o saguru." *Sekai* (August 1983): 40–43.

Tsutsui, William M. "W. Edwards Deming and the Origin of Quality Control in Japan." *Journal of Japanese Studies* 22, no. 2 (Summer 1996): 295–325.

Turner, Christeena. *Japanese Workers in Protest.* Berkeley: University of California Press, 1995.

Ueda Osamu. "Kigyō kan kyōsō to 'shokuba shakai.'" *Ōhara shakai mondai kenkyūjo zasshi,* no. 350 (January 1988): 48–68.

Upham, Frank. *Law and Social Change in Postwar Japan.* Cambridge, Mass.: Harvard University Press, 1987.

———. "Unplaced Persons and Movements for Place." In *Postwar Japan as History,* ed. Andrew Gordon. Berkeley: University of California Press, 1993.

Veblen, Thorsten. "The Opportunity of Japan." In *Essays in Our Changing Order.* New York: Viking Press, 1943.

Vitols, Sigurt. "Restructuring in the German Steel Industry: The Role of Industrial Relations." Unpublished paper, 1997.

Watanabe Kazuo. *Labor Relations: A Japanese Business Novel.* Translated with an introduction by Tamae Prindle. New York: University Press of America, 1994.

Watanabe Osamu. *Gendai Nihon no shihai kōzō bunseki: kijuku to shūhen.* Tokyo: Kadensha, 1988.

———. "Gendai Nihon shakai no ken'iteki kōzō to kokka." In *Ken'i teki chitsujo to kokka,* ed. Fujita Isamu. Tokyo: Tokyo University Press, 1987.

———. *"Yutaka na shakai": Nihon no kōzō.* Tokyo: Rōdō junpō sha, 1990.

Watanabe Tatsuo. "Kōkan shōji no kaisha kaisan ni itaru made no keii to sōhyō zenkoku kinzoku rōdō kumiai to no taisaku ni tsuite." Unpublished ms., 1980.

Williams, Raymond. *Marxism and Literature.* Oxford: Oxford University Press, 1977.

Williamson, Hugh. *Coping with the Miracle: Japan's Unions Explore New International Relations.* London and Hong Kong: Pluto Press with Asia Monitor Resource Center, 1994.

Woodiwiss, Anthony. *Law, Labour, and Society in Japan: From Repression to Reluctant Recognition.* London: Routledge, 1992.

Yamamoto Kiyoshi. "Daikigyō no rōshi kankei: 'fuomaru' kikō, 'infuormaru' soshiki." In *Gendai Nihon shakai,* ed. Tokyo daigaku shakai kagaku kenkyūjo. Vol. 5. Tokyo: Tokyo University Press, 1991.

———. "'Infuomaru soshiki' ni kansuru hito kōsatsu (1, 2): Kō denki ni okeru jirei o chūshin to shite." *Shakai kagaku* 42, no. 1 (July 1990): 206–262. Abridged English version: "'Japanese-style Industrial Relations' and an 'Informal' Employee Organization: A Case Study of the Ohgi-kai at T Electric." University of Tokyo, Institute of Social Science Occasional Papers in Labor Problem and Social Policy no. 8, December 1990.

———. "Sasebo jūkō rōdō sōgi (1979–80)." In *Nihon no rōdō sōgi (1945–80),* ed. Yamamoto Kiyoshi. Tokyo: Tokyo University Press, 1991.

Yamane Masako. *Jishu seisan rōsō: Tōshiba Anpekkusu sōgi 8 nen no tatakai.* Tokyo: Kodamasha, 1991.

Yonekura Seiichirō. *The Japanese Iron and Steel Industry, 1850–1990: Continuity and Discontinuity.* New York: St. Martin's Press, 1994.

Yoneyama Kikuji. *Gijutsu kakushin to shokuba kanri.* Tokyo: Kizawasha, 1978.

Yoshimura Muneo. *Jiritsu suru rōdō undō: shirarezaru infuorumaru soshiki.* Tokyo: Rōdō junpōsha, 1993.

Yoshizaki Shunichi. "Ishi ga nagarete ki no ha ga shizumu: Nihon kōkan inforumaru gurupu 'sōyū' no hankyō kōgeki ni hanron suru." *Rōdō undō,* no. 6–7 (1984): 5–25.

Index

Acorn Club (Shiinomi kai), 113, 125, 140, 181, 188; and strikes, 127, 138, 139, 142, 185; and unions, 83, 84, 115

AFL-CIO (American Federation of Labor–Congress of Industrial Organizations), 49, 50, 122

Allied occupation, 5–8; and corporations, 41; and education, 158; and general strike, 33; and pacifism, 200; reforms of, 5, 20, 22, 40; and unions, 22, 46; and war reparations, 33, 42, 197

All-Japan Private Sector Labor Union Federation, 136. *See also* Rengō

American Labor Review, 50

Anticommunism, 52, 82, 122, 126, 198

Aoki Fujio, 27

Asahi (newspaper), 190

Asano Ryōzō, 12, 29, 42, 43

Asano Shipyard, 43

Asano Sōichirō, 12

Asano zaibatsu, 12, 41

Asanuma Inejirō, 51

Asia Foundation, 49, 50

Atsugi Base, 18

Bargaining, 18, 34, 45; collective, 28, 56, 79, 80, 143, 145, 185, 198. *See also* Wage bargaining

Black market, 28, 30, 31

Boulware, Lemuel, 117

Bureaucrats, 54, 55, 56, 59, 60, 120

Capitalism: and cartels, 63; and competition, 114–115, 175, 213; and democracy, 2, 3, 45, 132; and government, 63, 193; as hegemonic system, 131; history of, in Japan, 202; and oppression of workers, 165; and recovery, 9, 36–39, 51, 52; reformed, 36; and science, 45; and socialism, 48, 122, 210; survival of, 195; triumph of, 19, 49, 56; and wage demands, 107. *See also* Corporate-centered society; Corporations

Central Labor Relations Commission, 109

China, 6, 15, 16, 46, 51

CIA (Central Intelligence Agency), 49, 135

Circles. *See* Cultural circles; Quality control circles

Coal industry, 6, 31, 57, 58, 59–60, 76, 120, 128

Cold War, 42, 45–51, 57, 83, 96

Cole, Robert, 170

Communism, 6, 50, 82, 138, 198, 201

Communist Party, 6, 7; purge of members, 46–47; and unions, 16, 22, 35, 43, 48, 49, 83, 88, 138, 185; and workers, 125, 185; youth groups, 179. *See also* Japan Communist Party

Competition, 52, 57, 61, 214; and education, 176, 200, 212; interfirm, 116, 118; international, 213; meritocratic, 176, 192

Comrades Club (Dōshikai), 83, 121, 126, 185

Consultation, labor-management, 49, 143, 145, 155, 197, 198, 202

Consumption, 52, 54, 213

Cooperation, 1, 10–11, 48, 49, 83, 182, 188, 189–190, 206; and banks, 61; *vs.* confrontation, 18–19, 45, 204; and informal